North West

Spain

Melissa Shales

Christopher Helm
A & C Black · London

For Penny and Dennis, with love

© Melissa Shales 1993

Christopher Helm (Publishers) Ltd,
a subsidiary of A&C Black (Publishers)
Limited, 35 Bedford Row, London WC1R 4JH

ISBN 0-7136-8061-X

A CIP catalogue record for this book is
available from the British Library

Filmset by Rowland Phototypesetting Ltd,
Bury St Edmunds, Suffolk
Printed and bound in Great Britain by
Butler and Tanner Ltd, Frome and London

Acknowledgements

Compiling this sort of book always involves huge numbers of people, who give generously of their time and expertise, without asking anything in return. I have been helped by too many people along the way to name them all, but I would like to offer them my grateful thanks. In particular, I have received constant assistance from the Spanish Tourist Office in London. Britanny Ferries, Iberian Airlines, RENFE, AVIS Rent-a-Car and the Paradores Nacionales have all given practical assistance in the form of transport and accommodation. Emma Valentine and Louise Dorey have helped both with research and by coming to the rescue of my shaky Spanish, and Stephen Fowler worked harder than anyone should have to on a holiday, driving me around the hairpin bends of the Picos de Europa.

The author and publishers are grateful to the Spanish National Tourist Office for permission to reproduce the photographs on pages 209, 216 and 222.
    All other photographs © Melissa Shales.

Contents

Introduction

When I first started work on this book, everyone sounded terribly enthusiastic about the area and said 'You'll love it, it's just like Wales.' I live in Wales, and love it dearly, but I see enough of it every day – and more than enough of the Welsh weather. My heart sank. It began to rise again on the voyage across when the Bay of Biscay, notorious for having some of the roughest seas in the world, lay in mill-pond calm. By the time I reached Pamplona, I was ready to drop, in some of the hottest weather I have ever encountered (and that includes many years of experience in the tropics). I began to think longingly and illogically of good, damp steady rain, but the sun continued to blaze.

I was lucky. This narrow strip along Spain's Atlantic coast didn't earn the name 'Green Spain' by accident. The region is made up of three distinct bands. To the north is a thin, relatively flat coastal plain. Inland comes a long string of high mountain ranges, which culminate in the magnificent Picos de Europa. South of these is the northern edge of the Castillian plateau. The coast and mountains are hit by the full force of the Atlantic weather. In summer this means that you are likely to spend at least some of your time in cloud and rain, although you would have to be very unlucky for your whole holiday to be a washout, while the winter can bring ferocious storms on the coast and deep, impassable snow in the high mountains. Only to the south will you find the burning heat we tend to associate with Spain.

Scenically, historically, architecturally and culturally, however, the area more than makes up for the vagaries of the climate. It is a region totally unlike any other, and one of the most beautiful in Europe. Ever-changing landscape leads from placidly green and fertile pastures to great rocky mountain crags, from sandy turquoise bays to bleak coastal cliffs dancing with spray, from vast plains of wheat to distant purple hill villages. Architecturally, it varies from massive, stupendous Gothic cathedrals to tiny, enchanting Romanesque chapels, from mellow stone palaces to elegant town houses with glassed-in balconies, and humble, slate-roofed fishermen's cottages. There are different languages and cultures, from the enigmatic Basques to the Celtic Galicians, all burning with intense patriotic pride. There are great cities and minute villages, paintings 15,000 years old, and modern sculptures. You can swim or ski, hike, cycle or ride, play golf or tennis, shoot or fish. And high in the remotest areas of the mountains, there are still bears and wolves and eagles.

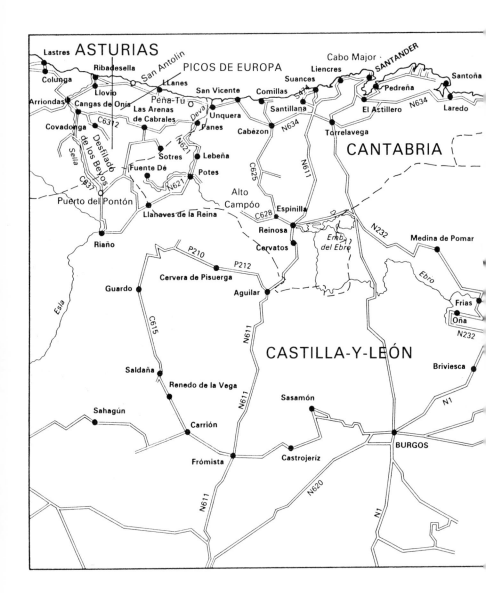

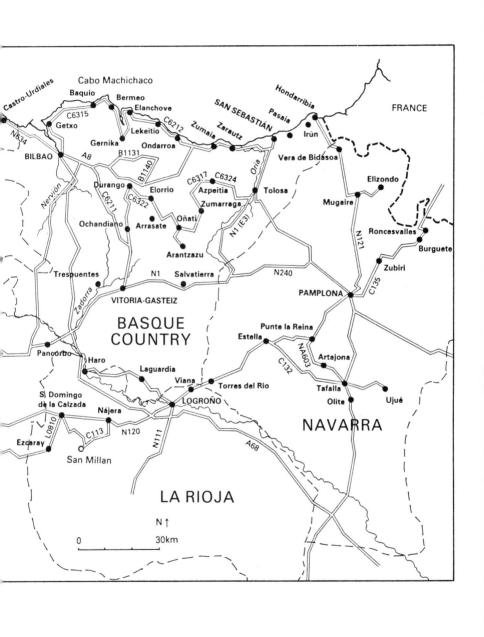

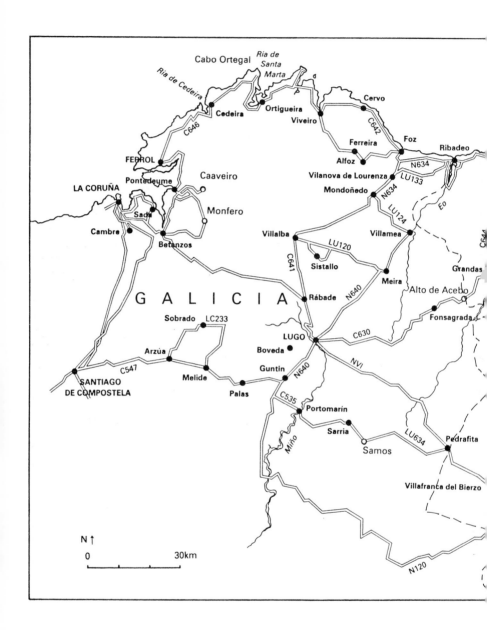

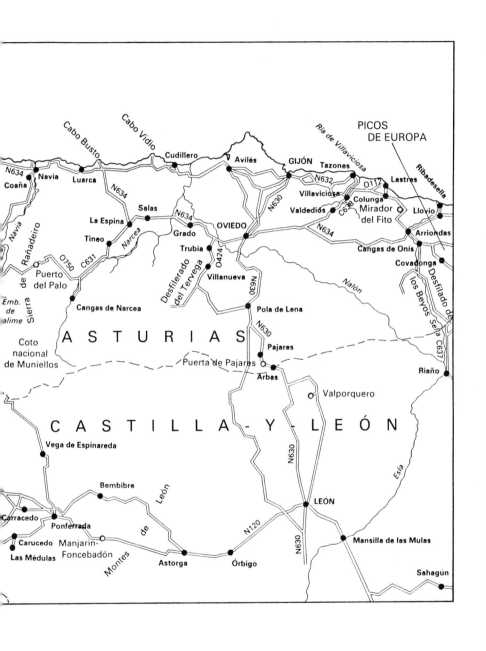

A 13th-century bridge at Cangas de Onís, in Asturias.

The main body of the book is written as a series of suggested routes. The two longest follow the coast, and at the southern boundary of the region, the famous Camino de Santiago, the great pilgrim route to Santiago de Compostela. Between them, at regular intervals, are a series of rather circuitous north-south routes designed to make the most of sites of interest as well as the magnificent mountain scenery. Where relevant, I have also added suggested side excursions. If you are short of time, however, there are plenty of large, fast, through roads, that will get you to your next destination without interruption. The seven different autonomous states, and their internal provinces are covered in alphabetical order, even though this is not quite logical geographically. Where a route comes to a screeching halt on the border of a province, I have cross-referenced it on to the adjacent relevant section. The only exception to this rule is the triangular route around the Picos de Europa, which is at the corner of three separate states. It is one of the most popular routes in the region, is approachable from every direction, and is not easily divided. I have therefore given it a separate chapter of its own.

Of necessity, the hotels and restaurant listings are by no means exhaustive, and tend to mention only those establishments that have a little something extra, whether in the quality of the food or the ambience. Those listed are mainly a little more expensive but, sadly, this is an area where money talks. Although relatively few Britons come here, it is a popular holiday area for the Spanish themselves, particularly amongst the wealthier citizens of Madrid, many of whom own holiday homes on the coast. As a result, the whole region is more expensive than other comparable areas of Spain, and in order to begin to get reasonable standards, you have to be prepared to spend that bit extra.

I have tried to make the book as comprehensive and up-to-date as possible, but there is always a gap between writing and publication and, inevitably, things do change. If you find any errors or alterations, or if you discover any wonderful new destinations, hotels or restaurants which you feel should be included in future editions, please do write and let me know. Your comments and suggestions will be gratefully received. Meantime, I hope you have a happy holiday, and find the area as beautiful and fascinating as I do.

Melissa Shales, Cardiff 1992

Section One
Practical Background

Getting there

It is extraordinary that north-west Spain is so little known – it is so easy to get there. Apart from the few *cognoscenti*, however, most northern Europeans prefer to fly over the top or, at least, drive straight through. For the few who do want to stay, the easiest way to get there from the UK is to take the ferry. The Brittany Ferries car ferry sails three times a week from Plymouth to Santander and back, year round. The crossing takes 24 hours, so it's advisable to book a cabin.

The ferry is expensive, so for those who decide not to take their car, it is just as cheap, and much faster, to fly. Iberia runs regular flights from the UK to the international airports at Bilbao, Oviedo and Santiago de Compostela, while British Airways also flies to Bilbao.

Access from France is just as easy, as the main road and rail links between Paris and Madrid both cross the border at Irún, near San Sebastián, offering motorway driving the whole way, and plenty of trains and coaches. There are also several other crossing points in the western Pyrenees, where smaller roads wind across the mountain passes, providing infinitely more picturesque routes for those with cars and time to spare.

Documents

UK citizens can enter on a full passport or British Visitor's Passport, while their national identity card is sufficient for nationals of all other EEC countries. Visas are required by citizens of Australia, New Zealand and some other Commonwealth countries. USA nationals can enter the country for three months without a visa. Work permits are no longer required by EEC citizens, although other foreign nationals wishing to work here still need one.

Getting around

BY CAR

Anyone wanting to tour the area should take a car. There is plenty of public transport but it is slow and many of the most beautiful areas are remote and virtually impossible to reach unless you have unlimited time. If you wish to hire, Avis, Hertz and Europcar all have offices at Bilbao and Santiago airports, near the ferry port in Santander and in many of the major towns and will arrange to have a car to meet you if you book ahead through their central booking offices. Iberia offers some good fly/drive deals using the main national chains of Atesa and Dial Spania. You will need an International Driver's Licence unless your own licence is accompanied by an official translation, stamped by a Spanish consulate. Minimum driving age for foreigners is 18. Third Party Insurance is compulsory, but a Green Card (if you are driving your own car) will be far more use. As the Spaniards tend to imprison participants in an accident and then ask questions, it is also recommended that you get a Bail Bond. This and the Green Card are available from either the AA or RAC.

Driving is on the right and is easy on the whole, with good, uncrowded roads, recently improved by a massive programme of road building, widening and straightening. There are some stretches of motorway, but these are tolled and very expensive. Roads marked N (national routes radiating out from Madrid) or C (major regional roads) are good, fast and free, so use these instead. The area is very mountainous, some of the smallest roads are impassable in winter and even the best roads must climb the passes. Don't be too ambitious in setting your schedules.

Only in and around the major cities will you find the normal clutter of rush hour in narrow streets (four times a day, because of the siesta), but even this, if noisy, is not a real difficulty. Parking in the cities can be a problem, however.

Seat belts are compulsory outside built-up areas, as are crash helmets for anyone on a motorbike. You may not use full headlights in a built-up area but you must use dipped headlights on motorways no matter how well lit. Motorbikes must used dipped headlights even during the day. You should carry a spare set of bulbs and warning triangles with you. Speed limits are 60kph in built-up areas, and, out of town, 90kph on second category roads, 100kph on first category roads and 120kph on motorways, unless otherwise indicated. The drink-drive limit is low, with heavy penalties that can include the withdrawal of your driving licence. If you pay your fine on the spot, you get a 20 per cent discount. Be sure to get a receipt.

Fuel is no longer a government monopoly, but the prices are still regulated and there is little variation between different companies. Petrol comes in two grades, Regular and Super. At the time of writing, it costs about 92 ptas per litre. Most foreign cars run on Super. Unleaded and diesel are both easily obtainable. Garages are few and far between and it is illegal to carry jerry cans of fuel in your car, so it is important to keep filled up, especially once you are outside the major towns.

BY RAIL

A look at a map will show a good rail network fanning out across this area, but as with all Spanish transport, things are not as easy as they seem. For a start, there are two guages and two companies. RENFE runs the wide-guage lines that carry the major routes south, while FEVE runs the narrow-guage trains along the coast and all suburban lines. To complicate matters further, they usually run from different stations, often with a great chunk of city between them. Local maps usually mark the different stations, but will often neglect to tell you to which company they belong. You cannot get RENFE information from a FEVE station and vice versa and FEVE stations will often be able to give you only local information, so pre-planning becomes a nightmare. Trains, except for commuter services into main cities, are also infrequent, from one a day on some of the major links, to one every couple of hours on regional lines.

RENFE offer a series of 8-, 15- and 22-day Tourist Cards, from £65 for eight days in second class, purchasable only by non-residents outside the country (available in the UK from Victoria Station, Thomas Cook and Wasteels Travel Agencies). These are wonderful if you are planning to include the north in a much wider journey, but they are not usable on FEVE trains for those concentrating on this area. There are no FEVE passes, but prices are reasonable. Young people's Interail cards are usable on all trains, but the Interail card for those over 26 is not valid in Spain. A supplement on RENFE and Interail passes will have to be paid on express trains and for overnight accommodation on sleepers. (There is a great difference in comfort and cost between a couchette (*literas*), a bed (*coche-cama*), and a tourist-class bed when booking a sleeper, so make sure you use the right word.)

BY BUS

Buses provide the best network of public transport across the region with regular services between major towns and several every day to all but the smallest villages. They are all clean, comfortable, uncrowded and efficient and the drivers all carry a plentiful supply of plastic bags for those that can't cope with the twisty mountain roads. Luxury coaches have lacy curtains and a video machine playing elderly British and American films dubbed into Spanish – and charge you some 50 per cent more for these privileges. They are not recommended.

The biggest problem with the buses is finding them. The system is completely deregulated with numerous different companies. Santander is a shining example, however – its smart new station has clearly labelled bays and proper information boards. In the other major towns, different companies use different stations (again unmarked), or, if they are in one building, there is rarely a combined timetable or information office and you have to queue at the different windows of each company, first of all to get the information and then to get your ticket. Several different companies will run services along the major routes, with prices that vary by as much as 75 per cent and nothing to tell you, until you reach the top of the queue who is running the next departure. All in all, catching a bus is a very slow process and it is worth buying your ticket ahead of schedule.

In the small towns and villages the bus traveller's life gets even more interesting as there is nothing to tell you where the bus stop is, let alone where and when the buses go. The few times I have been given definite information by the local tourist office it has always been wrong. The bus stop is usually a local bar, so ask around until you find the right one and even then, don't rely on the information given to you by the barman. He probably doesn't know and will pull figures out of the air. Ask everyone you meet and take a consensus. If possible, ask the driver of another bus.

UNDER YOUR OWN STEAM

Cycling is very popular in this area, but mostly amongst the ultra-fit, with racing bikes, cycle shorts and aero-dynamic helmets. If you wish to go cycle-touring, remember that you will spend a good part of your time on roads as steep as those you find in the Alps.

Hitchhiking is possible, but follows the same rules as elsewhere in Europe. Women shouldn't hitch alone and hitching on the motorways is forbidden.

BY BOAT

For those who prefer to travel by boat, the coast is well stocked with marinas. A brochure listing their facilities, *Instalaciones Nauticas en Guipuzcoa, Vizcaya, Cantabria y Asturias*, is available from the Spanish Tourist Office, as is the more detailed *Guide to Yacht Clubs and Marinas in Spain*, of which Volume IV deals with the north coast. Galicia is covered separately.

When to go

Weather

Because of the Atlantic, the climate along this coast and in the mountains is totally different to that of the rest of Spain. You certainly can't rely on the sun, and will inevitably experience some rain and grey days, even in midsummer. I have found that these are generally outnumbered by those with glorious sunshine and blue skies, although it is almost always a bit hazy. The temperature seems to hover through the summer in the high 20s centigrade, very occasionally shifting into the 30s and even 40s away from the mountains. The winters are grey, damp and mild, with occasional violent storms, whilst up in the mountains, heavy snow can cut off the passes for months on end.

Once over the mountains there is a dramatic and instant shift to the harsher weather of the Castillian plateau, marked by a very visible shift in the vegetation from dairy pastures to vineyards. Here, there is little rain, the summer sun is ferocious and the winter bitter.

There is a fledgling ski industry, but for general tourism, the area is good at any time between late April and early October. Relatively few British travellers come here, but it is very popular amongst the Spanish and French. The Spaniards have their holiday from mid-July to mid-August, while the French are on holiday through August. Advance booking is crucial during this period. At other times, it is reasonably easy to find hotel rooms, although the paradors are almost always full.

WEATHER CHART

The following chart gives average monthly temperatures and rainfalls for La Coruña and Santander. Both cities are on the coast. Weather conditions in the mountains are very different, particularly in winter.

La Coruña			Santander		
Temperature		Rainfall	Temperature		Rainfall
Max	Min		Max	Min	
F/C	F/C	In/mm	F/C	F/C	In/mm
J 55/13	45/7	4.7/118	53/12	44/7	4.7/119
F 55/13	44/7	3.2/80	54/12	44/7	3.5/88
M 59/15	47/8	3.6/92	58/14	47/8	3.1/78
A 61/16	48/9	2.6/67	60/15	49/10	3.3/83
M 64/18	51/11	2.1/54	62/17	53/11	3.5/89
J 68/20	55/13	1.8/45	68/20	58/14	2.5/63
J 71/22	58/15	1.1/28	71/22	61/16	2.1/54
A 73/23	59/15	1.8/46	72/22	62/16	3.3/84
S 71/22	57/14	2.4/61	70/21	59/15	4.5/114
O 66/19	53/12	3.4/87	65/18	54/12	5.2/133
N 60/15	49/9	4.9/124	59/15	49/10	4.9/125
D 56/13	46/8	5.3/135	55/13	46/8	6.3/159

FIESTAS

There are literally hundreds of fiestas from Easter onwards and you would have to work hard to miss them all. The two biggest in the region are the Fiesta of San Fermín in Pamplona (made world-famous by Hemingway) which is in the first two weeks of July and the Festival of Santiago (St James the Apostle) on 25 July. He is the patron saint of Spain and this is a national holiday, the focal point for many local fiestas. The biggest by a long way is the two-week celebration leading up to the feast day itself in Santiago de Compostela.

TIME

Winter time is GMT + 1. Summer time is GMT + 2. The clocks change on the last Sundays of March and September.

Money

The currency is the *peseta*, divided into 100 *centimos*, although these are rarely used now.

Inflation is officially tagged at 6 per cent at the time of writing, but tourist inflation has been running much higher since Spain joined the EEC, with massive rises in hotel and restaurant prices, to bring the region into line with the rest of western Europe. For some reason, the north is also more expensive than southern Spain, and there are none of the cut-price packages which are the hallmark of the south.

There are three tiers of IVA (VAT). Items such as books, medicines, etc are at 6 per cent; the standard rate is 13 per cent (this includes most hotels and restaurants); and the luxury tax (which includes the more upmarket establishments) is 28 per cent. It is never included in the marked price. A service charge is automatically included in restaurant prices, although not shown as a separate item on the bill. Tipping is normally 10%. A small tip is usually expected for bar service.

Eurocheques are the easiest way to take money to Spain, as you can use them like ordinary cheques. You will need to produce your passport as well as the cheque card for ID. There are plenty of cash machines that will take the cheque card as long as you remember your pin number. Travellers' cheques are also widely accepted, as are all major credit cards. The only exception is at garages, where you must pay cash. It can be difficult to change large denomination notes.

There are no currency restrictions, but foreigners may be asked to prove that they brought the money into the country before exporting, especially if large amounts are involved.

Clothing

Smart casual is the norm. The Spaniards are very fashion-conscious, and expect a reasonable standard of dress as a matter of courtesy. They are not formal however – even some casinos no longer require a tie, although they won't accept jeans or trainers. A few of the churches still forbid sleeveless tops and shorts, but none ask women to cover their heads any more. Topless sunbathing is rare but perfectly acceptable on the beaches, but men and women are expected to be properly dressed in town.

Cottons and polycottons are the best option for the summer, with a sweater for the grey days and the mountains, a jacket for the evenings, a hat for the mid-day sun and either a lightweight raincoat or an umbrella for downpours. If you are planning to go walking in the Picos de Europa, you should take lightweight hiking boots or shoes with a good grip and ankle support. It is possible to manage the easier trails in sandals, but it is very tiring to do so.

Laundry and dry-cleaning services are slow and there are very few launderettes, so be prepared to wash things yourself and rig up a line in your room. Take crush-resistant fabrics or a travel iron.

Accommodation

At the top end of the market, there are four- or five-star 'business' hotels in all the main industrial cities, of a similar quality and cost to business hotels the world over, while most of the major cities have at least one glamorous five-star hotel. Those in León and Santiago de Compostela are particularly worth mentioning. Both were originally pilgrim hospitals built by Ferdinand and Isabella and are magnificent buildings that are tourist sights in their own right. Both are part of the parador chain.

By far the most popular hotels amongst tourists are the paradors, of which there are a good sprinkling across the region. Many people actually organise their tour around the locations of the paradors. Started under Franco, they are government-owned hotels, usually three-star, which were designed originally to bring tourism to new areas. This means that although many of the major tourist cities do have one, there are exceptions, such as Burgos and Pamplona. Some are new buildings, but the majority are converted castles, palaces and even monasteries, often in spectacular settings. Internally, they range from pleasant to stunning, but are always comfortable. If I have any complaints, they are perhaps that a uniformity of style has wiped out too many of the idiosyncracies of the original buildings, and that the quality of the food generally doesn't live up to the promise of the menus. Prices are moderate to expensive, with a single room supplement of up to 75 per cent. They are well used, so early booking is essential. Keytel International is the official UK booking organisation, and Brittany Ferries operate a sail/drive voucher system in conjunction with their Santander crossing.

Lower down the scale, there are a range of two-, one- and no-star hotels (H), residential hotels (HR), pensions (P) and fondas (F) (in descending order), ranging in price from inexpensive to moderate. The hotels are generally smarter, and are beginning to spruce themselves up to meet the standards elsewhere in Europe, but I have found very little difference between pensions and fondas. The star rating seemed arbitrary, depending more on size than on quality. These small places are littered throughout the towns and villages and the local tourist offices will be able to provide a comprehensive list and a map to help you find one. It is worth booking ahead if you plan to stay in high summer or over fiestas, but during the rest of the year, you should have little trouble in finding accommodation. Rooms are simple, with a shared bathroom in all but 2-star hotels and above, but have washbasins, a wardrobe, table or chest of drawers and are often in old, attractive buildings. They can be charming, with friendly owners, and only once did I find one which was not spotlessly clean.

Finally, if you run into trouble finding accommodation, or if you wish to stay with a family, look for the *casas particulares*, or rooms in private houses, which are generally very modestly priced. Again, the tourist offices can give you a list of landladies, and many of the pension owners have sources that they use regularly for the overflow.

All the cheaper places are quite happy for you to inspect the rooms before deciding whether to stay there. There are no problems about sharing a room with someone of the opposite sex, as long as they are registered, and many have rooms with three and even five beds for families or groups travelling together.

CAMPING

Campsites are plentiful and pleasant, particularly along the coast and in the mountains. These are also graded into four classes, with Luxury, first and second all taking caravans as well. Some also have self-catering bungalows on site. Camping outside the sites on public land is forbidden. The national tourist office publishes a map of campsites throughout the country, which also has a list with categories and phone numbers on the back. They are all well signposted but, as ever, those serving major towns are a little distance from the centre.

ELECTRICITY

The electricity supply is 220V/50 cycles in most places. Check, if in doubt. Plugs are two-pin, so you will need a travel adaptor.

Health and insurance

As Spain is a member of the EEC, British citizens are covered by the reciprocal health agreement and can get free health care in the country. Fill in Form E1.11, available from DSS offices and Post Offices. I would still recommend taking out full holiday insurance cover, however, to cover all other eventualities such as delays, lost luggage, theft or, in case of serious illness or accident, the cost of transport back home. This is available through any travel agent at a reasonable cost. Read the small print carefully as many policies exclude water sports, climbing, riding etc, and skiers will always need a special ski policy.

No vaccinations are required and the food and water are quite safe. A basic medical kit should include mosquito repellent, travel sickness tablets, a good sun block and after-sun cream as well as basics such as plasters and analgesics.

By law, one chemist in each town will stay open after hours. A notice giving the name and address of the duty chemist should be posted on the doors of all the other. If you have to call a doctor or visit a hospital, you will be expected to pay even at public establishments, unless you can produce Form E1.11. Make sure you get a receipt for all medical treatment to claim against insurance.

Security

If you don't look after your possessions properly there is a danger of theft, although it is not greater than anywhere else in Europe. Don't leave anything lying around, cars unlocked or luggage in the back of the car in full view. The safest handbags are those with zips and shoulder straps that can be slung diagonally, and it is advisable not to carry wallets in back pockets. If using travellers' cheques, keep the numbers separate from the cheques. Women may experience some hassle, but very much less than on the south coast, and it is generally good-natured. Just be sensible and remember that most of the big towns are ports, so don't wander into the rougher areas on your own at night.

There is an added security risk from the activities of the Basque Separatist Movement, ETA, in the Basque Country and the surrounding areas, but it is a minor one. You will see plenty of graffiti, and hear stories of bombs, but these are few and far between. Only a tiny handful of people are involved and they don't target tourists. You would have to be extremely unlucky to be caught up in an incident and shouldn't let the thought of it trouble you.

If you do run into trouble, or anything is stolen, you must report it to the police and get a copy of their report for the insurance claim. The police are generally very much better now although they are still trying to live down the terrible reputation they gained under Franco and you will find few Spaniards who have anything good to say about the Guardia Civil. Formed in 1844 to control banditry, the Guardia ran out of control, terrorising the people, until they were brought under civilian rule on Franco's death. They are still used as rural traffic police and are the main law enforcement body outside urban areas. In town, there are Municipal Police, who handle the day-to-day running of the place, while official guards, riot police etc belong to the Policia Nacional. In the Basque Country, these have been replaced by a regional Basque police force. Confused? So are they: one Basque woman complained to me that there was no law and order because none of these different forces knew precisely what their duties were, and they were all so jealous of each other that they spent their time squabbling between themselves instead of doing their jobs! As a rule of thumb, report anything in town to the Policia Municipal, while road accidents should be reported to the Guardia Civil. All policemen are heavily armed.

Communicating

Phoning

When phoning into Spain from abroad, the country code is 34. Regional codes are all prefixed by 9, but this should be dropped if phoning from abroad.

STD service is available throughout Spain and to most places in the world. When phoning abroad from Spain, dial 07 and wait for a high-pitched tone before dialling the country code, the local code (without the zero) and the number. If you wish to make a reverse charges call (cobro revertido), dial the international operator.

Hotel phones are most convenient, but are expensive, as they are allowed to charge up to 300 per cent of the standard rate. For a cheaper call, use a public phone marked conferencias urbanas, interurbanas y internacionales. Most public phones take 5, 25 and 50 peseta pieces which should be placed in the groove at the top of the box. Make sure you have a good supply of 50 pta coins if you are phoning abroad.

In major centres, there are cabinas telefónicas at the telephone company offices, in which the operator will dial the number for you and you pay once the call is complete.

International country codes:
Australia 61, Canada 1, Eire 353, France 33, UK 44, New Zealand 64, USA 1.

Post

A poste restante service (Lista de Correos) is available free of charge at all post offices. In larger towns you will need to specify a particular post office. Take your passport with you for identification when collecting mail. All post offices have external slots and there are plenty of boxes (yellow) for posting out of hours. Stamps are also available from larger hotels and tobacconists.

TELEGRAPH OFFICES
Usually within or attached to the post office. Larger ones may also have a public telex and/or fax machine. In major towns, the main telegraph office will sometimes stay open in the evenings, on Sundays and during fiestas.

Shopping

Although there is the normal array of department stores and familiar chain names in the cities, supermarkets are still rare, and those that there are tend to be small. Food shopping is still usually done every day or two days from small grocers and specialist shops – much more fun for the visitor. Everything is metricated. Food is sold in grams and kilos and drink in litres. (There is a metric conversion chart on page 258.) Food bought this way is very reasonably priced. Do remember not to buy too much at any one time unless you have access to a refrigerator as things will quickly deteriorate in summer.

Most good bookshops will have a few English language titles – usually an eclectic mixture of classics (school and university texts) and the more lurid potboilers. A few newsagents will stock foreign language newspapers and magazines, one or two days out of date and very expensive. There are no home-grown English-language publications in this region.

Shoes and leather (bags and jackets) are of a comparable price to those in UK High Street shops, but the quality for the price is often much better and these can be a good souvenir buy. Spanish women are generally smaller than those in northern Europe, so you may not find women's shoes beyond size 39.

There are some souvenir shops, although as this isn't a major tourist region, they tend not to line the streets as in the south. Most obvious are those in major pilgrimage centres, where the shelves are full of light-up plastic Virgins and other such delights. There is some attractive pottery, but on the whole souvenirs are of poor quality. If you want to bring something home, stick to food and drink. First-pressing olive oil, *chorizo*, cheese, and wine all make good presents.

Opening hours

The Spanish live on a different time-scale to northern Europe and the only way to survive is to adapt. In some of the major cities, some offices are trying to change to a 9–5 working day, amidst protests from workers, but elsewhere, the working day revolves around the *siesta*, a three-hour break to avoid working in the worst of the heat. Meals, in the evening, are also later than we are accustomed to: few Spaniards sit down to dinner until about ten (2200). Some establishments will shorten the siesta in winter, and close correspondingly earlier in the evenings.

Banks: October to April: 0830–1630, Monday to Thursday; 0830–1400, Friday; and 0830–1300 on Saturdays. June to September: 0830–1400, Monday to Friday only. Closed public holidays. There are often 24-hour exchange offices (*cambios*) at major points of entry.

Post offices: 0900–1400, Monday to Friday, and 0900–1300, Saturday. Closed Sundays and public holidays.

Restaurants: Breakfast 0730–1100; lunch 1300–1600; dinner 2100–2330.

Shops: varied, but roughly 0900–1300 and 1500–1930, Monday to Saturday. Many food shops open Sunday mornings, and major department stores stay open through the siesta. All towns will have a market – daily in large cities, weekly in small towns and villages. Ask the local tourist office where and when it is. These normally operate from around 0730 to 1400.

Monuments: 1000–1400 and 1600–1930. These times vary, so check for each individual site.

Public holidays

1 January (New Year's Day)
6 January (Twelfth Night)
Good Friday
Easter Sunday
1 May (Labour Day)
Corpus Christi (second Thursday after Whitsun)
24 June (Feast of St John)
29 June (Feast of St Peter and St Paul)
25 July (Feast of Saint James)
15 August (Feast of the Assumption)
12 October (Columbus Day)
1 November (All Saints' Day)
8 December (Feast of the Immaculate Conception)
25 December (Christmas Day)
Maundy Thursday and Christmas Eve are also sometimes taken as holidays. In addition, every region has up to four variable days to celebrate the feast of its local patron saint and other important occasions. If the feast day falls at a weekend, it will be turned into a long weekend.

Food and Drink

Food

The north-west has been called the gourmet centre of Spain, but either whoever christened it hadn't tasted good food, or the rest of the country is worse. This is not the place to go if you want to eat really well, especially if you are a vegetarian or don't eat fish. The range is limited and, on the whole, good ingredients are massacred. Having said that, if you are prepared to pay, you can usually expect one good course out of three. Stick to the sea-food where possible and you will fare better than most.

Tapas

These traditional bar snacks used to be offered free with drinks but are now generally expensive, and are not a good way to try and fill up if you are on a tight budget. It is better, for a light meal, to look for *raciones*, larger portions of the same types of things – calamares, sausage, cheese, prawns, omelette etc. They are simply and well prepared on the whole and a couple of these with some bread make a good, reasonably priced meal. Another snack alternative is the *bocadillo*, a chunk of baguette with a choice of fillings. I would suggest taking some picnic implements and buying your own ingredients, when possible. There is a good choice of sausages and cheeses, and wine and mineral water are plentiful. The shops are loaded with wonderful fruit in season, although for some odd reason, it never seems to get as far as the restaurants. The best meals I have had in Spain have all been picnics.

Restaurants

Restaurants are no longer cheap, but there are ways of cutting down the cost if necessary. The *menu del día* is usually very reasonably priced. At the lower end of the market, it will usually be a fish soup (*sopa de pescado*), which is good, beef (*ternera*) or hake (*merluza*) served with a small quantity of chips and tomato salad, which isn't, and *flan* (creme caramel) or icecream, plus a half bottle of wine. The *plato combinado* is a one-plate meal often with a bizarre mix of fish and meat and frequently topped by a fried egg.

To eat reasonably well, you should expect to pay up to twice as much as the cost of the menu del día, but even then you will not find great improvements in

A narrow backstreet in Potes, in Picos de Europa

quality or variety. The ambience too often leaves something to be desired. The Spanish socialise in bars and even the better restaurants are often tucked round the back in uncomfortable, dark, airless rooms. The British yen to eat outdoors is considered bizarre.

BEST OPTIONS

What to eat? Fish soups, or *entremeses* (a plate of mixed hors d'oeuvres – called 'hot and old entertainments' in my favourite menu translation) to start. If you feel starved of greenery, which you may do about a week after arriving, try the vegetable soups (*sopas de verdura*). As a main course, it is often difficult to avoid hake or beef, and virtually impossible to avoid the chips. On the coast, however, there is a wonderful array of different sea-foods, and if there are several of you, and you are feeling extravagant, try a *mariscera*, a vast, stunning array of mixed sea-food that includes crab, (ordinary, soft-shelled and spider), lobster and langoustine, clams, mussels and other shellfish, along with an array of white fish. The Atlantic coast is much less polluted than the Mediterranean and you are still relatively safe eating seafood. Deserts range from dull to dreadful, unless you enjoy *flan* or are happy with perpetual ice cream.

Specialities to look out for include: *bacalao* – salted, dried cod; white asparagus, in season; *chorizo* – a salami-style pork sausage; and *morcilla* – the local black pudding. *Jamón Serrano*, a slightly stronger flavoured version of parma ham, does not come solely from this region, but it is delicious. In season, suckling pig and lamb are on offer at a price, particularly in the Burgos area, while in the Picos de Europa, there is usually at least one game dish on the menu – wild boar, venison, or one of a variety of game birds.

TRADITIONAL REGIONAL DISHES

There are a wide variety of traditional dishes on offer, but the most common and most famous include:

chipirones en su tinta – squid cooked in its own ink (the only black dish in the world, according to proud locals)

caldo gallego – a simple, but delicious Galician soup of cabbage and potato

fabada – a mountain stew of butter beans with *chorizo*, *morcilla* and pigs' trotters

cocido – similar to *fabada*, but substitute chickpeas for the beans.

The cheese you will usually be offered is *manchego*, the Spanish equivalent of cheddar in all-purpose popularity, but the north, particularly in the mountains, is a dairy region, and there is a wide range of local speciality cheeses, many of which are delicious, if hard to find. The most famous is the pungent *cabrales* from the foothills of the Picos.

Finally, it is traditional on Sunday mornings to have *churros y chocolate* for breakfast. *Churros* are hooped strips of dough, deep fried in olive oil, and served with small cup of sickly strong hot chocolate, designed for dunking, not drinking.

Drink

In the sphere of drink the local specialities of the north-west really come into their own. The mountains of Cantabria and Asturias are cider (*sidra*) areas, with a variety of local brands, mostly very light, slightly sparkling and with a delayed kick. *Sidrerias* or cider bars are a whole sub-culture of the food and drink industry here, and have even produced their own, apple-based cuisine.

The higher slopes of the mountains are home to *Oruja*, a 'warming' liqueur designed for cold mountain nights. It stops you breathing on the first sip and knocks you out on the second and after that, it is rather difficult to tell what it tastes like. Another liqueur worth watching out for is the infinitely more pleasant Patxarán, distilled from blueberries, that is a speciality of the Basque regions.

Elsewhere, however, wine is paramount. No wine lover would visit the north-west without heading towards La Rioja, home of Spain's best and most famous wines. The region is particularly known for rich, Burgundy-style reds, (*tintos*), aged in oak casks which give them a distinctive vanilla flavour, but local *bodegas* are now also making lighter reds, (*claretes*), and a growing range of whites and rosés (*rosados*). Rioja wines, which are more alcoholic than the French ones, are normally drunk mature, but in the province itself, you can also buy the cheaper young wines. For more details, see the box on page 245.

Reading the wine label

All the better Spanish wines are divided into a series of 30 regions, each controlled by a *Consejo Regulador*. These industry watchdogs make sure the wine comes from the region it claims, and from recognised varieties of grapes. They also oversee every aspect of production and quality control, and only those wines which meet their rigorous standards can be labelled as *Denominación de Origen*. The better bottles will also be issued with individual numbers.

Wines are also split into different categories, dependent on their ageing process. The very best of the blue riband wines are labelled *Gran Reserva*. These have to be made from vintage years, and have been aged for at least three years in an oak cask and three years in the bottle. *Reserva* wines are not quite as good, but they come from specially selected harvests and must have been aged for a minimum of three years, at least one of which must have been in an oak cask. A wine from a vintage harvest that has not been aged in this way will be labelled *Cosecha*, followed by the date. A *Viño de Crianza* is a wine from the normal harvest which has been aged for three years, one of which is in an oak cask. A normal wine which has not been aged this way is labelled *viño del año*. *Contiene Varias Cosechas* (CVC) means that the bottle contains a wine blended from several different vintages.

If you specify which wine you would like, you can order Riojan wine everywhere in Spain, for a higher price, but outside Rioja the house wine will always be a local one. Galicia, Navarra and the Basque country are all wine-growing regions. Of these local wines, the one to look out for is Txacoli, the tannin-strong wine of the Basque Country, which grows on you while there, but, like Greek retsina, palls quickly once out of its native setting.

Beer (*cerveza*), the other common drink, is always lager.

History

c1,000–650 BC Greeks and Phoenecians founded trading colonies throughout the south and east of the peninsula, naming the original inhabitants Iberian. The Celts arrived in the north, bringing iron and the potter's wheel, and settled in Galicia.

241–219 BC The Punic Wars between Rome and Carthage (the Phoenecians) were fought across the Iberian Peninsula in a territorial struggle which Carthage lost, adding all the Phoenecian territory in North Africa and Iberia to the Roman Empire.

c200 BC-200 AD From the start of the second century BC, the peninsula, now called Hispania after a small hare unique to the area, officially came under Roman rule, and was divided into two provinces, Hispania Citerior (all territory east of the Iberus) and Hispania Ulterior. It actually took nearly 200 years to bring the entire area under Roman domination. By the first century AD, Romanisation was complete. Augustus Caesar re-organised the area into three provinces, Baetica in the south, Lusitania in the south-west, and Tarraconensis. Iberian troops were integrated into the army, and were granted full citizenship of Rome in return for their service. Most of the major towns on the peninsula were founded during this period.

In the north-west, the garrison at Legio (León) was reduced from three legions to one by 74 AD, as Roman law and order took over. Iberian gold and silver mines, many of them in Galicia and Asturias, were, by now, helping to fund the further expansion of the empire. However, a greater number of people in this area were allowed to retain their native names, traditions and family structures, as long as they submitted to Roman law, while the mountain peoples (in the Picos de Europa) remained contained but unconquered throughout the period. The visible influence of Rome on this area is therefore considerably smaller than in many other parts of the empire.

c200–400 The pressure of the Germanic tribes on Rome's northern boundaries coincided with the splintering of imperial authority in Rome itself, leaving the other provinces, Hispania among them, open to attack. North African tribes mounted a series of attacks on Baetica from 171 to 210, while from c260 to 297, there were several attacks on the east coast by the Franks.

In 284, Diocletian became emperor of Rome and, for a while, restored confidence and authority, strengthening both the economy and the provincial garrisons (the imposing town walls of Lugo date to this period).

In 312, Constantine adopted Christianity, which already had a strong hold on the Iberian peninsula, as the state religion. The first great ecclesiastical buildings began to appear while the aristocracy began to leave the cities for ever larger and more luxurious country estates. By the end of the century, the empire had split in two.

c400–700 In 409, a combined army of some 200,000 Huns, Vandals, Suebi and Alans under Visigothic leadership invaded Hispania across the western Pyrenees. The Vandals settled in Baetica for a while before moving on to north Africa. The Suebi took control of Galicia and started campaigning from this base against Lusitania and Baetica. Rome had to appeal to the Visigoths for assistance against these incursions in 415, 446 and 449. Only Tarraconensis was even theoretically still under Roman rule when the western empire officially ended in 476.

Hispania was now broken up. The eastern empire of Rome retained Cartagena, Malaga and the Balearic Islands as the province of Spania. Galicia remained under Suebi control until they were defeated by the Visigoths in 585. The Vascones, Cantabrians and Astures of the northern mountains remained independent, raiding Frankish and Visigothic lands on both sides of the Pyrenees. The rest of the peninsula became a province of the Visigothic empire until the Visigoths were defeated by the Franks in 507 AD and pushed back across the Pyrenees.

The towns continued to decline into small, heavily fortified settlements while the power of the churches continued to grow, with the bishops taking over much of the urban civil administration. Many of the now crumbling Roman buildings were torn down for re-use in building churches and monasteries. In 587, the Visigothic King Reccared converted to Christianity and this once more became the state religion, with the king ruling through a council of bishops.

c700–1266 In the Moorish Invasion of 711, a force of 7000 Berbers led by Tariq invaded the peninsula, landing at Gibraltar. He had been sent by Musa, North African governor of the Caliphate of Damascus, to help the sons of King Witiza, King Roderic's predecessor, recover the throne they felt was theirs by rights.

Roderic was an unpopular king whose army – made up almost entirely of conscripts and slaves, many of them Jews who had refused to convert to Christianity and had been enslaved as a result – was both unwilling and inefficient. By the time he faced the Moors near Medina Sidonia, on 19 July, 711, another 5000 Berbers had arrived to join the original force. Roderic was killed and his army routed. By 714, the Moorish occupation of the country was complete, with again, only the mountain dwellers of the north-west retaining their independence.

By the tenth century, many Berbers had intermarried, much of the population had converted to Islam, local languages and Arabic had replaced Latin and the last vestiges of the Roman lifestyle had disintegrated. Those Christians who refused to convert were allowed to continue with their own religion and laws in exchange for taxes. Many nevertheless chose a very Arabic lifestyle, becoming known as *mozarabs*. The Jews were also given freedom of worship and many now returned to the country. The Roman towns were rebuilt and others founded in a flurry of magnificent architecture, while a much wider range of crops was introduced, many of which are still farmed in Spain today.

Meanwhile, the Visigothic nobility had fled north to join the Cantabres and Astures in the mountain fastness of the Picos de Europa. From here, in 722, the tribal leader, Pelayo, who claimed descent from the Visigothic kings, won a resounding, if largely symbolic victory against the Moors at Covadonga and was proclaimed king of Asturias-León. Charlemagne followed his disastrous defeat at Roncesvalles in 778 by capturing Gerona in 785 and Barcelona in 801. A further Christian victory in 939 near Logroño settled the border between Christian and Islamic states along the line of the Duero and Ebro Rivers, and to the south of the Pyrenees, leaving the territory covered in detail by this book outside the Moorish state with which most people associate early medieval Spain.

Over the years, three major Christian power bases grew up along this line; Catalunya in the east, Aragón and Navarra in the centre, and Asturias-León to the west. By the mid 11th century a series of judicious alliances and marriages had brought Navarra to the fore with the rulers of the other Christian states paying homage to its king. A century later, the power base amongst the Christians had shifted again. In 1035, Sancho III of Navarra left his second son, Fernando, the country of Castilla. Fernando spread his territory east – taking León; west – to include Navarra; and south – exacting tribute from the reigning Muslim leaders. He split the territory amongst his sons, but after further fighting, the second son, Alfonso, gained supremacy as Alfonso VI of Castilla and León. For a brief moment, in 1085, he even captured Toledo, although he lost this again a year later.

By the late 11th century, in-fighting and the loss of the war loot from their northern raids had split the Moorish kingdom and they no longer had the strength or unity to repulse the Christians to the north. They called on assistance from north Africa, bringing in a new, but short-lived dynasty. By 1266, only Granada remained under Islamic rule. This was to remain in Islamic hands until 1492.

Alfonso's daughter, Urraca, succeeded to the throne of Castille and León in 1109, but on her death in 1126, the lands were again divided, leading to decades of civil war. In 1143, Urraca's nephew declared himself King Alfonso I of Portugal, but the boundary between Spain and Portugal was only finally agreed by Alfonso III of Portugal and Alfonso X of Castilla-León in 1267.

Meantime, Urraca's second husband, Alfonso I of Aragón, was fighting the Moors in the east, with the help of the Knights Templar, re-conquering Zaragoza and reaching far enough south to campaign in Andalusia in 1125 and 1126. In 1212, Alfonso VIII of Castilla, Pedro II of Aragón, and Sancho VII of Navarra finally joined forces and their combined armies, together with French troops and the military orders won a decisive victory at Las Navas de Tolosa. By 1266, only Granada was still Islamic. The rest of the peninsula was made up of four kingdoms of Portugal, Castilla-León, Navarra, and Aragón-Catalunya, all Christian, and their ruling families all closely related.

1266–1516 Portugal, its borders now defined, remained aloof from the territorial squabbling in the rest of the peninsula, and has retained its borders to this day.

The doorway of the 12–13th-century church of San Pedro de la Rua in Estella, Navarra

Although it came under Spanish influence again for a short time in the 17th century, it has also managed to hold onto its independence.

Navarra stayed within the French sphere of influence until it was conquered by Castilla in 1512.

Aragón-Catalunya became a loose, almost federal system of principalities, under the dynasty which had ruled here since 1137. With a series of kings who towed the line laid down by the egalitarian nobility, it remained stable until 1348, when

27

The pilgrim route to Santiago

When the tomb of St James (see page 202) was rediscovered in 813, it quickly became a site of pilgrimage, surrounded by tales of miracles and military victories. By the 11th century, Santiago had been declared a holy city, equal in stature to Rome or Jerusalem. By the 12th century it was drawing up to two million pilgrims a year.

Passenger ships landed pilgrims at Soulac in France or in Valencia or Catalunya, or took them straight to La Coruña, a stone's throw from their destination. There were four main land routes from France, starting in Paris, Vezelay, Le Puy and Arles, the first three joining together to cross the Pyrenees at Roncesvalles, while the fourth crossed further east at Somport and joined the main route at Puente La Reina in Navarra. A few followed the coast as far as Mondoñedo, in Galicia before turning inland, but the vast majority took the safer route to the south of the mountains through Burgos and León, the route still known today at the Camino de Santiago.

The pilgrims wore a heavy cape, sandals, a broad-brimmed felt hat turned up at the front with a scallop-shell, a small bag or scrip for their possessions and a long staff with a water gourd attached. The origin of the scallop as St James's symbol is confused. One version says that as the boat containing his body reached the shore, a man was riding along the beach. His horse took fright and plunged into the sea. When it reappeared, both horse and rider were covered in the shells. In the other version the pilgrim rider, the Lord of Pimentel, had to swim across a river and again came up covered in shells. The scallop-shell symbol is woven into the architecture of every church connected with the pilgrimage. It has even landed on the dinner table as the famous Coquilles St Jacques.

From the beginning of the 11th century, the Benedictines and Cistercians became so involved in the organisation of the route that it became known as the Camino Francés. They built roads, hospices, way stations, monasteries and hospitals to provide the pilgrims with food and water, rest and medical aid, as well as churches. Meanwhile, the Knights Templar and a special order of the Knights of Santiago marked and guarded the road.

The boom in religious building brought early Romanesque style south from France, refining it in such churches as San Martín de Frómista in Palencia and the Cathedral of Santiago itself. In 1130, a French monk from Poitou, Amerique Picaud, wrote a life of St James, the Liber Sancti Jacobi also known as the Codex Calictus. One of the books describes the people, customs, landscape and most famous sights to be found along the main routes, together with practical information for the would-be pilgrim.

By the mid-16th century, the Protestant break-away, the political map of Europe and the route's now appalling reputation for crime conspired to stem the flow of pilgrims to a trickle and shortly afterwards, with the loss of the relics, it stopped entirely until the late 19th century.

Today, the pilgrim route is again operating, although few follow it to the letter. Pilgrims still stop to have their 'passports' stamped at major churches en route, and, on the 25 July, patient queues in front of the Cathedral of Santiago, wait to touch their fingers to the worn prints in the pillars, and kiss the statue of St James.

---

devastating plague, closely followed by a series of dreadful harvests sent the economy into a tailspin. Castilla invaded in 1356, leading to ten years of war. In 1412 the dynasty collapsed and a junior branch of the Castillian royal family, the Trastámaras, were invited in to take the throne.

The power struggle continued, with Prince Carlos fighting his father, Juan II.

When Carlos died in the early 1460s, Catalunya offered itself to Enrique IV of Castilla. A decade of outright civil war followed from 1462, won eventually by Enrique's daughter, Isabel. In 1469, Juan II's son, Fernando II, married Isabel I of Castilla, and in 1472, they combined their kingdoms to create modern Spain. After Isabel's death, Fernando remained as regent over her lands for his grandson, Carlos, until his own death in 1516.

1516–1700 Carlos I was the son of Juana of Castilla and Philip of Burgundy and grandson of Fernando and Isabel. Not only had he inherited some 17 titles from his father, but he was also heir to the crown of the Holy Roman Empire. Brought up in the Burgundian court, he spoke only French and arrived in Spain following his coronation in 1515 surrounded by Flemish advisers – a less than popular move. He was still involved in negotiations with the Spanish nobility when news of his grandfather's death was followed closely by that of his own election as the new emperor, Charles V. He was crowned in Aachen on 23 October, 1520.

In 1523, Charles obtained the right to elect all bishops in the Hispanic kingdoms, including the New World. In 1525, he defeated his longstanding rival, Francis I of France, forcing him to relinquish his claims to Milan and Naples, the Duchy of Burgundy and several towns in northern France. Later the same year, he married Isabel of Portugal, sealing a strong alliance with his closest neighbour. Spain's domination of Europe was at its height.

The Brave New World In 1492, backed by Fernando and Isabel, Christopher Columbus sailed the ocean blue. Shortly afterwards, Hernán Cortes claimed Mexico for Castilla, while in 1521, Magalhaes claimed the Philippines for Spain. Ten years later, Francisco Pizarro claimed Peru. By 1540, one and a half million square kilometres of the Americas, together with Cuba and Santo Domingo in the Caribbean, were under permanent Spanish rule, producing vast quantities of gold and silver, together with spices, pearls, sugar and indigo. From 1560 onwards, regular convoys travelled between the East Indies, Central America and Sevilla. Over the next century, the riches flowing east from the colonies continued to mount, turning Spain into the wealthiest state in Europe, as well as one of the most influential.

The administration involved in this vast colonial enterprise was a formidable affair and changed the face of both bureaucracy and education as some 32 new universities were founded to create a new class of professional civil servants. These, in turn, led to a massive growth of literacy and sparked off a new age of magnificent literary and artistic achievement best known in the works of writers such as Cervantes and de la Vega, the architecture of many of Spain's great cathedrals, and the paintings of El Greco, Murillo and Velázquez.

A Chaotic Old World In Europe, chaos continued with a constant succession of wars and rebellions. Spain's huge, permanent and very expensive army drained away most of its new found colonial wealth, but even this was not enough. Spain had grown too big, too unwieldy and too threatening. The rest of Europe was suspicious of her power. In 1588 came the famous defeat of the Armada launched against England, while, from 1618 onwards, there was almost constant war with

France. The Dutch managed to win their independence and Catalunya, Aragón, Naples and Sicily all rebelled. In 1655, Britain and France joined forces with Portugal against Spain. In 1659, a negotiated treaty with France, that included the marriage of Louis XIV to Felipe IV's daughter, Maria Theresa, lost many of Castilla's French territories. In 1668, Portugal finally gained full recognition of its independence.

On top of this, the 17th century was marked by a series of devastating plagues and droughts that wiped out nearly a third of the population of the peninsula, while Felipe III, in yet another effort to distract people from the disasters at home, expelled some quarter of a million *moriscos*, leaving vast areas of the country with no one to work the land. Desperate kings sold favours and titles, in an attempt to hold onto power, but only succeeded in creating a nobility too powerful for their successors to contain.

1700–1789 Shortly before he died, childless, in 1700, Carlos II named the French Philip of Anjou as his heir, supported by the Castillian Council of State and France. Civil war erupted, sparked by the rival claims of Archduke Charles of Hapsburg, brother of Emperor Joseph. In 1702, the United Provinces and Britain declared war on France in support of Charles' claim. The War of the Spanish Succession lasted until 1714, when Charles succeeded his brother as Emperor and Philip, now Felipe V, the first of the Bourbon kings, was finally allowed to take his throne on condition that he gave up any rights to that of France. At a peace conference at Utrecht in 1713, to which Spain was not even invited, she was stripped of the Netherlands, Naples, Milan, Sardinia, Tuscany, Mantua, and Sicily. England took Gibraltar and Minorca (leading to claims for Gibraltar's return that are still a bone of contention today).

Although Spain had been ruled as an entity for some time, it was Felipe V who finally turned it into one nation, stripping Aragón and Valencia of their regional charters in 1707, Mallorca in 1715 and Catalunya in 1716. Only Navarra and the Basque Country retained any degree of autonomy. The different provinces were all given Castillian law and a military governor and chief justice appointed by the crown. In 1749, Carlos III extended this system to the colonies.

By this time, however, the colonies were no longer so dependent on imports from mainland Spain and the Spanish trans-Atlantic monopoly had been broken both by the English and a large number of 'independent' vessels. Spain's defeat in the Seven Years War, which ended in 1763, lost her Florida and all territory east of the Mississippi River, and some territory in Honduras. Twenty years later, she managed to regain West Florida and Menorca and to pin down British interests in what is now Belize, but she had failed to obtain a firm decision about her claim to the Malvinas (Falklands) and Gibraltar remained in British hands. The golden age of Spanish imperialism was at an end.

In Spain itself, state control over the price of wheat was abolished in 1765 and hoarding and uncontrolled price rises led to severe riots in March 1766. The government used the Jesuits as a scapegoat, and took the opportunity to expel this uncomfortably powerful sect.

1789–1868 In 1789 came revolution in France. Carlos IV, believing that he had the support of his nobles and would be facing a weak and disorganised enemy, went to the aid of his royal relations. By 1795, he had learned better, and several Spanish towns were under French control. Carlos was forced to sue for peace, and had to concede the Spanish section of the island of Santo Domingo. As soon as Spain signed the treaty with France, Britain declared war on Spain. Spain lost Trinidad in 1797 and the naval battles of Cape San Vicente the same year and Trafalgar in 1805 finished her as a sea power. Between 1801 and 1802, Spain added to the confusion by declaring war on Portugal.

In 1807, Napoleon and Carlos agreed that they should invade Portugal together, an action which would necessitate French soldiers crossing Spanish territory. The French troops arrived, under Marshal Murat, but instead of passing through, garrisoned several major towns. Carlos was forced to renounce his right to the throne and in July, 1808, Napoleon declared his own brother as King José I of Spain. The people rose against the French invaders and five years of bitter fighting began. The Duke of Wellington led an expeditionary army that came to include Spanish, Portuguese, German and Dutch as well as the British, against Napoleon's forces, while the peasants banded together in guerrilla groups. It was 1813 before a decisive victory at the Battle of Vitoria broke Napoleon's hold on Spain, King José retreated back to France and the Peninsula Wars came to an end.

Many Spanish cities were left without leadership as the occupying forces retreated, in some cases taking the pro-French nobility with them. Local councils grew up to fill the gaps, banding together to form a Junta Suprema Central which eventually found its home in Cadiz. Under the presidency of the Count of Floridablanca, the junta set up an interim government. In 1812, this drew up a constitution that allowed the king executive power, but also laid down the foundations for an elected parliament. In December 1813, Napoleon agreed to give the throne back to the Bourbons and Fernando VII returned triumphantly to his kingdom. Fernando, a firm believer in absolute monarchy, declared the new constitution null and void as soon as he returned, reinstituting the Inquisition and conducting an increasingly tyrannical witch-hunt that lasted for 20 years. With French assistance, he finally regained his absolute authority within the peninsula, but was unable to do the same with the colonies, which finally broke away as independent states in December 1824.

In 1830, Fernando had his first child – a girl, the Infanta Isabel. Earlier that same year, he had endorsed the French Salic Law that forbade the succession to a woman. He now tried to change his mind, but his brother, Don Carlos, refused to accept Isabel's right to the throne. When Fernando died in 1833, his widow, María Christina, took the throne as regent on her daughter's behalf, while the officers of the Royalist Volunteers, an army of 120,000 men, threw their support behind Carlos. Civil war broke out. The army, the state administration and most of the people backed Isabel's claim, but even so the war was protracted, with the Carlists resorting to guerrilla action. It was 1839 by the time María Christina finally won, but the issue did not die. Even today, there is still an active Carlist movement in Spain.

Meanwhile, the industrial revolution was gathering momentum, in Spain as in the rest of Europe, with the introduction of a mail service, the telegraph, and, most importantly, the railways. Coal and steel began to rival agriculture as wealth creators and a whole new social structure was being forced on the country by the new breed of industrial rich.

In order to finance her large army, María Christina had to accept the liberal banner and a whole series of reforms. A parliamentary system was brought in with the Crown as chief executive, a senate appointed by the monarch and an elected congress representing the people, although fewer than six per cent of the population were given the vote. The feudal system of land tenure gave way to the open buying and selling of land, and hiring and firing of labour. Shortly afterwards, a royal decree disentailed church and municipal land and relieved the nobility of the burden of showing their title deeds. The idea was that this would free land for smallholders, but in practice, it resulted in the creation of even larger estates. The peasants were, on the whole, in a worse position than ever.

The military began to take over many of the functions of state until it had a grasp on virtually every aspect of the country's administration. In 1844, a new force was created to deal with the property laws. This was la *benemérita guardia civil* which, although it was envisaged initially as a police force, responsible to parliament, soon became a paramilitary wing of the army. As it grew, from 5500 on its creation, to nearly 20,000 by the turn of the century, it took more and more responsibility upon itself, hated and feared by the people for the brutal methods it used. In many ways, it was the *guardia* which was responsible for putting Franco into power and keeping him there and, even today, with its power severely curtailed, it is still regarded with deep mistrust by the large majority of the Spanish people.

1868–1936 On 29 September 1868, a military coup ousted Isabel II, who fled the country. General Francisco Serrano took her place as regent to an empty throne. In 1870, General Juan Prim y Prats offered the crown to a new king, Amadeo I, from Savoy. Amadeo struggled on for three years, but all real power was still in the hands of the military and in 1873, he too abdicated. In 1874, republican government was tried, but with rebellions by the Carlists, the Cubans and in Cartagena, this also failed. In September, Isabel's son, a military cadet, was called to the throne as Alfonso XII. A civilian government with a two tier parliament was reinstated and a new constitution signed in 1876.

The Labour Movement In 1900, the population was 18.5 million. By 1930, it was 23.5 million. More and more people drifted off the land, creating a whole new class of urban labourers ripe for the teachings of Marx, the French Socialists and the anarchist, Bakunin. The city streets began to ring to the sound of marches, strikes, and riots.

The Socialists gained their first parliamentary seat in 1910. Although unions had been legal since 1887, it was 1911 before they grew their teeth, with the creation of the Confederación Nacional del Trabajo, which was joined in 1919 by the Federación Nacional de Agricultura. The CNT remained the largest single voice in workers' politics until 1936.

From 1912 onwards, Spain was involved in a war in Morocco. It stayed neutral during the early years of World War I, however, selling to both sides and booming economically until the German blockade of the North Atlantic took hold in 1917, when recession set in almost overnight. As the economy reached its lowest ebb, news arrived of the Russian revolution. The unions, the military, left wing politicians and the industrialists joined forces to dissolve the Cortes. A general strike followed, the first of a series of crises to hit the country as political viewpoints polarised, and riots, strikes and assassinations rocked the cities.

Towards the Civil War In July, 1923, a disastrous defeat in Morocco led to the massacre of nearly 21,000 Spanish troops. On 13 September, with the support of King Alfonso XIII, Don Miguel Primo de Rivera, the Captain General of Catalunya, declared himself head of a military directorate. By 1926, he too was in trouble. In 1929, the socialists broke off the coalition, and in 1930, Rivera resigned. In 1931, after a strongly republican vote in the municipal elections, Alfonso XIII abdicated and fled the country.

A republic was declared, with Don Niceto Alcalá-Zamora as President of the Provisional Government. In May, the church came out in opposition to the republic and the Monarchists began to work openly towards restoring Alfonso as king. The republican backlash was violent, with riots in the streets and churches burned. When the government announced plans to secularise all schools and cemeteries, legalise divorce, ban religious fiestas, withdraw state financing from the church and expel the Jesuits, relations deteriorated to the point of no return. In October, the government collapsed and a new minority government took over, led by Azaña. In August, 1932, General Sanjurjo led a failed coup attempt.

Strikes rose to record levels and as the republican government relied more and more heavily on emergency powers, the workers turned towards hardline revolutionary ideals.

By November 1933, a new, popular right wing organisation, the Confederación Española de Derechas Autónomas (CEDA), had grown up amongst the landowners, Carlists, monarchists, industrialist and the church. In October, 1934, it looked as if CEDA was going to form the new government, sparking a new wave of strikes and riots. When the Asturian miners took up arms, the army, under the leadership of Don Francisco Franco, brutally crushed the rebellion.

1936–1939 The Asturian rebellion finally forced the left and centre to work together. A wide-ranging, left-wing alliance, the Popular Front, fought the elections of January, 1936, winning an overall majority to form an all-Republican government, with Azaña at its head.

Civil War Violence mounted, with fatalities on both sides. On 13 July, a group of Republican police officers killed the leader of the opposition, Don José Calvo Sotelo, in revenge for the death of one of their comrades. A group of young army officers in Morocco, led by General Sanjurjo, used Sotelo's death as the trigger for the coup they had been planning. On the 17 July, they called for an uprising, claiming to be stepping in to restore law and order and, eventually, the monarchy.

Germany and Italy provided ships and air cover to ferry the colonial army back to the mainland. The Nationalists moved swiftly northwards, heading for Madrid and a five-month-long battle to control the capital. The Republicans received foreign aid only from Russia, while the French and British stood aside and watched. The communist movements and intellectuals in other countries rallied however and by October, the first of the volunteer International Brigades arrived in Spain. Some 35,000 foreigners fought for the Republicans until the Brigades were disbanded in 1938.

The Carlists were firmly behind the Nationalists from the beginning. By August 1936, they controlled about a third of the country. In November 1936, Italy, Germany and Portugal recognised the Nationalists as the official government of Spain and offered arms, finance and troops. The Nationalists also had troops from north Africa and their own foreign volunteers. The monarchists were persuaded to

Franco

Born in 1892 in El Ferrol, Galicia, Don Francisco Franco y Bahamonde was one of four children of a free-thinking naval supply officer and a devoutly Catholic mother. At the age of 14, he was sent to school at the Military College in Toledo, where he had an undistinguished career, but was instilled with a deep love of duty, Spain and the empire. In 1912, he went to Morocco to fight in the increasingly bitter civil war. Said to be utterly fearless in battle, and surviving against all odds when badly wounded in the stomach, both his reputation and rank rose rapidly. By 1926, he was a Brigadier-General, the youngest in Europe since Napoleon. Following a spell as Director of the Military Academy in Zaragoza, in 1934, he was called in to break up the Asturian miners' strike, a task he accomplished with breathtaking efficiency, at the cost of some 2000 lives. Shortly after this, the nervous Republican government effectively exiled him to the Canary Islands.

Initially undecided about the coup, he only committed himself at the last minute and was still in the Canaries when the Nationalists rebelled in July 1936. He had a complicated journey home, calling in the Germans for the first military airlift in history to get himself and his army into mainland Spain. From the start, he controlled the whole professional army, but on 1 October, at Burgos, he was declared

Commander-in-Chief of all the Nationalist Forces. In January 1938, he declared himself the Head of State of all Spain, with the honorific title of *El Caudillo de Dios*, literally the 'appointed of God'.

A strong admirer of both Hitler and Mussolini, he offered to take Spain into the War on the Axis side in exchange for land in Africa on which to rebuild the Spanish empire, but was humiliatingly snubbed by Hitler. In spite of this, in 1941, he sent a division of 47,000 men to fight alongside the Germans. Meantime, he was also tightening his grasp on Spain. Over half a million Republican supporters were put into concentration camps, where an estimated 200,000 were massacred. He kept detailed files on any liberals, atheists and communists and was so anti the Freemasons that he built himself a replica Masonic Lodge as a constant reminder of the evil to be stamped out.

In 1942, he revived the Cortes (parliament) but reserved for himself a veto over its decisions. In 1947, the Cortes voted to declare Spain a kingdom, with Franco as Regent for life. He remained an outright dictator until his death on 20 November, 1975, after an illness lasting nearly 18 months. To the end, he remained convinced that he really had been sent by God to save Spain and be the Father of the Spanish people.

delay the restoration until the war was over, and the church, everywhere but the Basque Country and Catalunya, happily gave them its support.

From the start, General Franco was in charge of the main professional army. On 1 October, 1936, he was given full military command. On 17 April, 1937, Franco's brother-in-law, Serrano Súñer, announced the formation of a single, civilian umbrella group covering all the different Nationalist interests, the Falange Española Tradicionalista y de las Juntas Ofensivas Nacional Sindicalistas – the Falangists.

The Republicans were split by too many different issues, as each faction fought for its private goals. By the time they finally organised themselves into a unified force it was almost too late. By mid 1938, the Nationalists had broken through, cutting Catalunya off from other Republican areas. In September, Russia withdrew her support from the Republicans at the same time as Germany was increasing hers for the Nationalists. In January 1939, Barcelona fell. A month later, Britain and France recognised the Nationalists as the sole and legitimate government of Spain. When Madrid finally fell towards the end of March, the war was over and Franco was in control of the country.

1939–1975 Franco became head of state, with absolute authority. He ran the country on military lines. Any person or area which had supported the Republicans was severely punished, with many being shot and others sent to labour camps. All educational materials were revised while some 6000 teachers were shot and another 7000 imprisoned. Those artists and intellectuals who did not choose to leave were forced into exile. The press was brought under state control and heavy censorship imposed, while witch-hunts for 'reds' also wiped out almost all the Jews and Freemasons in the country.

Upper-class education was handed back to the church, while divorce was declared illegal and religious marriage made compulsory. A privatised, corporate system was introduced in industry with *sindicatos*, one for each major branch of the economy, replacing the unions, with supervised collective bargaining and, of course, no strikes.

At the beginning of World War II, Franco declared a policy of non-belligerence, later amended, to coincide with the start of the Allied North African campaign and the entry of the United States into the war, to a 'benevolent' neutrality which allowed the allies to use bases on Spanish soil.

From 1942 onwards, opposition to Franco began to gather around Alfonso XIII's son, Don Juan de Borbón. Franco held it off through the war years, but in 1946, international pressure was added. In March, he closed the French border, and in December, the newly formed United Nations passed an anti-Franco resolution, cutting off diplomatic links with Spain. On 26 July, 1947, Franco held a plebiscite, and as a result, declared Spain a kingdom with himself as 'Regent' for life. It worked. In March, 1948, the French border was reopened, and in August, Don Juan sent his son, Juan Carlos, to school in Spain, to be brought up as Franco's successor. In 1953, the United States and the Vatican both signed treaties with Spain, and in 1955, Spain became a full member of the UN and the 1946 resolution was rescinded. Franco finally had international credibility, and access to the financial aid he needed.

35

Main architectural styles of Northern Spain

Pre-Romanesque/Visigothic 7th-9th centuries. The best surviving churches, clustered around Oviedo, are small hall churches, without transepts, built from roughly hewn stone without mortar. Inside a profusion of high, narrow rounded arches, are set on heavy columns. The decorative work is often sophisticated.

Mozarabic 10th century. The Mozarabs were Christians who fled north from the Moors, but had soaked up some elements of Moorish design. Mozarabic churches can be found mainly in Castilla-y-León. The outstanding features are the horseshoe arch, external gallery, and square, open-arched belfry towers often built of brick.

Romanesque 11th and 12th centuries. The pilgrim route to Santiago de Compostela was largely responsible for bringing the Romanesque style to northern Spain. The churches vary from minute hermitages to cathedrals; the style is fairly simple, solid and elegant, in the form of a Latin cross, with three aisles, transept arms and three apsidal chapels. Rounded arches are used, with barrel vaulting in the nave and oven vaulting in the apsidal chapels. Earlier churches use dog tooth decoration on the arches and elaborate geometric designs on the capitals, while later design introduces sculpture with fabulous beasts, scenes from everyday life and Biblical stories.

Mudéjar 11th–15th centuries. As the Reconquista began to take hold many Arab craftsmen remained and turned their attentions to building for the new lords. This is best seen in the ornamentation, particularly the elaborate, geometric stuccowork that graces a few ceilings, such as the Gothic cloister at the Convent of Las Huelgas Reales, in Burgos.

Gothic 13th–15th centuries. Brought south by the monastic orders, the Gothic style is recognisable immediately by the use of the pointed arch, the pointed spire, and in later churches, the flying buttress. The decoration of capitals continued, but the pillars themselves were carved into ribs, while the vaults were covered with ribs, stars and bosses. To the north, the emphasis was on height, and light, with slim columns holding up huge expanses of stained glass. However, the Spaniards generally favoured a heavier, more solid style, with the length of the nave broken by choir screens and chapels. Outside, almost every available inch was decorated.

Plateresque 16th century. This peculiarly Spanish style marked the beginning of the Renaissance, with its neo-classical forms, and uses the flat-fronted building as a canvas on which to carve immensely ornate, but delicate designs, incorporating Italian-style friezes and medallions. It takes its name from its similarity to the filigree work of silversmiths.

Baroque 17th-18th centuries. Although still based on the simple, square forms of neo-classical design, the decoration began to get more elaborate. On the whole the best of the Baroque is found in paintings, choir stalls and massive gilded retables. Human figures are larger than life, while the surrounding ornamentation includes twisting barley sugar columns, vine and floral wreaths. The even more flamboyant work of the 18th-century Churriguera family gave its name to the *Churrigueresque* style.

It was a time of famine and feast, with nearly 20 years of intense poverty followed by a boom in the 1960s. By the early 1970s, however, things were going wrong again, with high urban unemployment, and galloping inflation. The international oil crisis brought Spain to its economic knees and political opposition was again growing in strength with the Basque and Catalan separatist movements resorting to violence, an increasing number of industrial strikes and even the Catholic Church distancing itself from Franco. Franco died on 20 November, 1975, leaving Spain in chaos.

1975–1992 On 22 November 1975, Juan Carlos was declared King of Spain. He had kept very quiet over the preceding years and was now walking a political tightrope, but Franco himself had named him as his successor, so he was inevitably associated with the Falangists. He immediately set about reforming the country.

In July, 1976, he appointed Adolfo Suárez as Prime Minister. In November, the Political Reform Act disbanded the last Francoist Assembly, and in December, a huge majority backed the reforms in a referendum. A Royal Decree in March 1977, called for a June general election, which was won by the centre left. In April 1977, Juan Carlos's father, Don Juan, officially gave up his right to the throne, and in 1978, the Carlist Pretender, Carlos Hugo de Borbón-Parma, also came to terms with the new order. A new constitution was drawn up in 1978. Spain joined NATO in 1982, and the EEC in 1986.

There have been problems along the way, with coup attempts in 1978 and 1981, both led by Colonel Tejero. The Basque Nationalists in particular have continued their campaign of violence, although their influence and activities have died down considerably since the introduction of regional autonomy. On the whole, however, Spain has entered a new era of stable, democratic government, with an improving economy and liberal lifestyle.

Spain Today

Geography

Spain, the third largest country in Europe, (after France and European Russia), covers an area of 581,000 square kilometres, and takes in most of the Iberian peninsula, the Balearic Islands and the more distant Canary Islands, off the African coast. It has a coastline nearly 4000km long, split between the Atlantic and Mediterranean, and hangs below the rest of Europe, attached by an isthmus only 440km wide, along which runs the Pyrenees, one of the highest and most inaccessible mountain ranges in Europe. This, together with the fact that it is separated from Africa by the Straits of Gibraltar, only 13.4km wide at its narrowest point, has meant that the country's development has been very different to that of the rest of the European mainland.

Physically too, the country is very different from the rest of Europe, its narrow coastal belt giving way a few miles inland to a high plateau laced by formidable mountain ranges. The average altitude of the country is 660m above sea level, second in Europe only to Switzerland. Seventeen per cent of the land is above 1000m and only 18.5 per cent is under 200m, the best altitude for agricultural production. The highest peak is Mulhacén, in the south, at 3482m.

The North West

In the north-west, the Cantabrian Cordillera follows the length of the Atlantic coast, reaching a peak of 2648m with the Torre de Cerredo in the Picos de Europa, to join the western extreme of the Pyrenees. These have proved over the years to be an extremely effective defensive barrier, cutting off several of the many invasions which Spain has faced, allowing the inhabitants of the area to develop independently from the rest of the peninsula. They also act as a major weather barrier, ensuring a totally different climate along the coastal strip, known because of its green pastures as the Costa Verde or Green Coast, to that found in the majority of the country.

Many visitors to the Costa Verde remark that the scenery reminds them of parts of Wales or Cornwall. This is perhaps with good reason. This stretch of the Spanish coast, bordering the notoriously stormy Bay of Biscay, shares an Atlantic climate with southern Britain. Although the latitude makes the coast generally warmer than Britain's, it is similarly damp, with frequent gentle rains in summer. The winter brings occasional violent storms, but rarely any snow and the temperature on the coast remains mild.

The northern shore is a continuous strip of rolling hills leading down to low cliffs, punctuated only by small bays and river valleys. Further west, the Galician coast becomes wilder, its river valleys pulling back to form a series of rías or low fjords.

Inland, the coastal area is lush and green, perfectly adapted for small-scale, intensive agriculture, while some of the northern slopes of the *cordillera* are still heavily wooded. In 1918, the first National Park in Spain was created in the area surrounding Covadonga. This was later joined by other parks until, today, much of the Picos range is protected land. It is a rich area of rare flora and fauna in which live some of the last brown bears, wild cats, wolves, mountain goats and wild boar to be found in Europe. Sadly, however, numbers are still decreasing and it is highly unlikely that you will see any of these species without specialist assistance and a great deal of time and energy. Nevertheless, there is still a wonderful variety of wild flowers, smaller animals and birds, including a number of raptors – enough to keep any amateur naturalist happy for weeks.

As the mountains peak, the forest gives way to scrubland, scree slopes and rocky crags, with their attendant mountain extremes of brilliant sunshine, thick mist, and heavy winter snowfalls. On the south slopes you drop immediately into an almost Mediterranean dryness caused by the rain shadow. The temperature rises several degrees and the slopes become arid – bare, rocky expanses where goats browse amongst the olive trees. A little further south again and the land levels out onto the northern edge of the Castillian plateau, with its vast purple and gold acreages of wheat and vines.

The Population

Spain now has a stable population of about 38 million, of whom some 40 per cent now live in the major cities. In the country as a whole, the migration away from the land is still continuing. In the north west, however, the fertile farmland has ensured there is still a large farming community, many of them still peasant farmers working traditional smallholdings. There are also some dozen large cities in the area, resulting in a greater population density here than in any other area apart from the Mediterranean coast.

The area's isolation from the mainstream of Spanish development has also ensured a more complex racial and linguistic structure than in much of Spain, with several different traditions still going strong and four languages still in common usage. Of the different groups, the Basques are the most famous, thought to be the last remnants of the peninsula's pre-Celtic inhabitants, with a language seemingly unrelated to any other European tongue. In the centre of the area, the Asturians have a strong local dialect, *bable*, based loosely on Castillian Spanish, while to the west, the Galicians, descended from the Celts, speak *gallego*. The common

39

A shrine at Covadonga, in Asturias.

language, however, is Castillian Spanish, which everyone, even in the remotest areas, speaks to some degree.

The Economy

Farming and fishing

The traditional occupation of the coastal villages has always been fishing and this is still one of the last places in Europe where there are significant fleets of small inshore fishing boats, catching a wide range of shellfish, octopus and squid as well as such Atlantic staples as cod. As everywhere else, however, the decline in fish stocks due to overfishing and pollution and the temptation of easy pickings presented by tourism are slowly killing off this traditional lifestyle. But for the moment, you can still see the fleets come in and watch the fishwives spreading the nets on the quays for mending. You can also still get delicious seafood, caught an hour before it landed on your plate, if you find the right restaurants in the harbour areas.

Inland, the grass is a lush, vivid green, and much of the area is given over to small scale, intensive farming. The Basque Country in particular is noted for its dairy herds, while further west, the deciduous fruit orchards have made Asturias famous for its cider, sidra. This is also one of the main vegetable growing regions of Spain, with cabbages and beans alongside potatoes and other root crops. Recent reforestation has also brought commercial pine and eucalyptus cultivation to the area. To the south of the mountains, you are into the heartland of La Rioja, the most famous of Spain's wine growing regions.

Industry

The early gold and silver workings in Asturias were followed by later discoveries of major iron and coal deposits which have turned the north west (with the exception of Galicia) into one of the most heavily industrialised regions of Spain. The low grade brown coal mined in Asturias is still the country's main domestic fuel supply. The three main ports in the area – San Sebastián, Bilbao and Santander – all have their attendant areas of industrial development, belching black smoke into the atmosphere and tragically, now producing the first visible signs of pollution both in the sea and in the national parks to the south. The worldwide recession in heavy industry also hit the area, producing widespread unemployment, which only the Basque Country escaped by a deft transfer to the building and service industries. Since Spain joined the EEC in 1986, however, a large injection of community cash into the area has been improving communications and is beginning to build up alternative sources of income. Amongst the possible solutions, tourism is seen as one of the most promising and Spain has recently begun a campaign to attract more foreign tourists to the area. Hopefully the vagaries of the climate should ensure they will never be able to achieve the same level of interest and development that they have in the south. So far, they seem to be content to appeal to lovers of nature and history, leaving the coast to the Spaniards who have traditionally holidayed there for a century or so.

Politics

In 1978, the King and the leaders of the four main political parties agreed a written constitution, which has been in existence ever since. It may have more flowery words than hard facts, but the form – and the fact that everyone had a hand in creating it – have meant that no one has yet found any reason to want to alter it.

Today, therefore, Spain is a democratic monarchy with a written constitution. The King is the hereditary Head of State, but is answerable to Parliament (the Cortes). This has two chambers, the Congress and Senate, both elected. The country is run by a Prime Minister, as leader of the majority party, and a Cabinet. There is universal suffrage for everyone over the age of 18. The current government, which seems stable and popular, is moderate Socialist.

As various regional Nationalist movements became more and more vocal, nearly a quarter of the 1978 Constitution was given over to the setting up of a series of Autonomous Communities. Euskadi (the Basque Country) was one of the first to be given its Statute of Autonomy, in 1979. Galicia, Asturias and Cantabria followed in 1981; La Rioja and Navarra in 1982; and Castilla-León in 1983.

The whole of Spain is now divided into 17 Autonomous Communities. Each has its own President, Governing Council, Legislative Assembly and Supreme Court. It has responsibility for health and social services (within a national framework), housing, agriculture, forestry, freshwater fishing, planning, tourism and sport. Foreign affairs, defence, trade, shipping and aviation, off-shore fishing and the administration of the law remain with central government. Remaining responsibilities, such as education, have been negotiated separately with each Community, and the balance is different in each case.

Spain has been a member of NATO since 1982, and the EEC since 1986. In 1992, it reached perhaps the pinnacle of its modern achievement, with Madrid as the European City of Culture, Expo '92 in Seville, and the Olympic Games in Barcelona.

Life in modern Spain

On the whole, life is sweet. There is still a large, relatively poor peasant community, and fairly high urban unemployment, but the ecomony is now stable, growth is above the European average, and a great deal of investment is being pumped into the country's infrastructure. Donkeys are giving way to tractors and carts to cars.

The Spaniards have also grown used to freedom remarkably quickly. There is no longer any censorship and there is full freedom of speech and religion. The newspapers become increasingly searching, year by year, and there is a rapid and inspiring growth of artistic achievement, whether in literature or fashion, music or painting. Women have been given equal rights, including the right to divorce, and they are rapidly catching up with their counterparts elsewhere in Europe. Urban society is sophisticated, ambitious and, if anything, too liberal, for along with all the other freedoms came the sexual revolution, a rapid increase in crime, and the use of drugs. It is hard to recognise the repressed, deeply religious and backward-looking country of only 20 years ago.

Section Two
Asturias

Asturias claims, with some justification, to be the birthplace of modern Spain. It is a status recognised at the highest level, and of all the Autonomous Communities in Spain, this is the only Principality. In 1388, King Juan I granted his son, Enrique, the title of Prince of Asturias in honour of his marriage to Catherine of Lancaster, daughter of John of Gaunt. Since then, the title has traditionally always belonged to the heir to the throne.

It is a long thin state that runs along the coast of the Cantabrian Sea, bordered by the Eo River to the west and the Deva River to the east, and covering a total area of 10,564 square kilometres. It has a population of around one million, of whom nearly three-quarters are clustered in the industrial heartland around the cities of Oviedo, Gijón and Aviles. The rest of the state is sparsely populated by small coastal fishing villages, tiny mountain hamlets and remote farms.

Geography and history have always gone hand in hand in this dramatically beautiful region. The coastal strip, 345km long and never more than 25km wide, is richly fertile agricultural land, buffeted in winter by heavy Atlantic storms, but the rest of the time receiving gentle rains and warm sun that keep it lush and green. Many compare it to the other Celtic lands of Cornwall, Wales and Ireland and there is a great similarity in the sloping pastures and apple orchards that lead down to rocky shores, punctuated by small bays of gleaming sand and gaily painted fishing villages. Behind this strip however, the massive mountains of the Cordillera Cantábrica rise like a sheer wall against the sky. Nowhere are you out of sight of this rocky fortress, a wild land of gushing rivers and deep gorges, of snow-capped crags and vast tracts of ancient forest. It is a place where eagles fly and bears and wolves still roam (albeit in minute numbers), and where people still live in houses designed by the Celts 2000 years ago.

It is these mountains that shaped the early history of the region, with wave after wave of attackers turned back by their impenetrable bulk. The Romans colonised the plains to north and south, but had to leave alone the Astures tribe, from which the state gets its name. The Visigoths set up a coastal kingdom here, but when the Moors attacked, they too fled into the mountains, and it was from here that the

Christians eventually turned and fought back. At the Battle of Covadonga in 722 (see page 238), they won their first victory and soon afterwards, the Moors abandoned the coast. The first capital of Christian Spain was created at Cangas de Onís, and from here the Reconquista headed south. As the Moors were gradually pushed back across the Castillian plains, however, Asturias lost its importance and was incorporated into the new kingdom of León, becoming little more than a rural backwater. It remained that way until the 18th century when the industrial revolution created an insatiable demand for coal and iron, both of which were present in huge quantities in the central mountains. Both had been mined since Roman times, but now, as in the Welsh valleys, the landscape was transformed and the rivers ran black. First the accessible layers were stripped away from the hillsides and as those were exhausted, tunnels were dug deep into the earth. Railway lines were pushed up mountains and through tunnels to carry the ore, and massive port complexes were built at Gijón and Aviles to cope with the trade. Around these grew up vast complexes of heavy industry, manufacturing everything from steel to munitions. In the turbulent 1920s and 30s, the Asturian miners became politically active, amongst the first to form unions and take industrial action. On 5 October, 1934, violence spilled over, the miners invaded Oviedo and set up a revolutionary government. On 11 October, troops arrived, headed by the young Colonel Franco, brought back from Morocco to deal with them. It took him another four days, but he broke up the revolution in a particularly brutal fashion, in an episode approved by his superiors but which earned him early notoriety elsewhere. Although it was another 18 months before the coup, this is recognised today as the opening skirmish in the Civil War.

Like other great mining areas, Asturias has suffered in recent years as pit after pit closed, although the heavy industry is still active on the coast. Today, the mountains are, for the most part, green and calm again. Asturias is now looking to its rural heritage, and almost forgotten crafts, hoping to build back prosperity not through mass market tourism but by appealing to those who love the wilderness.

Although part of the Picos de Europa is in Asturias, the range is situated on the border of three states. As it can be approached from every direction, is one of the most popular in the region, and is not easily divided, I have given it a separate chapter to itself. See page 231.

Oviedo

Twenty-eight km from the coast, Oviedo was first founded in 757, when King Fruela I built a fort to guard the mountain pass of the Puerto de Pajares. It failed to do its job a few years later, when the arrival of the Moors resulted in the total destruction of the fledgling town. When Alfonso II (the Chaste), who reigned from 792 to 842, moved his court here from Cangas de Onís in 810 AD, he had to start again from scratch, to rebuild the fortifications and equip the city with churches and palaces. For a short time, until the reconquest of León in 1002, it shone as the capital of Christian Spain, and there are still several churches in and around

the city dating from this glorious period, together making up the single greatest concentration of pre-Romanesque architecture in Spain.

Since then, although it remained the capital of Asturias, like the rest of the state, Oviedo shrank back into obscurity until the industrial revolution gave it a fresh lease of life. It was sacked again by the French, under Marshal Ney in 1809, suffered enormous damage during the miners' revolt of 1934 (see page 45), and was a battleground for some 18 months during the early part of the Civil War. As a result, relatively little of its historic past has remained intact, and it is really quite astonishing that there is still so much to see.

Today, Oviedo is a thriving industrial and administrative centre, with a population of around 190,000 and a healthy sense of its own importance. The surburbs and environs are generally pretty ugly, but don't let that deter you, for the modern city centre is elegant and sophisticated, full of wide boulevards, chic shops and cafés, while the tiny old city, centred around the cathedral, is crammed with interest. Everything in the centre is within easy walking distance, and navigation is surprisingly easy.

The geographical centre of the city is taken up by a huge, roughly square park, the **Campo de San Francisco**, on what were once the grounds of an old monastic hospital. Filled with mature, shady trees, and formal walkways decorated by sculptures, this is where the whole city turns out in its finery for the *paseo* (a traditional evening stroll, with its origins in the marriage mart). The modern city centre is directly to the north of the park, while the centre of the old city is just down the hill to the north east. Walk along the Calle de San Francisco from the Plaza de la Escandalera and you will pass two fine old palaces. On the right is the 17th century **Palacio de Toreno**, which now houses the Institute of Asturian Studies, while on

46

the left is the 18th century **Palacio de Camposagrado**, now the High Court. At the far end of the road, you come out into the beautiful **Plaza de Alfonso II el Casto**. In the square are several other fine buildings, including the 17th- to 18th-century **Palacio de Valdecarzana**, and the 15th-century **Casa de la Rúa**, the oldest house in Oviedo. In the right-hand corner is the small **Church of San Tirso**, originally founded in the 9th century, although one window in the east wall is all that now remains of this early church.

All these pale into insignificance however, as directly ahead is the west front of the **Cathedral**. The first church on this site was built by Fruela I in 765, but was completely destroyed by the Moors, although a local architect, Teoda, did manage to save the archives. Work on the next basilica, dedicated to San Salvador, began during the reign of Alfonso II in 802. Only a tiny portion of this remains intact, and that has been heavily restored. The current cathedral is an almost pure product

A monument by the Campo de San Francisco in central Oviedo

of the flamboyant High Gothic era, begun in 1388 and completed during the bishopric of Cristóbal de Rojas (1547–1556). Built of a mustardy yellow stone, the west front is almost entirely 16th-century, and owes its rather lopsided appearance to the fact that it was never completed. There are three portals, all of different heights, the work of Pedro de Bruyeres in 1512. While there are six 14th-century figures of the Transfiguration over the central door, most of the sculpture niches are empty. The beautifully carved doors themselves date to the 18th century. Construction of the 70m high South Tower, with its delicate fretwork spire, began in 1508 under Juan de Badajoz, but was only completed in 1556. The North Tower has never been built.

Inside, the church is in the form of a Latin cross, lined on both sides by numerous small chapels, mostly overblown Baroque creations laden down by ornate decoration. Unusually, however, the line of the nave has been left open, giving it a light and airy feel, and a clear view through to the vast wooden altarpiece on the High Altar. The work of Gerald of Brussels and Juan de Balmaseda in 1525, its many panels tell stories from the life of Christ. Of all the chapels, two are worth particular attention. The first on the left as you enter is the Chapel of St Eulalia, patron saint of Asturias, whose body is now entombed in a massive Baroque shrine. Behind the north transept, the Capilla del Rey Casto is on the site of the original Visigothic church, and contains the pantheon of the Asturian kings. The tombs are still there, but the evil genius who insisted on all the 18th century 'improvements' scrubbed off the names while giving the chapel the Baroque treatment, so no one knows who is in which tomb.

A door in the south transept leads through to the cloister. Just on your right is a 12th-century tower, itself built onto the former palace of Alfonso II. The lower level of the cloister, which has some fine capitals, is the oldest part of the current cathedral, built from the late 14th to mid-15th centuries. The arcaded upper storey is an 18th-century addition. The Chapterhouse in the east wall now houses the recently restored 15th-century choirstalls.

Up the steps in the east wall, you come to the entrance of the minute Camara Santa, the real jewel of the cathedral and one of the main reasons for visiting Oviedo. Built originally by Alfonso II in the 9th century, it too formed part of his palace. It is on two levels: the upper being the Chapel of San Miguel, which was remodelled in the 12th century, the lower, the crypt of Santa Leocadia, which housed the relics of the Cordobá Martyrs, Santa Leocadia and San Eulogio. The whole thing was blown apart in 1934, but the treasures and original artworks were rescued and painstakingly restored, while the chapel itself has been rebuilt as an exact copy of the original. The east wall of the upper chapel is covered by six marvellous 12th-century pillars, each sculpted with the elongated forms of two of the apostles. Between them steps lead down to the crypt, which now houses the cathedral treasury, a small but glowing feast of gold. Pride of place is taken by the Cruz de los Angeles, commissioned by Alfonso II for the cathedral in 808. It gets its name from a popular legend that it is so beautiful, it was made by the angels themselves. Made of wood, covered in gold leaf and ornamented with pearls and precious stones, it bears an inscription on the back 'Received complacently, let this which is offered by Alfonso, humble servant of Christ, remain in honour of

God. May anyone who dares remove me from the place where I have been willingly donated be struck down by a bolt of divine lightning.' Considering that it is still here, after all that the city has been through, it is obviously a threat that works. The other, stunningly beautiful cross, made of gold, encrusted with precious stones and figured with animals and floral decoration, is the Cruz de la Victoria, donated in 908 by Alfonso III. Other treasures include a gold chest inlayed with agates, donated by Fruela I in 910, a 12th-century travelling altar with ivory inlaid doors, an ivory Gothic diptych and gold and silver plate.

Leaving the Cathedral, head north along the Calle Aguilla, and turn right past the 18th-century National Archives building, then first right again, past the Convent of San Pelayo, built between the 11th and 18th centuries. You are now on the Calle San Vicente, which leads past the west end of the cathedral. On your left, in the Plaza Feijoo, is the 16th-century **Church of Santa Maria la Real de la Corte**. Fray Benito Jerónimo Feijoo (1676–1764) is buried here. A Benedictine monk, philosopher, theologian and reformer, he was one of the leading thinkers of his generation. Behind the church are some of the few remaining fragments of the 13th-century city walls.

Keep going along the road, and a few yards on, directly behind the cathedral, you come to the **Archaelogical Museum**, housed in the cloisters of the former Monastery of San Vicente. This Benedictine foundation dates right back to 761 and the earliest days of the town, although nothing survived the Moorish invasion. Work on the existing building began in 1493, while work on the cloister, designed by Juan de Badajoz, began in the 1540s. The upper gallery was finally completed in 1775. It was here that Feijoo lived and worked and his cell is on view to the public. The small but well-displayed museum collection has artifacts from the paleolithic right through to the Visigothic era, including some beautiful pre-Romanesque capitals, a Roman mosaic floor, and Asturian coins and musical instruments.

Continue along the Calle San Vicente and turn right into the Corrada del Obispo. On your right, tucked in next to the cathedral, you will see the Romanesque tower of Santa Barbara. A small alley with a covered bridge leads through to the Calle Santa Ana, where you turn left for the **Fine Art Museum**, opened in 1980, and housed in two adjoining buildings, the 18th-century Palacio de Velarde and 17th-century Casa de los Oviedo-Portal, both beautifully restored. While the museum concentrates on the work of Asturian artists, it has also received works from the Modern Art Museum in Madrid, and the Royal Academy of Fine Art in San Fernando, and the result is an excellent, beautifully displayed and wide-ranging collection. Highlights include The Annunciation by Juan van der Hamen (c1625), the triptych of the Adoration of the Magi, attributed to the Master of the Legend of the Magdalena (c1520) and the galleries devoted to the works of modern Asturian artists including Evaristo Valle (1873–1951), and Nicanor Piñole (1878–1978).

From here, walk down through the back streets and through the archway under the arcaded, 18th-century Town Hall into the Plaza Mayor. Just off to the left is the 16th- to 18th-century **Church of San Isidoro**, and a short way beyond that, you come out into the 18th-century **Plaza y Mercado del Fontan**, where the market is still held today. From here it is only a couple of blocks back to the park and your starting point.

You must not leave Oviedo however without seeing the several superb pre-Romanesque churches scattered around the outskirts of the city. Two of the finest are grouped together on **Mount Naranco**, about 4km north west of the city centre, reached along the Avenida de los Monumentos. Both belong to the reign of Ramiro I (842–850). The **Church of Santa María del Naranco** was originally designed as part of the king's summer palace, with baths and halls on the ground floor, and an audience chamber above, but it was converted into a church within a few years of its completion. It is a magnificent high-sided rectangular building that used slender, elegant round arches and barrel vaulting a good two centuries before they are found anywhere else in Europe. The lower level is now the crypt. The upper level is lit by huge bays, with two arched balconies that open out over wonderful views across Oviedo to the Picos de Europa. For the first time too, the decoration is an integral part of the structure with pillars decorated with the Asturian rope motif, with some Corinthian capitals, and others decorated by floral and animal designs, while the interior walls are covered by a series of delicate disc medallions showing strong Byzantine influence.

The **Royal Chapel of San Miguel de Lillo**, nearby, has suffered a little over the centuries, firstly when one section collapsed in the 13th century, and later when the east end was rebuilt in the 17th. It is a much more solid building, cruciform in shape, but still with the characteristic height, three times the width of the nave. The façade has a wide arched doorway, with a huge decorative window above, flanked by two smaller ones. The arrangement, seen here for the first time, became common throughout the Romanesque and Gothic periods. Above all here, it is the detail of the decoration which is so superb, with primitive reliefs, possibly inspired by Roman or Byzantine work, showing vividly mobile circus scenes complete with acrobats and animal tamers.

Just to the north of the city centre, near the A8 motorway to Gijón, is the **Church of San Julián de los Prados**, also known as San Tullano. Built during the reign of Alfonso II (812- 42), it is the earliest surviving pre-Romanesque church in Spain, as well as the largest. Built originally as part of a private house, it is high, narrow and solid, with two porches on the outside. Inside it has a wide nave and two side aisles separated off by massive columns. Three square apsidal chapels, vaulted in brick, form the east end. The church is lit by large latticed windows. Most impressive of all however are the remains of the original Roman-style frescoes which still survive, enabling experts to reconstruct the decoration which would originally have covered every internal surface.

The Coast Road East – Oviedo to Unquera

This route starts with a visit to the city of Gijón, but then winds its way east along the coast road towards Santander, with occasional side trips to points of interest. As ever in northern Spain, there are plenty of churches, but the way to enjoy this is to dawdle on the clifftops and in the tiny brightly coloured fishing harbours.

*

The doorway of a house in Gijón

Leave Oviedo heading north along either the N630 or the A8 motorway, signposted Gijón. This coastal city, about 20km away, is your first stop.

Like so many of the towns in northern Spain, **GIJÓN** has grown rapidly over the last century, since a railway line through to the inland coalfields turned it into a booming port and centre for heavy industry. Today the population is about 265,000, and the largely modern city sprawls out along a wide bay, broken by a small peninsula on which stands the tiny old town. Originally colonised by the

51

Romans, who called the town Gigia, it was later a Visigothic centre, and was occupied briefly by the Moors in the 8th century. The harbour was first founded by Charles V in 1552, and it was here that the ragged remnants of the defeated Armada fled for shelter in 1588. The docks were later enlarged in 1766, and 1859. By the end of the 19th century, however, they could no longer cope with the volume of traffic or the massive new breed of merchant shipping, and a whole new harbour complex was built at El Musel, just to the west of the town. This is now the sixth busiest port in Spain, and is still growing.

The city has also suffered over the years. In 1395, a disastrous fire almost completely destroyed it, and it was badly damaged again during the Civil War. As a result, while parts of the city are attractive, there are few specific sights of real interest, and your time here would be best spent wandering the streets and the beach.

Start your tour on the eastern edge of the city, which is marked by the Canal del Rio Piles. To the right of the canal are the World Trade Centre, and the 'Pueblo Asturias', which houses two small museums, one ethnographic, one with a collection of bagpipes from around the world. Along the left bank runs the huge **Parque Isabel la Católica**, one of the most attractive parks in the region, a haven of mature trees, rich floral displays, and formal avenues, with two small lakes in the southern section. In the corner behind the lakes is the parador and just behind this stand the vast sports stadium, the Estacio de el Molinon, and the Plaza de Toro (bullring).

The northern edge of the park leads onto the massive sweep of **San Lorenzo**

A street fountain in Gijón

beach, a heavily built up and, in some ways, surprisingly popular holiday destination. Unlike the other great beach cities of Santander and San Sebastián, there are no gracious façades here, but rather a collection of ugly modern buildings. However, the area is lively and popular with the young. At the far end you will see the peninsula of the old town, now more usually known as the Cimadevilla, or Fishermen's Quarter. The Town Hall stands on the sea front, just in front of the elegant but unfinished Plaza Mayor. A small street leads north from here into the shady, triangular Plaza Jovellanos, and directly opposite you will see an mellow 16th-century stone building, the **Casa de Jovellanos**. Gaspar Melchor de Jovellanos was born in Gijón in 1744, and became a lawyer, encyclopedist, historian, philosopher, poet and statesman, one of the leading Spanish thinkers of the 18th century. He wrote on economic reform, founded an educational institute in Gijón, and in 1808, joined the anti-French General Council. He died in Puerto de Vega in 1811. His family home is now a museum and art gallery dedicated to the works of Asturian artists.

From here, a road to the right leads up to the remains of the **Roman baths**, which have a well-preserved section of hypercaust, and the **Church of San Pedro**, completely rebuilt in 1954. Wander up the hill through the maze of narrow streets and decaying cottages to the vast complex of the tobacco factory, then turn right. A path leads out onto a wide green space on the clifftop, the **Cerro de Santa Catalina**, where there are a few remnants of city fortifications, which date back to Roman times. Walk round, and down on the other side of the isthmus and you come out beside the fishing harbour, the site of the original city harbour, now a vibrant mass of small, elderly multi-coloured boats. As you come back round to the edge of the old town, and the Plaza del Marques, you will see on your left the magnificent Baroque façade of the **Rivillagigedo Palace**, flanked by two massive towers. Built originally in the 15th century, and altered in 1702, this is, without doubt, the grandest building in the city. Just beyond this, the Jardín de la Reina marks the centre of the modern city. Follow the harbour round to the far end and the area rapidly deteriorates from sophistication to sleaze as you enter the vicinity of the modern port, closed off to the public behind high walls.

Leave Gijón heading east on the N632 towards Villaviciosa. Four kilometres out of town, at Somío, are the Universidad Laboral, a college of higher technology and agriculture, and the Evaristo Valle Museum, dedicated to the works of this magnificent 20th-century artist. Keep going along the N632 as far as Venta de las Ranas, where you turn left and then right and follow the small road up to the coastal village of **Tazones**, a small pretty fishing village with a charming harbour and a lighthouse overlooking the mouth of the Ría de Villaviciosa and the Playa de Rodiles, one of the most popular local beaches, on the opposite bank. Follow the road round along the bank of the ría, through El Puntal, where many locals keep their pleasure boats, to the small Church of San Andrés de Bedriñana. Built originally in the 9th century, it was almost completely rebuilt in the 16th, but still retains a few fragments of its Mozarabic design. Villaviciosa, at the foot of the ría, is 2km further on.

In the middle ages, **Villaviciosa** was one of the most important towns in Asturias.

In 1270, it was given its charter and the right to hold a Wednesday market, by Alfonso X. When the town was virtually destroyed by fire in 1484, the Catholic Monarchs, Ferdinand and Isabel, paid for the rebuilding. In 1517, Carlos I arrived in Spain to take up his throne, landing here unexpectedly and by accident (they should have been in Santander). It caused great excitement locally, and the event is still commemorated by a memorial in one of the local parks. Today, the town is a small, but lively centre with a population of about 16,000, which makes its living from tourists, fishing, but above all from apples. This is the undisputed centre of the Asturian cider country, with the roads lined by orchards and cider mills. The whole centre of the old town is protected as a national monument and there are a number of attractive old mansions. On the Plaza Mayor, the 13th-century Church of Santa María, with a Romanesque portal and Gothic rose window, is worth a visit.

Two other churches, a little way inland, also merit side excursions. The first is the Church of San Juan de Amandi on the O121, about 2km from the centre. Built in 1155, it was restored in 1755 and the belfry was added in 1831, but it has a beautiful arcaded portal, some fine capitals and a lovely frieze in the arcaded apse. It is one of the best remaining examples of Romanesque architecture in Asturias. At **Valdediós**, 9km to the south-west, on the C638, the Church of San Salvador was first consecrated in 893 AD, and has been little altered over the years. Built as the style changed from the Asturian pre-Romanesque to Romanesque, it has been little altered over the years and is simple but enchanting, with fine capitals, some decorated with Asturian cordwork, some with Mozarabic influence, and several primitive sculptures. Beside it is the Cistercian Monastery of Santa María, known locally as 'El Conventín'. The church was built between 1218, while the three-storey cloister was built in stages in the 15th, 17th and 18th centuries.

Leave Villaviciosa on the N632, still heading east. After about 10km, a small road off to the left, the O112, leads to Luces and **Lastres**, a charming fishing village with a maze of narrow streets and steps that seem to cling to an almost vertical hillside. Surrounded by several good beaches, and within easy access of several large cities, this is rapidly turning into one of the more popular holiday playgrounds along this stretch of the coast.

Follow the road along the ría, from where there are superb views along the coast, to Colunga and turn back onto the N632. About 2km on, turn right to **Gobiendes** and the early 10th-century Church of Santiago, which has some interesting windows and fine twisted columns topped by Corinthian capitals. It also has some 19th century additions and a bell-tower built in 1918. Head south from here along the C637, a pretty road which climbs into the hills to the 658m **Mirador del Fito**, from where there is one of the finest views in the area, extending for miles along the coast, and across the Cornión Massif of the Picos de Europa. The road south from here winds its way through the chestnut forests of the Cordillera de Sueve, much of which is set aside as a nature reserve, to Arriondas, on the Sella River. Turn left onto the N634 and follow the road along the river, said to be one of the best salmon rivers in the region, to Llovio, where a small road to the left leads back along the ría to the coast and Ribadasella.

Although there is evidence of people living here for over 20,000 years, the 'modern' town of **Ribadasella** was founded shortly after the Moors left the north coast following the battle of Covadonga in 722 (see page 238). It remained a royal town until about 1440 when it was granted to Diego Fernández de Quiñones by Juan II. The old town is almost completely cut off from the open sea, tucked safely away from winter storms behind Monte Corbero, along the serpentine ría. This natural harbour soon became a vital and busy port, with the crown paying to repair defences in order to provide a safe haven for naval vessels. By the 18th century, it was a major trading centre, but as ships grew in the late 19th century, the harbour was abandoned for deep water anchorages, and today, it is left to the fishermen. It is an immensely appealing town, with a number of fine old houses crammed into its narrow streets, while there is an excellent view over the ría from the Santuario de la Virgen de la Guía, the tiny chapel on top of Monte Corbero.

Across the bridge, the sea front itself has a completely different atmosphere, with one of the longest beaches in the region. In high summer, this area is thronged with holidaymakers and more and more tourist developments are rapidly filling in all the available building space.

On the western edge of the town is the **Tito Bustillo Cave**, with one of the finest collections of prehistoric cave paintings on the coast (see also page 130). Numbers are limited, but 400 people a day are allowed in, so you have a much better chance of getting in than at most of the other caves. In high summer it is advisable to go early. There are three main passages in the cave system, which was used as a dwelling in the middle Magdalenian period of the Stone Age (c20,000 to 15,000 years ago). Many of the pictures are very faint now, but they are still fascinating, created by a variety of techniques, including line drawing, block colour and engraving. Most are pictures of local animals, including several horses, deer, and bison, but there are also several drawings of the female vulva, thought to be used as ritual fertility symbols.

Although it is the height of the tourist season and therefore busy, the best time to be here is in late August, when the local festival kicks off with the Procession of Santa Marina, the patron saint of fishermen. Her statue is taken from the local church, processed around the town with music and dancing, then a fleet of gaily decorated fishing boats gather to take her out to sea on a short voyage around the local fishing grounds. On the last Saturday in August, there is also a major and hugely popular international kayak race along the Sella River from Arriondas to Ribadasella, ending in a romería in the small hours of the morning.

Leave Ribadasella on the N632 heading east towards the pretty little village of Nueva, where you rejoin the N634. Several small side roads lead down to the sea and popular swimming beaches. About 10km on, you will see the recently restored 13th-century church of the Romanesque Benedictine **Monastery of San Antolín de Bedón**. Eleven km after this, you come to Llanes.

Another coastal fishing and tourist town, though much larger, with a population of around 15,000, **Llanes** has a very similar story to Ribadasella. Founded in the 8th century, following the Moorish retreat, it gained its charter in 1206, but remained royal land until given to Diego Fernández de Quiñones by Juan II in

A festival at Ribadasella: the Santa Marina procession

The fishing harbour at Llanes

1440. Until the 18th century, it was a major centre for deep sea fishing, particularly for cod, and whaling. Since then, the town has sunk back into obscurity, and is only now beginning to climb into a new incarnation as a tourist centre, although the tiny size of its beaches should perhaps guarantee that there will never be a mainstream destination. Meantime, it is one of the most attractive of all the small towns along the Cantabrian coast, with several markedly different areas, all within easy walking distance of each other. The main centre of town, with a lively collection of shops, small hotels and cafés is a little way behind the harbour, away from the sea. The fishing harbour itself is bright and noisy, with several excellent fish restaurants along the quay. In a vain attempt to stop the harbour silting, a sluice gate and harbour wall was built in the 1920s. This proved to be utterly useless, but it's a good place to sit and watch the fishing fleet come in and unload. It is also the local teenage hang-out in the evenings. On the small hill behind this are the tiny alleys and old cottages of the fishermen's quarter, interspersed with a few grander mansions. Wander through here and down to the far side of the hill, and you come to the Gothic Church of Santa María and the ruins of the old castle. Further along from here is a small sandy swimming beach, and on the far side of that, is the formal clifftop walk of the Paseo de San Pedro, from where there is an excellent view over the town.

Leave here along the small coast road to Cué and Andrín, both tiny, pretty villages, with an excellent view along the coast. The road loops round to rejoin the N634, and the main route east. About 4km on, at Vidiago, an almost invisible

Traditional Asturian culture and crafts

More perhaps than in any other corner of north-west Spain the isolation of the mountain villages and tiny fishing ports of Asturias have kept a traditional folk culture alive and well. Festivals, *verbenas* (outdoor dances) and *romerías* (pilgrimages cum picnics) abound. In high summer it is hard to move without meeting yet another cheerful, noisy procession of dancers and musicians in scarlet, black and white national dress, with full skirts, knee breeches and floppy hats. The girls dance while the men play the pipes and drums, or run down a crowded street, a vast log on their shoulders, to the cheers of the crowd. Behind, with incense and ceremony come the gilded and flower-decked local saints, being taken on their annual walkabout or even on a thanksgiving voyage round the local fishing grounds.

Of all the local festivals, the largest and most exciting is the annual canoe race from Arriondas to Ribadasella (see page 55). Others worth watching for include the Fiestas de l'Amuravela in Cudillero on 29 June; the Fiesta del Pastor (the Shepherds' Feast at the Covadonga Lakes on the Feast of Santiago, 25 July); the Fiesta Vaqueira (Feast of the Wandering Shepherds) at Luarca on the last Sunday in July; the Fiesta de San Roque at Llanes on the 16 August; and the Day of Asturias in Gijón on the last day in August.

For the moment, although probably not for long, traditional crafts are also still in demand for real use, not just to satisfy the tourist trade. Metalworkers make anything from hunting horns or cow bells to knives and farm tools. Chestnut and hazel wickerwork baskets and hampers are still used in preference to plastic bags and boxes, while the traditional black pottery of Llames de Mouro is currently undergoing something of a renaissance. Above all, though, the Asturians work in wood, building their houses and boats from it, making musical instruments such as the small local bagpipes, violins, tambourines and castanets. They carve wooden statues for their churches and even wear wooden shoes – farmers often preferring clogs in the muddy hills. A favourite souvenir is an inlaid boxwood penknife from the Taramundi area.

sign marks the start of the footpath up through the woods to the Bronze Age megalith of **Peña-Tú**. The walk takes between 20 and 30 minutes. The rock itself stands about 10m high, and is decorated on one side by engravings and paintings, thought by some to be Celtic funerary symbols. At Pimiango, 10km on from here, a small road on the left leads down to the shore and **Pindal Cave**, dramatically sited on a cliff ledge overlooking the sea. The roof of the wide, shallow cave is covered in thin stalactite needles, while the walls in its depths are covered by rock paintings of animals, including one of an elephant. Like others along the coast, they are thought to be 15–20,000 years old.

Shortly after this, the road reaches the Deva River and Unquera, which marks the border with Cantabria.

For a description of the route east to Santander, see page 122. For a description of the Picos de Europa tour, see page 231.

The Coast Road West – Oviedo to Ribadeo

This route rejoins the coast at Avilés then heads west towards the Galician border along the main coast road, with regular short detours to sights of particular beauty or interest.

Leave Oviedo on the C634 or the A8 motorway, heading north to **AVILÉS**. This is the third and smallest of the three large industrial cities of central Asturias, having grown rapidly over the last century from a small fishing port to an industrial centre with a population of 90,000. The whole of the city centre has been declared a national monument, but sadly this is not the place to linger in appreciation of historic beauty. In the 1950s, a massive industrial complex, complete with coke furnaces, steel mills and port, was built within walking distance of the historic district. Just its sheer size is impressive, but the result is that a pall of grime hangs in the air and the buildings are all a sickly yellowy-black with soot.

There is some evidence of prehistoric and Roman habitation in the area, but the known history of Avilés begins in 1085, when the town was granted a *fuero* (charter) by Alfonso VI. In 1155, Alfonso VII confirmed its rights to independence, in gratitude for the town's assistance against the church and nobility. In 1188, however, Fernando II back-tracked and gave a third of the town and its port revenues to the church of Oviedo, creating a bitter enmity between the two towns that lasted until the 16th century. Over the centuries, the city has always been connected with the sea, producing several notable sailors, the most famous of whom was Pedro Menéndez de Avilés who, in 1565, founded the first town in the United States, San Agustín in Florida. The main sights of interest are all in the old town, within easy walking distance of each other.

Start your tour in the triangular Parque de Muelle, opposite the FEVE railway station beside the river. Turn left from here onto the Calle de la Ferreria to find the **Church of San Nicolás de Bari**, which is now run by the Franciscans. Originally built in the 12th century, it still has a 12th-century portal, but was almost completely rebuilt in the 17th century. Pedro Menéndez de Avilés is buried in the chancel, and there are several fine side chapels. Keep going up the road and off to your right, a block on, is the **Palacio de Valdecarzano**, which has a beautiful, late 13th-century façade. Another block on and you come to the elegant, arcaded **Plaza de Espana**, a small, but very beautiful square that is the real centre of the old town. Just off to the left, at the corner of the Calle del Rivero, is another fine mansion, the 17th-century **Palacio del Llano Ponte**, with a scalloped relief frieze on the façade; it is now used as a cinema. At the centre of the plaza is the 17th-century Town Hall, while to the right is the early 18th-century Palacio del Marques de Ferrera. Go past this into the Calle San Francisco and on your left, you come to the **Church of San Nicolás de Bari**, with a small garden beside it containing a beautiful 18th-century fountain, the Fuente de los Canos de San Francisco, the water pouring from the mouths of a row of sculpted heads, interspersed by coats of arms. Formerly dedicated to San Francisco, the church is essentially late Romanesque and still retains its 13th-century portal, some arcades and one 13th-century fresco inside. There are also several fine Gothic tombs and a Renaissance cloister.

From here, turn left onto the Calle de Galliana, and walk through its fine arcades, before turning back down the road, to the Plaza de España. Take the Calle de la Fruta back down the hill towards your starting point. On your right, two blocks down, you come to the **Palacio de Camposagrado**, which has an ornate 17th-century Baroque façade, and houses the School and Museum of Ceramics.

The last point of interest, just to the north of the Parque de Muelle, is the Romanesque **Church of Sabugo**, in the old fishermen's district, in which you can see the stone table and benches used for meetings by the local navigators.

Leave Avilés heading west, on the N632. About 3km from the town, you reach the rapidly growing resort town of **Salinas**, which has one of the longest beaches in Asturias. From here, the road continues on, past the airport, to **Soto de Barco**, a small village on the bank of the Narlón River, where you will see the ruins of the Castillo de Don Martin. Just across the bridge from here, a small road leads off to the right, up to the coast, lighthouse and the **Hermitage of Espíritu Santo**, from where there is a wonderful view across the mouth of the river, and for miles along the coast. Follow the road round, back to the N632, and continue on for about a kilometre, until another turning off to the right leads to the charming little fishing village of **Cudillero**, its old red-tiled cottages clambering up the walls of a steep-sided river valley to peer down on the tiny harbour. Although the Town Hall is housed in an old castle, there are no buildings of real architectural note here, Its setting makes this one of the most attractive villages on the coast, however, and although there are plenty of beaches within reach, the lay of the land makes it almost certain that it will not be targeted for major, ugly tourism development.

Loop back onto the N632, and a little further on, yet another small road on the right leads to a huge, beautiful beach, the Concha de Artedo. At the far end of this, reached by car from a separate slip road signed to Riegobajo, a lighthouse stands at the end of a peninsula, Cabo Vidio, with superb views along the rugged coastline for about 20km in each direction.

Back on the N632, keep going west, for about 20km, with the road travelling above a long series of beaches which extends virtually the whole way. The easiest access is along another small road on the right, signposted to Busto, which leads to the next lighthouse peninsula and viewing point at Cabo Busto. This route returns to the main road west, now the N634, for the last 12km into **Luarca**, at the mouth of the Negro River.

In the opposite direction, the N634 heads south to La Espina, to join the route from Oviedo to Lugo (see page 62).

The centre of an administrative district, Luarca is today one of the largest and prettiest towns along this stretch of coast, with a population of around 20,000. New development is rapidly spreading out across the gentle hills nearby, but this does not affect the charming old town centre, which snakes back from the coast, along the line of the river, crossed by no less than seven bridges. Although there are few traces left, humans have lived in this valley since prehistoric times, making their livelihood from fishing, as they still do to this day. The town received its charter from Alfonso X in the 13th century, but did not really begin to flourish until the 17th, when it became a trading centre with the Americas, and a regular place of safety from the pirates who roamed the area. Numerous men sailed from here to the New World, some returning with fortunes to build grand houses, emblazoned with coats of arms. The town is centred on the Plaza de Alfonso X, on the river bank, hidden from the sea. In the streets around, keep an eye open for several particularly fine buildings, including the Palacio del Marqués de Ferrera, with a heavily restored 13th-century tower, one wing dating from the 15th to 16th centuries, and another dating from the 17th to 18th; the Casa de los Marqueses de Gamoneda, a neo-classical 18th-century town house; and the 19th-century Baroque Church of Santa Eulalia, which houses several fine 17th- and 18th-century retables.

Follow the line of the river towards the coast, and you come to the small fishing harbour, protected from the elements by sea walls. To the right, a walk leads up through the alleys of the old, slate-roofed cottages to the small cemetery and church, from where there is a superb view across the town and harbour.

Leave Luarca on the N634, heading west. About 10km on, a small road on the right heads back to the coast, past the tiny fishing port of Puerto de Vega, to **Navia**, a basically modern port town, with a few attractive old buildings, on the right bank of the Ría de Navia. Cross the ría and turn left immediately onto the C644, which winds down the west bank of the ría to **Coaña**. Just south of the town, you will reach the Castro de Coana, one of the finest prehistoric complexes in the region. Although probably the best preserved, with all the foundations and some of the walls intact, this is just one of a number of similar villages in the area. They belonged to the Astures tribe of the late Iron Age and early Roman period. Covering about one hectare, the *castro* is a heavily fortified village, with a solid stone wall surrounding the huddle of circular stone built huts.

Make your way back up to the N634 coast road and turn west again. There are excellent views of the ría and coast from the lighthouse at Ortiguera, reached via a small side road on the left, about 1 km on. Most of the tiny towns and villages along this last stretch of the Asturian coast are attractive, with whitewashed walls and slate-tiled roofs interspersed by a few old stone buildings emblazoned with coats of arms. Rich green fields pour down to the coast to end abruptly in low, ferocious rocky cliffs and hidden inlets. On good days the sea shines turquoise, on bad it gleams steel grey. The shore here is changing from the relative calm of the Costa Verde to the wildness of the Galician coast. The actual border is reached at the Ría de Ribadeo, the estuary of the Eo River. A small road on the right just before you reach Figueras leads down to the magnificent modern bridge which soars across the mouth of the river to Ribadeo. The older road meanders down the side of the ría to **Castropol**, a pretty town built out on a small peninsula in the ría. It has a 15th-century Church of Nuestra Senora del Campo, one of only a handful of buildings to survive a terrible fire in the 16th century, and a number of attractive 18th-century mansions, including the Palacio Valledor, the Palacio de las Cuatro Torres, and the Villa Rosita. Continue south to cross the river at the foot of the estuary.

For a description of Ribadeo and the continuation of the coastal route in Galicia, see page 177. For a description of the inland route from Ribadeo to La Coruña, see page 184.

Oviedo to Lugo via the Alto de Acebo

This route heads due west from Oviedo, curving round the northern slopes of the western Cordillera Cantábrica, a beautiful area rarely visited by tourists, to cross the border into Galicia at the Alto de Acebo. There are good routes connecting it to the coast from La Espina and Grandas de Salime. Distances are long and some of the roads mountainous, but there is little heavy-duty sightseeing, unless you wish to veer up into the mountains to remote monasteries and prehistoric sites.

Leave Oviedo heading west along the N634. After 12.5km, turn right along the Naln River to visit the pre-Romanesque Church of San Pedro de Nora (see page 65). Return to the main road and turn right towards Grado. You are once more on the pilgrim route to Santiago de Compostela, that great network of Romanesque roads that has so influenced northern Spain (see page 28). This is very much a minor branch, nowhere near as popular or as well-travelled as its famous counterpart to the south of the mountains, but some did prefer to stay closer to the coast, roughly following the line of this tour before crossing into Galicia.

Grado has two medieval towers and an 18th-century chapel, but it is a basically uninspiring town with little that warrants a stop. Continue on for about 7km until you see a small turning on the left signposted to **Doriga**. This little village has a fine, if somewhat austere palace with a 14th-century keep, drawbridge and a splendid galleried courtyard. There are also two small churches that have kept some Romanesque features. The village stands on the Narcea River, one of the two largest rivers in an area threaded by hundreds. It is pretty and peaceful and just to the south starts a stretch of tumbling water famed throughout Spain as one of the great salmon and trout fishing areas.

Turn right from Doriga onto the C633, which leads along the river back up to the main road, **Cornellana**, and the Monastery of San Salvador. The elegant, Italianate façade and monastic buildings to the right of the entrance were built in the late 17th century, but once you enter the church you find yourself in a classic Romanesque church with three aisles and three apsidal chapels. A door to one side leads into a lovely cloister, which has a Romanesque tower and relief carvings which tell the story of the church's foundation.

From here, continue along the road to the regional administrative centre of **Salas**, its population of about 9000 little bigger than in the glory days of the town, 600 years ago, when this was one of the larger stops on the northern pilgrim route. The little town has several fine old mansions and churches. Amongst the houses, look out for the 14th-century Torre de la Villa. In 1959, this was partially restored and attached by a covered way to the neighbouring 16th-century Casa-Palacio de Valdés Salas. Built by the Archbishop of Seville, who was also responsible for founding Oviedo University, it has a somewhat sobre façade, with two towers, a central courtyard and small chapel. The 17th-century Palacio de los Condes de Casares is another mansion built onto a 14th-century tower.

Of the churches, the most interesting is the early 16th-century Collegiate Church of Santa María. There are two fine retables inside, a Baroque work on the high altar, and one by Asturian artist, Luis Fernández de la Vega, in the Capilla de los

Malleza. The finest of all the artworks however is the alabaster tomb of Archbishop Fernándo Valdés-Salas, sculpted by Pompeyo Leoni between 1576 and 1582. Also in the choir are some reliefs and an inscription dated 951, taken from the small pre-Romanesque Chapel of San Martin, on the edge of the town.

Leaving Salas, continue west along the N634 to La Espina. The main road turns sharply north here, to join the coast road near Luarca, but this route turns left onto the C630 and heads south to **Tineo**. Another administrative and agricultural centre, with a population of 20,000, Tineo flows down the gentle slope of a 675m hill, with wonderful views out across the Narcea Valley. Take time for a stroll through the main streets of the town, where there are several fine mansions, including the Palacio de los Garca, with a 14th-century façade and round tower, and the Palacio de Mers, built in 1525, with a Renaissance façade flanked by two towers, and a fine interior courtyard.

From now on, the scenery along the route becomes increasingly wild and remote, but two to three thousand years ago, the region was a positive hive of activity. A number of Bronze Age burial tumuli, Iron Age forts, remnants of Roman camps and deserted Roman mines are scattered across the surrounding hills. Right across the area you will also see the *horreos* that are such a significant feature of the architectural landscape. Although all are built up on stilts to stop rats getting into the grain, it is around here that the style begins to change, from the wooden built, square, thatched *horreo* that is typical of eastern Asturias and Cantabria to the smaller, rectangular stone-built design of Galicia.

From Tineo, take the small road south to El Rodical, where you turn right to La Florida, and right again onto the C631, which runs along the bank of the Narcea River to **Corias**. The Benedictine Monastery of San Juan is one of the largest monasteries in western Asturias. It was founded in the 11th century but nothing remains of its Romanesque heritage and the existing church, which houses a couple of fine Baroque retables, dates from the late 16th century. The rest of the monastery was completely rebuilt by Herrera in a neo-classical style following a massive fire in 1763. Partly because of its sheer size, and partly because it shares an architect with the massive Madrid palace, it is nicknamed the 'Asturian Escorial'.

Cangas de Narcea is about 2km south of Corias, still on the C631. Similar in size to Tineo, with about 20,000 inhabitants, the town is tucked into a steep-sided valley. It acts as the regional centre and market town for the many tiny, bleak and isolated settlements of south west Asturias, and was also, in the Middle Ages, a pilgrim stop on the Santiago trail. Work on its Collegiate Church of Santa María Magdalena began in 1642. It has a single nave lined by small side chapels, while the tomb of its founder, Bishop Valdés Llano, is one of several below the high altar. Amongst the many grand houses, many emblazoned with coats of arms, that line the streets of the town, are the 16th-century Palacio de Omaña, in the square beside the church, and the Palacio de los Condes de Toreno, built in 1701, which now houses the Casa Consistorial.

In the mountains above here are a tiny group of brañas, Celtic style settlements built by the *vaqueiros de alzada*, a people who have traditionally made their living as wandering shepherds. With an obviously different ethnic heritage and a different language, there are fierce arguments about their origins, some claiming that they are outcasts who refused to support the Christian rebellion against the Moors, others that they were Moors captured and converted during the Reconquista, and still others that they are the descendents of Roman slaves. Always treated as second class citizens in the past, it is only the last century that they have been allowed to live, worship and be buried alongside the rest of the community. If you continue south for 25km along the bank of the Narcea River, you reach the **Coto nacional de Muniellos** (Muniellos Forest Reserve), a 50 square kilometre forest that is the largest surviving oak forest on the Iberian Peninsula. It also contains a number of other species of tree and is a wildlife refuge with small populations of wolves, bears and chamois.

To regain the route, retrace your steps from Cangas de Narcea north to Puente del Inferno. A small road on the left, sigposted to Puelo, joins the O750 which carves its way through a narrow, dramatic valley to the little village of Linares, where there are several attractive towered houses. Two kilometres on, a side road on the left leads to **Celón**, a tiny village where you can visit the lovely Church of Santa María, which has a Romanesque portal, a 14th-century Gothic statue of the Virgin, a 15th-century nave and Baroque retable.

The road leads on through Pola de Allande, heading west along the C630, with the road climbing steeply all the way into the Sierra de Rañadoiro, a mountain range that acts as a watershed between the Narcea and Navia River systems. About 10km on, you reach the top of the **Puerto del Palo**, the highest pass on the road, at 1146m. There are superb views from the top.

As the road falls again on the far side, it enters a desolate landscape which lasts almost until the road crosses the Navia River, about 40km on. Just to the left is the Embalse de Salime, where the construction of a hydro-electric dam has created a long, ribbon-like and remarkably beautiful lake, which wriggles its way back along the line of the Navia for about 24km. There are several good views of the lake, the dam wall, and the waterfall below it from the road, but it is also worth stopping at the power station. At the entrance there is a relief by Vaquero Palacios, while inside, it has been decorated with murals by Vaquero Turcios, both local artists.

A few kilometres further on, you reach **Grandas de Salime**. A charming town tucked between pine trees and pastures in a wide, gentle valley, this was an important place on a major crossroads, in the Middle Ages, and it became a main stop on the northern pilgrim route. Today, although it is a still a district administrative centre and market town, with a population of about 20,000, it is a sleepy backwater, with some pretty houses and one interesting church. Although virtually rebuilt in the 18th century, the Collegiate Church of San Salvador is originally 12th-century, and still has a Romanesque portal. There is also a fine Baroque retable on the high altar. A small Folk Museum in the Casa Consistorial, exists alongside a Handicrafts School, where you can see people learning the old crafts such as weaving, and woodworking. This route continues west from here, climbing to the 1030m Alto de Acebo which forms the border with Galicia.

To rejoin the coast, the C644 runs north from Grandas de Salime along the enchantingly pretty Navia Valley to meet the coast road at Navia (see page 61).
For the onward route from the Alto de Acebo to Lugo, see page 180.

Oviedo to León via the Puerto de Pajares

The fastest route south from Oviedo follows the N630 the whole way. This route detours through the mountains into the Somiedo National Park before rejoining the N630 for the climb over the pass into León.

Leave Oviedo on the N634, heading west for 12.5km until you reach the Nalón River. Turn right and head north for 2km up to the small pre-Romanesque **Church of San Pedro de Nora**, which stands of the bank of the Nora River. Built during the reign of Alfonso II, it is very similar in style and date to San Julián de los Prados in Oviedo (see page 50), although it has been extensively restored in recent years. The rectangular exterior is of rough stone, with an extended open entry porch and large, lattice-work windows. Inside, the high central aisle is supported on either side by lower, barrel vaulted aisles, and there are three straight apses behind the high altar. It is simpler than many other chapels of the same period with little decorative stonework and no remaining frescoes, but it is nevertheless still charming.

From here, retrace your steps, crossing the main road, onto the O424 to **Trubia**, an industrial town at the confluence of the Naln and Trubia Rivers. These days it is chiefly famous as a centre for manufacturing arms. The first cannon factory was set up here in 1794.

Keep going straight through the town and follow the O424 south along the riverbank for 8km to **Tuñon**, where you should stop off to look at the abbey Church of San Adriano. Originally built in 891, during the reign of Alfonso III, it was virtually rebuilt in 1108. It is nevertheless still clearly pre-Romanesque in style and boasts (in the main chapel) the earliest Mozarabic mural paintings in Spain.

Continue down the O424 to **Proaza**, where a medieval tower forms part of the 17th-century Palacio de los Gonzáles-Tuñon. This small village also marks the start of the **Desfilerado del Tervega**, a dramatic series of narrow gorges which lead up into the mountains of the Cordillera Cantábrica. Partway along, at the village of Caranga de Abajo, turn left and follow the western valley through to Entago and **La Plaza de Tervega**. At the far end of the village stands the Collegiate Church of San Pedro de Tervega, founded in 1070. Most of it is actually 12th-century, while the porch and tower are later additions. The church's architecture harks back to pre-Romanesque influences, with a narthex, tall, narrow nave and squared east end, and some magnificent capitals in a lively primitive style. There is a small museum in the cloister that contains, amongst other exhibits, various mummies of the Ponces de León family.

Turn right here up the Valdecarzana Valley to Villanueva and the small 11th-century Romanesque Church of Santa María, which has a number of marvellous capitals and a fine font.

This is at the heart of the Reserva nacional de Somiedo (Somiedo National Park), which stretches across the mountains to the Castilla-y-León border. At 304 square kilometres, it is one of the largest national parks in Spain, as well as being one of the richest in terms of its flora and fauna, with some 160 different species of animal and bird. It also includes the highest peak in the western Cordilleras, Peña Ubiña

Mountain wildlife

The Cordillera Cantábrica is one of the last great wildlife refuges of Europe, yet even here, many species survive only in tiny numbers and fragmented communities, barely clinging to existence. And while the ecologists are at work, and there are some areas of National Park, such as the Covadonga and Somiedo Parks, hunting is the real obsession of the local people and far more land is given over to hunting preserves. These do help preserve endangered species as stocks are regulated, but success is measured not by whether the community is growing, healthy and sustainable, but whether there are enough animals to allow you to shoot some.

The rarest of all the mammals in the region is the European brown bear. There are thought to be only about 80 left in Spain, of which nearly half live in the Somiedo National Park. There are also some in the Ancares de León and, supposedly, at Covadonga. They have been permanently protected since 1967. The Iberian wolf is also still present in small numbers. The target of vitriolic hatred by farmers over the centuries, and the subject of many, often supernatural legends, the wolf is now protected, but is still hated and feared, and on the rare occasions when the ban is lifted, enthusiasm for the chase is as great as ever.

The chamois (ibex or mountain goat) with its huge, backward curving horns, was so eagerly hunted that it actually became extinct in many areas of the mountains, and had to be reintroduced in the 1950s. Now, although the population is only a few hundred, there is already some limited hunting. Red and roe deer have also been reintroduced and numbers are slowly building up again, although these too are hunted. Perhaps the only large mammal present in plentiful numbers is the wild boar.

Amongst the many species of bird to be found, it is the raptors which most excite the imagination. There are numerous species from golden eagles to lammergeiers (bearded vultures), as well as several species of harrier (Hen, Montague and Marsh amongst them. Game birds include partridge, red-legged partridge, pigeon, turtle dove and quail. Amongst the rarest of all the birds however is the capercaillie or mountain cock, a rather odd creature that looks a little like a small turkey, crossed with a guinea fowl.

(2417m). As the road climbs, you find yourself on the fringes of a remote, beautiful mountain region where life seems to have frozen several centuries ago and old men sit carving in front of balconied wooden cottages. In the high pastures, rudimentary shepherds' huts can appear more like bundles of thatch or cairns of stones. The region has a population of around 20,000 in all, living in about 200 scattered villages and hamlets.

Several long distance footpaths traverse the park and a new road from Villanueva leads across the mountains to Somiedo, finally providing access to the very heart of the National Park and to the stunningly beautiful Saliencia Lakes.

This route back-tracks along the valley as far as Caranga de Abajo, where you turn right onto the O430, which meanders along the river through magnificent scenery, to Las Agueras, Santa Marina, Llanuces and Armada, finally connecting up with the main N630 south at Pola de Lena. Four kilometres south of the village, a steep footpath leads off the road to the last of the major pre-Romanesque churches in the area, **Santa Cristina de Lena**, built during the reign of Ramiro I in the late

9th century. To get inside, ask for the key from the house beside the bridge, before you start up the hill. From the outside, this church seems less sophisticated than others of the period, built of rough stone, with few decorative features, its rectangular nave surrounded by small porches or extensions on all four sides. Inside, however, it is beautiful, with typical corded columns and a vaulted ceiling. A three-bayed iconostasis, based on Byzantine design, with Mozarabic decoration, separates the altar chapel from the main body of the nave.

Continuing south, those who prefer an easier drive can pick up the motorway 6km on. This crosses under the mountains into León through a series of tunnels. The N630 winds its way up into the high mountains and to the border at the **Puerto de Pajares**.

For a description of the Puerto de Pajares and the onward route south to León, see page 166.

Asturias: General Information

Regional tourist office

Comunidad Autónoma de Principado de Asturias, Consejería de Obras Públicas, Turismo, Transportes y Communicaciones, c/ Gil de Jaz 10, 4ê, 33004 Oviedo (tel. (985) 254 611).

The Coast

CUDILLERO
Where to stay and eat:
Hotel Mariño, Playa de la Concha de Artedo, 33155 (tel. and fax (985) 590 186). Small, friendly modern hotel on the beach. The rooms have balconies with sea views, and the seafood restaurant is popular with locals. Cheap to moderate.
Hotel Aspiazu, Playa de Aguilar (tel. (985) 583 210; fax (985) 583 685). Small family-run hotel in a beautiful setting, with a river valley leading into a quiet cove. The restaurant specialises in fish, and there is also a cider bar. Cheap to moderate.

FIGUERAS DEL MAR
Where to stay and eat:
Palacete Peñalba, (tel. (985) 623 150). Standing in its own grounds, at the top end

of town above the port, this is an Art Nouveau masterpiece, built in 1912 by a disciple of Antonio Gaudí. Most of its original features and fittings, from the oval balconies to the tiled atrium are still intact and the whole place has been declared a National Artistic Monument. Moderate prices.

GIJÓN

Tourist Office, Marques de San Esteban, 1, 33206 (tel. (985) 346 046).

Where to stay:

Parador El Molino Viejo, Parque Isabel la Católica, 33203 (tel. (985) 370 511; fax: (985) 370 233). There is an old watermill somewhere on the premises, but the hotel has been so extended that today it is an uninspired, if attractive, modern white building. It is sandwiched between a main road and the sports stadium on one side, and a luxuriously green and peaceful park on the other, so ask for a room with a park view. Expensive.

La Casona de Jovellanos, Plaza de Jovellanos 1, 33201 (tel. (985) 341 264; fax (985) 356 151). Small hotel in a carefully restored old building, looking out over a leafy square in the heart of the old city. Expensive.

Hernán Cortés, Fernández Vallin 5, 33205 (tel. (985) 346 000; fax (985) 355 645). Large, comfortable if soulless hotel right in the centre of town. Cafeteria only. Moderate.

Where to eat:

Parador El Molino Viejo, as above.

Las Delicias, Barrio Fuejo, Somío, 33203 (tel. (985) 360 227). Four km from the city centre, in a residencial district, this is probably the best restaurant in Gijón, serving a mix of seafood and regional specialities. You can dine out on the terrace in fine weather. Expensive.

LASTRES

Where to stay:

Miramar, 33330 (tel. (985) 850 120). A simple but attractive hostel with attractive views over the fishing port. Bed and breakfast only. Cheap.

Where to eat:

Eutomio, c/ San Antonio (tel. (985) 850 012). Sea-food restaurant specialising in regional dishes, with good views over the fishing harbour. Cheap to moderate.

El Mirador, San Roque (tel. (985) 850 162). Simple tapas and cider bar with a limited menu of local dishes. Cheerful and friendly, with good views. Cheap.

LLANES

Where to stay and eat:

Hotel Don Paco, Posada Herrera, 1, 33500 (tel. (985) 400 150). A slightly faded 17th-century palace, with a remarkably grandiose dining room, right in the centre of the town. Cheap-moderate.

LUARCA

Where to stay and eat:

Casa Consuelo, Otur 33792 (tel. (985) 641 809; fax (985) 641 642). About 0.5km from Luarca on the N634, this is a simple family-run establishment, with good, basic rooms, food, and a sea view. Rooms cheap; food moderate.

RIBADASELLA
Where to stay and eat:
Gran Hotel del Sella, 33560 (tel. (985) 860 150; fax (985) 861 331). Large up-market resort hotel in its own grounds, beside the beach, with good views, a swimming pool and tennis court. Expensive.
Hotel La Playa, c/ de la Playa 16, 33560 (tel. (985) 860 100). A private mansion converted into a small, rather old-fashioned hotel right beside the beach. Cheap.
There are a number of small, cheap fondas in the centre of town, away from the beach.

VILLAVICIOSA
Where to stay:
La Casona de Amandi, Amandi (tel. (985) 890 130; fax (985) 890 129). A delightful small hotel in a 19th-century villa set in its own formal gardens. Bed and breakfast only. Expensive.

Inland and The Asturian Mountains

BESNES
Where to stay and eat:
La Tahona, 33578 Besnes-Alles, Peñamellera Alta (tel. and fax (985) 414 249). A small, rustic stone, wood and geraniums-type hotel, beside a mountain stream in a beech wood. The restaurant specialises in regional dishes and is popular with locals. Completely off the beaten track, 10 km west of Panes. Cheap-moderate.

CANGAS DE ONÍS
Where to eat:
Mesón del Puente Romano (tel. (985) 848 110). With an attractive setting and outdoor terrace right beside the old pilgrim bridge, this is noisy, popular, unpretentious and cheap.
A new parador is under construction in Cangas de Onís, but at the time of writing, there are no further details.

COVADONGA
Tourist Office, El Repelao, 33589 (tel (985) 846 013).
Where to stay and eat:
Hotel Pelayo (tel (985) 846 000; fax (985) 846 054). On a ridge overlooking the sanctuary, this is comfortable, if a bit boring, and has stupendous views and a good restaurant. Moderate-expensive.
For those with tents, there is a superbly sited camping site high in the mountains, at the lakes above Covadonga.

OVIEDO
Tourist Office, Plaza de Alfonso II El Casto, 6, 33002 (tel. (985) 213 385).
Where to stay:
Hotel de la Reconquista, Gil de Jaz 16, 33004 (tel. (985) 241 100; fax (985) 241

166). Wonderful 18th-century orphanage built round a series of inner courtyards, which now has its second incarnation as a very upmarket hotel run by the Ciga group. Expensive.

Regente, Jovellanos 31; 33003 (tel. (985) 222 343; fax (985) 220 596). Large, comfortable if uninspiring hotel, best for its location, a stone's throw from the cathedral. Bed and breakfast only. Moderate-expensive.

Where to eat:

Trascorrales, Plaza Trascoralles 19, 33009 (tel (985) 222 441). Rural decor in an old aristocratic town house, together with some of the best regional cooking around make this one of Oviedo's top restaurants. Expensive.

El Raitan, Plaza Trascoralles 6 (tel. (985) 214 218. An attractive restaurant with three dining rooms decorated with local folk items. Set menu only, with nine courses! Moderate.

Cabo Peña, Mequíades Alvarez 24 (tel (985) 220 320). Popular tapas bar with a limited menu of full meals and *raciones* large enough to provide a meal in themselves. Cheap.

For those who are screaming for something other than regional specialities, Oviedo has a Macdonalds and a couple of wonderful delicatessens that sell pizzas as well as icecreams and pastries.

PUERTO DE PAJARES
Where to stay and eat:

Hotel Puerto de Pajares, Lena (tel and fax (985) 957 023). Once a parador, built like a hunting lodge, this small hotel on a pass high in the mountains on the Castille border has wonderful views and a restaurant that specialises in hearty mountain fare. Rooms moderate; restaurant cheap-moderate.

SALAS
Where to stay and eat:

Castillo de Valdés-Salas, Plaza General Aranda, 33860 (tel. (985) 583 1037). A converted 16th-century castle in a small market town in the foothills of the Cordillera Cantábrica. Simple, but charming, with the rooms arranged around a cloistered courtyard. This is a possible stop for those who wish to explore Oviedo and Gijón without staying in the city. Cheap-moderate.

The Basque Country

Tucked into the fertile eastern corner of the Bay of Biscay, between the high peaks of the Pyrenees and the Cordillera Cantábrica, the Basque Country (País Vasco or Euskadia) must be one of the most famous regions of Western Europe. It has a proudly nationalist and vociferous people, seemingly unconnected by blood or language to any of their neighbours. The Basque language is totally unrelated to any other in Europe and seems also to be outside the whole Indo-European language group. Whatever its origin, it is certainly very old. The Basques themselves claim that they were the original inhabitants of the Iberian peninsula, stretching back in unbroken line to Cro-Magnon man (c15,000 BC). Others, thinking they can detect vague linguistic similarities with the native languages of North Africa, seek to link them with the Iberians who are thought to have migrated northwards from Africa several thousand years later.

Old traditions remain startlingly alive and no one is afraid to fight to keep them so. The presence of the massive port of Bilbao, large-scale iron mining in the hills and a reputation for hard work have also attracted in more and more industry to make this one of the wealthiest corners of Spain.

Above all, however, the Basques have gained their greatest reputation and wealth as sailors. In the 15th and 16th centuries, when they were described as 'better instructed than any other nation in the world in the art of seafaring', every one of the great maritime adventures had at least one Basque sailor in the crew.

The Basque nation actually spreads far further than the current state boundaries, into eastern Cantabria, most of Navarra and across the Pyrenees into southern France. When the País Vasco was given Autonomous status in 1979 however, part of the deal was that the state borders would remain on their current lines and that the most hotly disputed region of Navarra would remain as a separate state. All but the die-hard few are satisfied now that they finally have a separate homeland, although the rumbling violence of ETA (see page 72) still continues sporadically.

The state is made up of three provinces, has a total area of 7500 square kilometres and a total population of 2,200,000, of whom nearly half live in and around Bilbao. This is the capital of Viscaya (Bizkaia) province, an area of 2217 square kilometres along the western edge of the Basque coast, bordering Cantabria. The eastern coast is taken up by Guipúzcoa (Gipuzkoa) province, an area of 1977 square kilometres, with San Sebastián (Donostía) as its capital. The whole line of the coast is heavily populated, mostly by an almost continuous stream of small

The Basque struggle for autonomy

After centuries of peaceful co-existence, a minority of Basques supported the Carlist Rebellion of 1876 (see page 29) and as a punishment, the Basques' traditional privileges were rescinded. The majority, who had remained true to the crown, were outraged and the first seeds of discontent were sown. To this day, the two causes are linked, with many Basque nationalists sporting the red beret of the Carlists.

The first Basque activist was a man called Sabino de Arana Goiri, son of a Carlist, who spent much of his early life as an exile in France. He began by writing about the language, and coined the name *Euskadi*, (literally 'a collection of Basques') which has been used by all nationalists since as the name of their homeland. He went on to found the first Nationalist newspapers, campaigning for full independence, and separate development. He died in 1903, but in 1910, his followers started the Basque Nationalist Party (the PNV).

The region suffered severe punishment under Franco, leading to increasingly anti-Spanish feeling. In the late 1950s, a militant Nationalist movement began in the universities. In 1960, the slogan *Euskadi Ta Askatasuna* (Euskadi and Freedom) was seen for the first time as graffiti and in 1961, the movement made its first act of terrorism, trying to derail a train full of Franco supporters on their way to a rally. The violence has continued ever since. Since 1966, the movement has split six or seven times, and each time, the breakaway faction has renounced violence and eventually disintegrated, while the hard-line military branch has remained intact.

Since the granting of Autonomous Status in 1979, the political wing of ETA, Herri Betasuna, still has a powerful voice, but the military wing has lost much of its public support. Most Basques seem content with their current situation. The tiny hard core that is left is still sworn to fight for full independence however and, as in Northern Ireland, the cycle of violence and police repression seems almost self-perpetuating. The visitor to the region will see the signs and slogans everywhere and will probably notice a much stronger police and army presence than in other regions, but the violence is sporadic and limited, and after one disastrous campaign in 1985, ETA have formally sworn off targeting tourists.

Campaign posters for Herri Batasuna, the political wing of ETA.

towns and fishing villages, many of which are now doing double duty as tourist resorts. Few however have been as heavily and hastily developed as those on the Cantabrian coast to the west of Bilbao and most retain a great degree of their original charm. Inland, the rolling hills are rich agricultural land with contented dairy cows up to their ankles in emerald green grass, though the almost Alpine idyll is regularly interrupted by sudden patches of black industry. The southern boundaries of both provinces run along the high points of the mountains of the Sierra de Gorbea and the Sierra de Urquilla. These two ranges create the link between the Cordillera Cantábrica and the Pyrenees. They are much lower than their giant neighbours, rarely exceeding 1000m, and never higher than 1500m, but they are, nevertheless, imposingly high and dramatically beautiful.

To the south of this mountain ridge lies Alava (Araba), at 3306 square kilometres the largest and least populated of the three provinces, with a population of only 250,000. The vast majority of these live in Vitoria-Gasteiz which doubles both as the provincial capital and the state capital of the País Vasco. The terrain here is very different, with the southern slopes of the mountains in a severe rain shadow that leads to almost Mediterranean aridity. Within a few short miles you find yourself swirling out of Irish mists and apple orchards into rocky fields and olive groves roamed by dusty goats. As you reach the bottom of the mountains and the land flattens out to become the northern edge of the Castillian meseta, you head into a vast prairie land of wheat and vines. The southern corner of Alava is part of the Rioja wine appellation (see page 245).

For the tourist, the state offers a pleasing mix of sophisticated cities and remote villages, of pretty coast and lovely mountain passes, of old and new history and a distinct and visible culture. The region also prides itself on being the gourmet capital of Spain and food is a subject of obsessive interest amongst everyone from peasants to princes. Unfortunately, in my estimation, prices for the real gourmet cuisine are excessive and my long-running hunt for a truly superb Spanish meal was as fruitless here as further west.

The Basque language, Euskara, ranks alongside Castillian Spanish as an official language here, and all signs are written in both. Many towns have completely different names in the two languages, while others are spelt differently. As the Basque names are given on Michelin maps, I have used these and put the Spanish name in brackets afterwards. In all but a few villages, people will speak both languages, and will rarely expect the visitor to be able to converse in even survival Basque.

Bilbao

Most tourists and even guidebooks shy away from Bilbao, hands raised in horror at the industrial fug that traps it within a circle of ugliness. This is by far the largest city in north-west Spain, and the sixth largest in the whole country, with an inner city population of around 435,000, but a population of over a million in 'Greater Bilbao'. It is also the capital of Vizcaya province, the largest port in the whole of

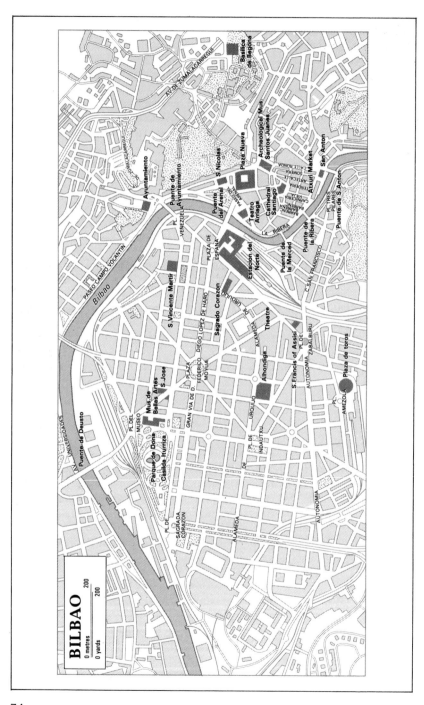

Spain, and one of the country's main industrial centres. If you are flying in, this is almost certainly where you will land.

Built along the twisting estuary of the huge Nervión River, the town received its charter in 1300 AD from Don Diego López de Haro, who is today honoured as the city's founder, the two wolves from his coat of arms incorporated into those of the city. In 1310, the town was given a second charter by Don Diego's niece, Doña Maria de Vizcaya, while in 1315, King Alfonso XI issued yet another, formally converting Bilbao into a trading post. For the next 500 years, it remained a small town similar to all the others along this coast, making its living from fishing and as a trading port, and squabbling with Santander over supremacy in the Castilian wool trade. In the early 19th century all that was to change. After centuries of peace, it was sacked by the French in 1808, and was besieged three times during the Carlist Wars, in the middle of the century. With strongly Republican leanings, it faced its last siege during the Civil War. Some 20,000 Nationalist shells poured down onto the city, flattening huge areas, before it eventually surrendered on 19 June, 1937.

The main catalyst for change came not from this century of warfare however, but from the Industrial Revolution when, in the 1870s, large-scale iron mining began in the hills behind the city. The docks grew to cope with the iron trade, the railway arrived to service them, and heavy industries based at first on iron and steel production grew up around the docks. Today, large-scale shipbuilding (including supertankers), chemical and fertiliser plants have all added to this immense concentration of giant factories. People flooded in to service the new industries and are still arriving from all over Spain. Vast new estates, many of them little more than slum tenements, sprang up to house the workers and the city was bathed in a pall of pollution.

Break in through the outer ring however and you find a vibrant city centre of attractive boulevards and pedestrian precincts, bursting with life and fascinating sights. More than in any other town or city in the region, you find yourself at the heart of the new Spain. After centuries of repression by the over-zealous Catholic church, a monarchy terrified of innovation and Franco's iron fist, the dam wall has burst and a positive tidal wave of new ideas is flooding into existence. Sadly, however, with this new freedom have come the new confusions, such as a growing drugs scene and, for some, sexual liberation run wild.

Right at the heart of modern Bilbao, on the east (right) bank of the river, opposite the gaily tiled façade of the Estación del Norte, is the old city. Commonly known as Las Siete Calles (Seven Streets), this was the original walled city, with seven streets, seven bridges, eight towers and two fortified gates. Today, much of it is given over to pedestrian precincts lined by small cafés, bars, restaurants and boutiques, and it is a lively place to come for a wander at the paseo hour. The southern end of the old city starts beside the Puente de San Antón and the heavily restored 15th-century **Church of San Antón**. The main door is a Renaissance work, dating from 1543, while inside the Chapel of Our Lady of Grief houses a Plateresque altarpiece with a statue of Piety by Guiot de Beaugrant. Just behind this is the vast indoor **Atxuri Market**, a magnificent place bustling with life and noise and colour that is well worth walking round, even if you can't think of anything to buy.

Head away from the river and cross the Calle Ronda, which follows the line of the old walls, and got its name from the rounds of the night watch. On the far side, you are in the original **Siete Calles**. Somera (literally meaning 'High St') has always been and is still the main meeting place for friends to gather. A tower house belonging to Martín Saez de Gueñes once stood on Artecalle, and it was here that three separate monarchs swore to uphold the Fueros of the Basque Nation – Henry IV of Castilla in 1457, Ferdinand the Catholic in 1476, and his wife Isabela, in 1483. Tendería is best known for its busy street market, while Belosticalle was the centre for leather and fabrics, Carnicería Vieja was the butchers' quarter, and the hotly competitive Barrencalle and Barrencalle Barrena were both lined by restaurants and inns. Both streets took their name from the castle of the Barondo family which stood here in the middle ages.

As you walk through these streets, you come out into the plaza beside the **Cathedral of Santiago**. With the town gaining quite a bit of prosperity from the lucrative pilgrim trade, the grateful townsfolk adopted Santiago as their patron saint, and, in the late 14th century, built him a suitable church. Work continued from 1379 to the end of the 15th century, but in 1571, the church was badly damaged by fire. The existing portal is an Isabelline work dating from 1581 to 1596. Still basically Gothic in form, the cathedral is chiefly famous not for the quality of its art, but for the fact that it has 24 altars – 18 in the main church and six in the cloister!

A block behind this stands the old Jesuit **Monastery and School of San André**. When, in 1774, the church of Santos Juanes was destroyed by fire, the parish was moved into this baroque church, and it was duly renamed as the Church of Santos Juanes. The monastic and school buildings behind now house the Museum of Basque Archaeology, Ethnography and History. The archaeology section, housed in and around the cloister, has a collection of finds from all over Viscaya, including finds from the excavation at the Santimamine Cave site (see page 79). The ethnographic collection includes displays of all major aspects of Basque life, such as fishing, weaving, ironwork, sports, local costume, ceramics and furniture. The history section includes collections of religious art, arms and a room dedicated to the Bilbao Consulate, which controlled local shipping from 1511 to 1829.

From here, a small road leads through to the large and magnificent **Plaza Nueva**, a huge arcaded square with 64 arches, that was built in 1830 as part of the first large-scale extension of the old city. This is now home to several smart cafés and bars, as well as to the San Tomás market. On the far side of the plaza, you come out into the Paseo del Arenal, beside the river. Just beside you is the 18th-century Church of San Nicolás de Bari, while on your left, standing alone in a small plaza is the elegant Teatro Arriaga, the city's municipal theatre, built in 1890 by Joaquin Rucoba. To the right, the paseo leads through a small garden area centred on a bandstand to the Town Hall, also built by Joaquin Rucoba on the ruins of the Convent of San Agustín, and opened in 1892.

Before you leave the right bank, head up the hill behind to the **Church of Nostra Senora de Begoña**. There are several ways up – on a winding main road for those in a car, in a lift, or up a long, flight of broad stairs lined by attractive houses and pilgrim crosses. Probably the best way to do things is to take the lift up, and walk down. The original hermitage on Artagan hill was founded after the Virgin made a miraculous appearance in a grove of holm oaks. An early 14th-century statue of the Virgin (now patron saint of the province of Viscaya) has been the centre of a minor pilgrimage cult here ever since. Designed by Sancho Martínez de Arego, building began on the current Gothic church in 1519. It was enlarged in 1588, while the spire is modern, built by José María de Basterra in 1907. Architecturally, the church is attractive, if not inspired, but it is a lively place, popular for weddings and you are likely to find plenty of festivities to watch. It is also set in attractive gardens which offer superb views across the river valley and the whole city of Bilbao.

Crossing the river, you enter an area known as el Abando (the Extension), a planned new town designed to house the overspill from the desperately over-crowded and rapidly growing city of Bilbao. Work first began in 1863 and today, in spite of its name, this is the main centre of Bilbao many times larger than the old town opposite. A block away from the Puente del Arenal, the Plaza de España (also known as the Plaza Circular) marks one end of the **Gran Via de Don Diego López de Haro**, the great boulevard that is the commercial and shopping focus of the city, with banks and consulates, department stores and cinemas. An imposing street with tall houses, shady pavements and an immense impression of wealth, this leads straight through the circular Plaza Federico Moyua, from which all the main roads fan out, to end back near the river (which has come round in a massive loop) in the circular Plaza del Sagrado Corazón.

Before you get this far, however, branch off to your right into the **Parque de Doña Casilda Iturriza**. Founded in 1945, this is not only the first but one of the largest and most beautiful of Bilbao's public gardens, with formal avenues and lawns, shade trees and a small lake. More to the point, however, in one corner stands the complex which houses the superb **Museo de Bellas Artes**. This is the combined collections of two separate museums, one covering classical, the other modern art. Allow plenty of time here, for the classical collection alone fills 31 rooms and there are many masterpieces, including works by El Greco, Goya, Breughel, Watteau, Picasso, Kokoschka and Francis Bacon, to name only a very few. Rooms 1–9 house paintings and sculptures of the Spanish school, from the 12th to 17th centuries; 10–12 have Flemish and Dutch works; and 13 and 14 house Italian works, all of the 15th to 17th centuries. Room 15 has French art of the 17th and 18th centuries while rooms 16–19 have a collection of Spanish art from the 17th to 19th centuries. Rooms 20–31 are dedicated to Basque painting and sculpture. The Contemporary collection is housed on the upper floor of the modern building, and there are also some 20 temporary and/or touring exhibitions each year.

There are also several other small museums in Bilbao, including one dedicated to the life and work of the musician, Arriaga. The Museum of Artistic Reproductions in Conde de Mirasol was originally part of the Art School, and houses 200 copies of great works of art from Ancient Greece to the present day, all of which live scattered in museums as far afield as London, the Vatican and Munich. As part of the Basque University at Leioa are two small museums of Basque Medicine and Basque Science History.

The Coast Road East – Bilbao to San Sebastián

This route hugs the curves of the coast, passing through a series of small ports and fishing villages, most of which have managed to remain attractive in spite of the growing pressure of tourism development. After the first few kilometres, the scenery is always good, with low, rolling green hills leading down to coastal cliffs and white sandy bays.

Leave the centre of Bilbao on the small road that leads along the right bank of the estuary to Getxo. The city has a total of 18,000 factories, employing about 300,000 people, and the vast majority line this 15km stretch of the estuary. It is a fascinating and eye-opening journey through the heart of the industrial complex on which the city is founded – grim, grey, dirty and desolate. Just before the river opens out into the estuary proper, you will see the **Puente Colgante** (the Hanging Bridge), a high iron transporter bridge that has become one of the city's major landmarks since its opening in 1893. Just beyond this, at **Getxo**, a promenade along the sea wall offers a superb view over the gigantic new container port of Abra and the enormous blast furnaces and steel mills behind it. At the far end of the promenade are the wind-breaks and lighthouses that mark the entrance to the port, while on the hills behind are a series of increasingly imposing, and often rather curious mansions, built as summer houses in the early 20th century by newly rich industrial magnates. As you turn the corner to find the open sea, at Sopelana and Plenzia, you find a surprisingly large number of people from Bilbao happily swimming off the beach. This is still the nearest, and one of the most popular beaches for daytrippers, although how they can venture into the water after driving through that industrial inferno is hard to imagine.

At Plenzia, turn left off the main road onto the C6315, through Gorliz and Arminza, from where a pretty road along the clifftops with lovely sea views leads to Bakio (Baquio), a small village rapidly growing in popularity as a resort. Keep going along the same road, past the Hermitage of San Juan de Gatelugache, which is perched on a rocky islet connected to the main coast only by a narrow stone causeway. Just beyond here, **Cape Machichaco** is the most northerly point on this stretch of coast, and there are superb views from beside the lighthouse.

A couple of kilometres on, still on the C6315, you come to **Bermeo**, the most important of the numerous small fishing towns along here, founded like many of the others on the whaling industry, and still incorporating a whale in its coat of arms. Set in a small bay, the town uses every available inch of space, with its colourful harbour lined by four and five-storey houses, all with glassed-in balconies. The dour 16th-century Ercilla Tower beside the harbour now houses a fascinating Fisherman's Museum, with exhibits that include a history of the fishermen's guilds, sailing instruments, models of traditional fishing boats and displays about their construction. There are also collections of equipment used both for fishing and on shore, and most poignantly of all, the various charms used to try and bring the boat home safely and with a good catch. Nearby, the 13th-century Church of Santa Euphemia was used by various kings and nobles to swear the fueros that provided the basis of common law. Also nearby are a few fragmentary remains of the old fortifications, and the Gothic church which is all that survives of the Convent of San Francisco.

As the road continues on, a lighthouse marks the entrance to the Ría de Gernika. Beside it, the little village of **Mundaka**, although also a fishing port, has a good beach and acts, in effect, as the resort area of Bermeo. From here, the road follows the west bank of the estuary down to **Gernika** (Guernica). Architecturally, this is a less than inspiring town, and most of it is downright ugly, but it is an immensely important place that acts as a symbolic focus of Basque Nationalism.

Traditionally, the Basque people have always been both thoroughly independent and impressively democratic, running their affairs through a structure of councils, starting at village level, while representatives of the various villages, districts and provinces would meet to discuss matters of mutual interest. The meeting-place would always be under a tree. As the early nobles and monarchs gathered power in the early Middle Ages, the Basques agreed to pay homage, only on condition that the ruler would abide by certain local laws and rights, which were codified and written down as *fueros*. The assembly tree at Guernica was one of only a few used for national assemblies and the town therefore became associated from the first with the national identity. Today meetings are held in an Assembly Hall above the town centre, but in its grounds the oak still grows. Strictly, it is the grandson of the 1000 year old Assembly tree, whose dead trunk is placed on view, carefully protected by railings. A sapling grown from the original line is always planted nearby to ensure continuity. Nearby, another building houses the National Archives, and a small Museum of Historic Documents.

Gernika's international notoriety comes from a different source however, as the site of one of the most horrific episodes of the Civil War. Both because of its symbolic status, and because of its fiercely Republican stance, the town was targetted for punishment by an irate Franco. On 26 April, 1937, when the people of the town and the local countryside had all gathered for the market, a German air squadron, backed up by naval shipping, bombarded the town for three hours, killing over 2000 people and flattening almost every building. It was a horrendous massacre, but it was also the first time that Hitler's newly powerful airforce had really shown its teeth, and the success of the raid is now considered to be a significant step on the road to World War II. Picasso painted a commemorative picture of the massacre, which is said to be one of his finest works. However, in spite of many representations by local people who would like to see it come 'home', the canvas still hangs in Madrid.

Turn north out of Gernika along the road that leads up the eastern shore of the estuary. About 3km on, a slip road on the right leads to **Santimamiñe Cave**, site of a number of Magdalenian cave paintings (see page 130). There have been numerous excavations here since the caves were first discovered in 1917, which have shown that the caves were inhabited for some 30,000 years. Finds from the digs are on display in Bilbao. The best of the paintings, including several charcoal sketches of horses, deer, bears, goats and bison are in one small chamber. Some are covered by a limestone film that has built up along with a number of splendid stalactites and stalagmites.

Just beyond this is the **Castle of Arteaga**. Built originally in the 15th century, little remains of the medieval fortress. Its current formidable battlements were actually the result of 19th-century rebuilding, when it was used as the home of Eugénie de Montijo, later the wife of Emperor Napoleon III. Turn left in the village and take the small road that leads around the headland, past Cape Ogono, to the crowded little hillside fishing village of **Elanchove**, which is now attracting attention as a resort due to the nearby Playa de Laga, a long and beautiful beach of pinkish sand.

The road continues east from here, back on the clifftops, to the larger town of **Lekeitio** (Lequeitio). Founded in the 15th century as a fishing and whaling port, this follows the now familiar pattern of Basque coastal towns. Set at the foot of Monte Calvario, its port is protected from the open sea by San Nicolás Island, which is connected to the mainland by a causeway at low tide. The attractive fishing harbour is surrounded by a huddle of houses with glassed-in balconies, interspersed by a few grand old houses such as the Casa de Adán. The Gothic Basilica of Santa María de Asunción is one of the finest in the region. Founded in the early 15th century, it was largely rebuilt between 1488 and 1508, with the addition of three tiers of flying buttresses. The belfry is 17th-century Baroque. In one of the side chapels, there is a small, but very beautiful High Gothic altarpiece depicting the road to Calvary, while the statue of the town's patron saint, Nuestra Señora la Vieja, stands in one of the north chapels. There are two good beaches nearby, one right beside the town, the other, the Playa de Karaspio, about 1.5km along the coast.

Still heading east, the road now becomes the C6212. Twelve km on, you reach **Ondarroa**, one of the largest towns on the Basque coast, with a permanent population of about 12,500. Another medieval fishing port surrounded by tall, brightly coloured houses, built on a loop in the Rio Artibay, this is still one of the main fishing centres in the region, its fleet of trawlers backed up by salting and canning factories. With two good beaches nearby, it is also growing in popularity as a summer resort. The old quarter of the town is charming, with an old bridge and the attractive Gothic Church of Santa María, built in 1492. The other church, Nuestra Señora de la Antigua, largely rebuilt in 1750, offers a good view of the harbour and coast.

A road south along the river valley via Markina-Xemein links up with the inland route from Bilbao to San Sebastián at Irubuzi (see page 82).

Just to the east of Ondarroa, still on the coastal C6212, you cross the border into the next province of Gipuzcoa (Guipuzkoa).

The next of the pretty fishing villages is **Mutriku** (Motriko), about 4km on, which takes its name from the Basque word *tricu* (hedgehog), because of the spiky rocks above. Sadly, as its popularity has grown, careless planning has allowed the construction of a number of unattractive buildings that are beginning to dominate and destroy the charm of the old harbour area. There are a fine beach, the Playa de Saturrarán, and an attractive 18th-century church.

The old town of **Deba** (Deva), another 4km on, is one of the most popular resorts in the regions and is already all but submerged under hotels and apartment blocks. There is a beautiful, but often crowded beach. The Church of Santa María la Real dates from the 13th century and still has a fine early Gothic portal. The cloister is 15th-century Gothic, and most of the rest of the church was rebuilt in 1629.

At Deva, the coast road joins the N634 that was, until the construction of the motorway, the main road west from San Sebastián. It has been straightened to some extent, but is still a slow, winding road that is used heavily by everyone hoping to avoid motorway tolls.

The next stop, **Zumaia** (Zumaya) is 15km on. In an attractive setting at the mouth of the Urola River, this began life as a Roman port, before its main growth in the 14th and 15th centuries as a fishing and whaling port. It is still a port town, with a busy, colourful harbour, but, with two good beaches nearby, it is also growing in popularity as a tourist resort. There are a number of fine mansions and several interesting churches here, including the 15th-century Church of San Pedro, which numbers amongst its art collection two beautiful triptychs, one of the road to Calvary, the other a Gothic gilded low relief of the life of St Christopher. Look also at the finely carved reliefs of the Descent from the Cross and the Flagellation near the High Altar. Other churches include the Sanctuaries of Arritokieta and San Telmo and the Convent of San José. The main reason to stop here however is to visit the Villa Zuloaga, the former home of Basque artist, Ignacio Zuloaga (1870–1945). Since his death, the house has been converted into a small museum displaying both his own works and those of his private collection, including five paintings by El Greco, and several by Goya. Attached to the house is the 12th Chapel of Santiago Echea, with a tiny cloister. An imposing, tree-lined esplanade leads from the town centre to the lighthouse.

From here, the C6317 leads south to Azpeita and the Sanctuary of Loyola, on the inland route from Bilbao to San Sebastián (see page 89).

This route continues east along the N634, passing some lovely sea views, to **Getaria** (Guetaria). This is one of the finest of the coastal villages, in a wonderful setting. From the coast road, you get a clear view of the island of Monte San Antón, which officially forms the end of this little peninsula, connected to the mainland by a breakwater. Because of its hunched shape, it is nicknamed *el ratón* (the mouse). Guetaria was the birthplace of Juan Sebastián Elcano, captain of one of the five vessels that sailed on Magellan's epic journey in 1519. Magellan himself was murdered in the Philippines and Elcano's ship was the only one to get home, arriving in 1522, after making the first circumnavigation of the globe. It was a feat for which he rarely gets any recognition, except from the people of his home town. The steep narrow streets of the fishing quarter lead up from the harbour to the Church of San Salvador. Founded in the 13th century, the church was virtually rebuilt in 1429, while the inner porch dates to 1605. The tower was started in 1526, but took some 150 years to build. Because of the steep slope on which it stands, part of the church rests on an arcaded alleyway. You can see into the crypt from here. Guetaria is perhaps best known for its fish restaurants and is a popular eating spot with San Sebastián foodies.

Zarautz (Zarauz), sprawled out along a stretch of flat land and with a wide, 2km beach became a prominent resort as early as 1855, when that indefatigable sea bather, Queen Isabela II (see page 92), arrived to try it out, trailing her retinue behind her. Today, most people come here for the increasingly wide range of resort hotels and apartments, golf courses, tennis courts and swimming pools, and of course, for the beach, from where there is a good view across to Guetaria.

In the past, the town had a more chequered history, first receiving its charter from King Fernando III in 1237 as a whaling port. The harbour was not a good one however and the town was forced to diversify to survive, becoming a major shipbuilding centre in the 15th to 17th centuries, and also creating small iron, weaving and tile-making industries. Generally fairly poor in terms of agriculture, it became a major producer of the 'green' Basque wine, Txacoli, and there are still several vineyards on the surrounding hills.

There are several fine buildings in the old town, including two 15th-century tower houses, the magnificent Torre Luzea, and the Torre Motza, both of which were private dwellings, although they also formed part of the town's defences and mark the line of the old walls. A third was incorporated into the 16th-century Palacio del Marqués de Narros. Other fine secular buildings include the 16th-century Palacio de Portu, now the Town Hall, and the Palacio de Makazaga in the Plaza Mayor, a fine example of Basque architecture at the transition from fortress to manor.

The parish Church of Santa María la Real was first built in the 14th century, but heavily altered in the 16th and is now a mix of Gothic and Baroque in style. It has a fine 16th-century altarpiece by father and son Andrés and Juan de Araoz from Onati, with a central figure of the Royal Virgin surrounded by the story of the Passion. Beside the church is a free-standing belfry, adapted from a medieval tower house. Other interesting churches include the Church of the Franciscan Fathers, built in 1610, which contains two fine Flemish Baroque altarpieces, and the Hermitages of San Pelayo and San Pedro Elcano.

Near the Torre Luzea stands a monument to the great Basque poet, Xabier Lizardi, who came from here. The town takes its Basque heritage seriously, creating a language school for Euskara and holding a Basque festival each September. In fact, if you wish to see traditional festivities, this is one of the best places to come, as the festival season starts in late May and continues virtually non-stop until mid-September.

From here, the road continues on through the little village of Orio, but it becomes increasingly built up and busy as the outskirts of San Sebastián gradually creep outwards.

For the description of the city of San Sebastián, see page 90).

The Inland Route – Bilbao to San Sebastián

This route winds its way through the northern hills of the Basque country, and the wonderfully lush green patchwork of fields and woods that characterises the region. It is far longer than the coastal journey, with several long stretches of mountain driving, interspersed by numerous historic sights. Access to the coast, or to the fast motorway and N634, is possible at various points along the way.

Leave Bilbao on the N634, signposted towards San Sebastián. Keep going for about 20km, much of it through uninspiring industrial areas, suburbs and commuter districts. At Amorebieta, turn left onto the C6315, signposted to Gernika. *(If you wish to join the coastal route or merely detour to Gernika, see page 79)*. Just outside Amorebieta, the road crosses a small pass with good views before joining Oca River valley. About 1km after the pass, turn right onto the B1131, signposted to Urruchua. This leads through Urruchua onto the high northern slopes of the 1029m Oiz Mountain. With a steep drop onto the coastal plain, this is known as the **Balcón de Vizcaya**, and there are wonderful views both across to Gernika and the coast, and the rich fields and heavily wooded hills of the hinterland.

About 7km beyond the official mirador, you come to the tiny **Puebla de Bolivar**, family home of the Bolivar family. At the end of the 16th century, the first Bolivar set sail for Latin America, aiming, like so many others of the period, to make his fortune. One of his descendants, Simón Bolivar (1783–1830), later became the greatest of the Latin American revolutionaries, claiming independence from Spain for his native Venezuela in 1821, for Colombia and Ecuador in 1822, for Peru in 1824 and Bolivia (which is named after him) in 1825. Given the title of El Liberator, he is revered and honoured throughout South America. A monument to him stands in the centre of this village, beside the amazingly solid Church of San Tomás and the cattle sales yard. Nearby is the humble mill (later a rementería or blacksmith's forge) which was the Bolivar family home. In 1983, this was converted into a small museum to celebrate the bicentenary of the Liberator's birth. There are displays about the village and its people, the nearby Collegiate Church of Cenarruza, and, of course, about the great man himself. The much grander, but virtually ruinous Palacio de Bolivar-Jauregui nearby belonged to a completely different family.

A small road to the right out of the village leads up to the isolated **Collegiate Church of Santa María de Cenarruza**, the only collegiate church in the whole of Viscaya. The abbey was first founded in 968 AD, although both abbey and church have been rebuilt or altered many times since then, and have recently undergone yet another restoration. According to legend, the spot for the abbey was chosen by an eagle, who swooped down on the grave of Santa Lucía de Garay, who was buried in Guerricaiz, and carried off her skull. He flew off and deposited the skull in the exact spot where the church was to be built. The eagle and skull are both depicted in the abbey's coat of arms, depicted on the side of the church. It also has a fine portal, a Plateresque altarpiece and a tomb, of Abbot Diego de Irusta, by Giot de Beaugrant.

Return to La Puebla de Bolivar and turn right onto the B1140 to Iruzubi. *(Go left from here to join the coast road at Ondarroa, see page 80)*. This route leads south over the 400m high Puerto de Trabacua. A few kilometres further on, past the charming villages of Elizondo-Berriz and Garay, the southern slopes of Mount Oiz offer another spectacular view, known as the **Balcón de Duranguesado**. After this, the road crosses under the motorway, and joins the N634. Turn right, and follow this into **Durango**.

This small industrial town on the Ibaizábal River is the administrative centre of an area known either as the Duranguesado, or the Merindad of Durango. *Merindad* is the Basque word used to describe the jurisdiction of a *merino* or judge of sheep-walks (areas of common land allocated to sheep-owners as grazing). It has also been adopted as the name of one of the most common breeds of sheep in the world, especially renowned for the weight of its fleece. Durango is also the home of the Basque television network. Stretches of the old walls still surround the town centre, which has to be one of the most attractive in the region. Only one of the town gates, the Arch of Santa Ana, is still standing, and that was rebuilt in the 18th century as a grand baroque monument, beautifully sited beside the old bridge.

The town has three churches of note. The Church of San Pedro de Tabira was the original parish church and is now the oldest in Viscaya, first built in the 9th century, although much of what you see today is the result of 14th- and 16th-century restructuring. It has two interesting tombs and a Plateresque altarpiece. The Church of Santa Ana, near the gate, has a wonderful altar, sculpted by Ventura Rodriguez in 1774. The Church of Santa María de Ulibarri has a curious hexagonal arcaded porch and a 16th-century choir. There are also many fine secular buildings, chief amongst them the Town Hall, which houses a series of fine Baroque murals and the arcaded Market Hall. Of the various monuments, look out in particular for the Kurutziaga Cross, a magnificent stone pilgrim cross erected in 1442. In the two main streets also stand monuments to the town's most famous sons, Friar John of Zumarraga, who became the first bishop of Mexico and founded the first University in America, and Pedro Pablo de Astarloa, an 18th-century scholar of the Basque language.

The local Art and History Museum is in the Palacio de Etxezarreta on Calle San Agustinalde. There are several sections, many of them largely used for reference, such as the council archives, dating back to the 14th century, and a large public library. The History Museum concentrates on local and regional artefacts, including remains from the period of the Carlist Wars, various religious items, and a portrait gallery. The Art Collection concentrates on contemporary work by Basque artists. There is also a more wide-ranging collection of drawings and engravings and some 20 temporary exhibitions are held each year.

For the route south from Durango to Vitoria, see page 101.

Leave the town along the C6322, heading south-east through Abadiño, a town famous both as an industrial centre and as a cattle-breeding district. A little further on, on the left, you will pass the Torre de Muntsaratz, a formidable early medieval tower that was home in the 12th century to the Infant María Urraca, an almost legendary local character known in Basque as Mari Urrika or the Dame of Amboto. A turning to the right leads down past the Amboto Rock into a lovely valley in which there are several tiny hamlets, such as Arrazola, that are becoming popular as places in which to buy second homes. The C6322 continues on along the Ibaizábal River valley. At Etxebarria, the Church of San Agustín contains several tombs of the Condes de Durango.

Elorrio, still on the Ibaizábal River, is now a backward little country town with a population of only 8000, but it was a busy centre in the 16th to 18th centuries and has a legacy of numerous fine Renaissance houses, many emblazoned with coats of arms. As a result, the entire town has been declared a National Historic and Artistic Monument. The parish Church of Nuestra Señora de la Concepción is a typically Basque 15th- to 16th-century hall church with finely wrought star vaulting resting on heavy round columns. It has a magnificent Churrigueresque altarpiece. In the grounds are 23 simple stone sarcophagi belonging to the Argineta family and dating from the 6th to 11th centuries.

Leave Elorrio on the road south-east to Arrasate (Mondragón). This climbs rapidly in a series of switchbacks to the 457m Puerto de Campanza, which marks the provincial border with Gipuzkoa (Guipúzcoa). A short while on, you reach Arrasate, a town most famous as the site of early iron workings and for being an early proponent of industrial co-operatives. *(If you wish to head south for Vitoria, turn right here onto the C6312 for a direct and very pretty road across the mountains).* Turn left onto the C6312, signposted to Bergara. 4km from the centre of town, at San Prudencio, turn right onto the road to **Oñati** (Oñate).

This small town, with a population of around 11,000, is set in the rich green valley of the Udana River, between rolling hills and the rocky, pyramidal peak of 1324m Mount Aloña. Its apt name means 'the place abundant in hills'. The town is one of only a handful in the Basque Country to have been owned by the nobility, first by a Señor, and later a Count. First mention of it is in a deed of gift from Count D. Ladrón to his son, Vela, in 1149, by which time it already appears to have been a thriving community. Initially, at least, the authority of the family was complete, but the history of town is one of an almost continuous ferment of civil strife, both between the Counts and the town, and between two of its leading families, the Garibays and the Murguías. Though the townspeople won the right to elect a mayor in 1389, for a long time afterwards, his appointment had to be confirmed by the Count, who would often choose a rival with more power, then sit back and leave the two of them to fight it out. The struggle for democracy grew fiercer in the 16th and 17th centuries, as did the family feud. For many years, the mayor was elected by the Garibays in even-numbered years, and by the Murguías in odd-numbered years. By the late 18th century, however, a free-thinking Count finally handed over the reins of power and the feud fizzled out. To celebrate, in 1783, the townsfolk built a magnificent new Baroque Town Hall, emblazoned with a coat of arms that uses the emblems of all three families. This is still, without doubt, the most imposing building in the small main square, but beside it stands the Palacio de los Lazarragas, an 18th-century mansion joined onto a 15th-century tower house that was once the residence of Carlos V, the pretender to the throne of Spain during the First Carlist Wars. The fountain in the square is one of eight installed in 1882, along with the town's first water supply.

A little way from the centre stands the imposing bulk of the University, founded by a local scholar, Bishop Rodrigo Mercado de Zuazola in 1548. It was the first university in Euskadi and remained the only one for nearly 300 years, offering degrees in canonical and civil law, medicine, philosophy, and literature. It closed early this century and is now used to house the provincial archives and as a School of Local Administration, run by the Basque Autonomous Government. The building is a splendid example of Plateresque architecture, with a basically simple outline with ornate decoration at the corners and a superbly carved main entrance by French sculptor, Pierre Picart. Inside, the chapel and cloister are particularly fine, both also decorated in the Plateresque style.

Opposite stands the parish Church of San Miguel, built in the late 15th century in the Gothic style, but remodelled, with Baroque additions such as the bell tower by Manuel de Carrera, in 1783. Inside, the finest art is in the side chapel of Nuestra Señora de la Piedad. Enclosed by a finely wrought iron grille, the chapel contains the tomb of Bishop Zuazola, the founder of the university, and a beautiful stone altarpiece, both Plateresque works sculpted by Diego de Siloé. The far more opulent Baroque main entrance, and the amazingly flamboyant gilded altarpiece behind the high altar are the work of a Navarrese artist, Juan Bautista de Suso. There is also a charming Plateresque cloister, built round and over Ubao River, while in the crypt is an elegant alabaster tomb of one of the Counts of Oñati.

The other important religious building is the Convent of Bidaurreta, founded in 1510 by Juan López de Lazarraga, accountant to Isabela the Catholic, for the Poor Clare nuns. The church is mainly late Gothic in style, with some Baroque additions, while inside, behind the high altar, there is an overblown Baroque altarpiece by Fray Jacinta de Sierra. The earlier, Plateresque altarpiece is now housed in one of the side chapels.

Before you leave the town, take the time to have a good wander through the streets, which are filled with a number of fine mansions, some of them converted from medieval tower houses, many of them dating to the 18th century. There are also several other smaller churches and hermitages in the vicinity.

From here, take the small road to the right to Arantzazu. This winds its way up through the Arantzazu River Gorge before climbing high into the thickly forested mountains to the **Monastery of Arantzazu**, a spectacular modern abbey in a wonderful setting. This is only the latest in a long line of hermitages and abbeys to be constructed on the spot since the 15th century.

In 1469, a local goatherd found an image of the Virgin lying in a thornbush beside a large cowbell. As was customary at the time, it was taken to be miraculous and a pilgrimage cult rapidly grew around the little statue. Unofficially the patron of the Basque people, in 1918, Andra Mari de Arantzazu (literally 'St Mary of the Thornbush') was appointed Patron Saint of Guipúzcoa. Her cult still flourishes unabated and the narrow road up the mountain is almost always busy with the cars of the faithful or the curious.

The first religious house on the site was run by nuns, but as increasing numbers of people became interested in making the trek into this remote spot, the citizens of Oñati and Mondragón paid both to build the road and to construct the first male monastery. Numerous orders came, including the Mercedarians, Franciscans, Dominicans and Hieronymites. From 1514, however, the Franciscans settled here permanently and it is they who still run the monastery today.

Work on the modern abbey, designed by architects Sáinz de Oiza and Laorga, began in 1950. Built of a sombre grey stone and cement, with square towers covered by diamond-faceted stones to represent thorns, it is an impressive complex that some love and many loathe, but which leaves no-one indifferent. Perhaps even more dramatic than the building itself are the magnificent works of modern

The monastery of Arantzazu at Oñati

art that adorn it. On the west front is a powerful frieze of figures by Oteiza, while the four west doors, designed by Chillida, are themselves abstract masterpieces. Inside, there are wonderful, mosaic-style stained glass windows by Fray Xabier de Eulate. Most impressive of all however is the massive curved wooden altarpiece by Muñoz. High up, in a central niche, sits the tiny Romanesque figure of the Virgin, on a pedestal made from the thornbush, the cowbell still hanging from one of the branches.

Before you head back down the mountain, continue on the road up to the mirador just above. The view over both the mountains and the monastery is wonderful, while a footpath for the energetic leads up the last 200m to the 1549m summit of Aitzgorri Peak, the highest in Guipúzcoa. From here, there is a superlative 360° panorama which, on clear days, stretches across six provinces of Spain, one of France and a stretch of the Cantabrian Sea.

To continue the route, you have to wind your way back down the mountain to Oñati before turning right towards Zumarraga. The road climbs out of the valley up to the 521m Alto de Udana, from where there is a fine view back across the town to the east and Mount Aloña to the south. Follow the road round, via Legazpiao, to Zumarraga, and turn left onto the C6317. This wriggles its way along the Urola River valley to **Azkoitia**, a small country town with a wide array of churches and a number of fine mansions. Chief amongst the churches are the parish Church of Nuestra Señora de la Asunción, dating from the 16th to 18th centuries, the 17th-century Convent of Santa Cruz, and the 16th-century Monastery of Santa Clara. Amongst the civil buildings, the finest is the Palacio de Insausti, which stands near the parish church at the entrance to the park. It was here, in 1748, that Don Francisco Xabier de Muniber founded the society that was to become the influential Basque Sociedades Económicas de Amigos del Pais (the Royal Basque Society of the Friends of the Country).

Six km further on, you reach **Azpeitia**, an attractive town framed by the twin peaks of Mounts Erlo and Xoxote. The parish Church of San Sebastián is said to have been founded originally by the Templars, but today appears as a classic 16th-century hall church, with a portal sculpted by Ventura Rodriguez. Inside you can see the font at which Ignatius de Loyola was christened. Opposite this, the Casa de Antxieta is a wonderful 15th-century tower house with a Mudéjar-style façade of delicately patterned brickwork. Take time to wander around the town which has a great many other fine buildings, both secular and religious, such as the Casa de Basozabal, the Town Hall, the Puente de Amube, and the Convento de la Concepcin.

Turn right out of the town centre along the well-signed route and follow the tourist coaches down to the **Monastery and Basilica of San Ignacio de Loyola**, a vast, opulent shrine to the saint who founded the Jesuit order (see box opposite). The church was designed by Italian architect, Carlos Fontana, on the orders of Mariana of Austria, wife of King Felipe IV, and was built between 1686 and 1738. The approach is made along a wide tree-lined avenue that frames the enormous, 65m dome of the church, flamboyantly decorated by Joaquin de Chirruguera. As you reach the end of the avenue, the full imposing length of the complex is revealed, the relative austerity of the long neo-classical wings only serving to accentuate the elaborate rotunda.

Inside, the church is entirely given over to the one, massive, echoing dome, said to be large enough for a congregation of 4000. The floors throughout are elaborately patterned in multi-coloured marbles, while each of the small side chapels is richly furnished with painted and gilded art. Most staggering of all however, is the minutely detailed sculpting that covers literally every available surface of the dome.

Behind the church, enclosed within the monastery walls, is the Casa Santa, the Loyola family home, in which the saint was born and lived for many years. It was originally built as a typically Basque tower house in the 13th century, but after the

San Ignacio de Loyola

Born in 1491, Iñigo López de Loyola was the youngest of 13 children and a member of a minor aristocratic family best known locally for their quarrelsome and somewhat dubious past, a family of black sheep in which this one white one stood out like a beacon. In the course of one feud, in 1456, his grandfather had nailed a proclamation to the door of Azpeitia church that read 'We shall wound and kill you and do you all the harm and evil we can.' All in all, the name Loyola, which means 'muddy ground', was considered to be remarkably apt.

Young Ignatius began his adult life as a soldier, but was wounded during a siege of Pamplona in 1521. While recuperating at his family home, he was given time to think and reflect and eventually received the call of God. In 1522, he left home and spent the next eight years either living in retirement, studying and writing, or going on numerous pilgrimages, from Arantzazu to Jerusalem. In 1530, he went to Paris to study, meeting up with the other great Spanish saint of the period, St Francis Xavier. They were ordained together in 1537, before travelling to Rome.

In 1540, Loyola received permission from the Pope to found a new religious order, the Society of Jesus. He drew up the somewhat spartan constitution and rules and became its first Vicar-General. Francis Xavier was one of the founder members. The order, better known as the Jesuits, rapidly grew to be one of the largest, richest and most powerful in the world, its members renowned for their theological knowledge, missionary zeal, and, for some time at least, as enthusiastic supporters of the Inquisition. By 1773, their power was so threatening to the Spanish and Portuguese thrones that the order was dissolved forcibly by the Marquis of Pombal. It was reformed in 1814 and still exists today, primarily as a teaching order.

St Ignatius died in Rome in 1556 and was canonised, along with Francis Xavier, in 1622. His feastday is on 31 July.

somewhat rash proclamation by Loyola's grandfather in 1456, the house was attacked and the top storeys knocked down, with the full blessing of King Henry IV. When the family eventually got permission to rebuild, they were allowed to do so only if they didn't build in stone. The result is an almost Moorish façade of gaily patterned red brick. Inside, Ignacio's private rooms have been converted into a series of lavishly decorated and overpowering chapels oozing gilt from every crevice.

Return to Azpeitia to continue along the route. (If you wish to join the coastal route turn north onto the C6317, signposted to Zumaya, page 81). Turn right onto the C6324, signposted to Tolosa. This is a beautiful road that winds its way through the mountains, via the pretty little village of **Regil**, where the Gothic parish Church of San Martín has a fine 15th-century altarpiece and a statue of San Martín on horseback, dated 1713. The large building opposite is the old University. As you continue on, through the 532m Puerto de Zelatun to Vidana, there are some wonderful views across a patchwork landscape of rocky crags, beech forest and emerald fields.

Tolosa was once an important trading cross-roads and, for some years, capital of Guipúzcoa province. Now a built-up industrial town that is the centre of the Basque paper-making trade, there are still several fine buildings in the old town. Chief amongst them are the 17th-century Church of Santa María, the 16th-century

Church and Convent of San Francisco, the Town Hall, the Palacio de Idiaquez and the Palacio de Atodo. Beside the Town Hall stands the Confectionary Museum, dedicated to the production of sweets and pastries before the introduction of electricity. Concentrating on Basque specialities, there is a wide range of kitchen equipment on view, used for making everything from wafer-biscuits to cakes, ice-cream to sweet alcoholic drinks.

In Tolosa, the road joins the main N1 to head north along the increasingly built-up Oria River Valley to San Sebastián.

San Sebastián (Donostia)

'A headland on the right, a headland on the left, two gulfs, an isthmus in the middle, a mountain in the sea; at the foot of the mountain, a City: *Voilà Saint*

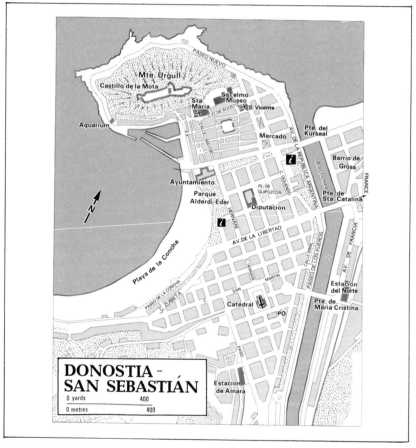

A fish stall in the market at San Sebastián

Sebastien! . . .' This description, written by Victor Hugo in the mid-19th century, is still remarkably apt. The city might have sprawled outwards, but its geography is virtually unchanged and it still has the immense charm that, for nearly a century, drew to it like a magnet the beautiful, rich and powerful of Europe.

Although it started life as a haphazard collection of Basque farms and small holdings, the convenient position of the bay near the French border soon made this small community a popular stopping point on the northern pilgrim route to Santiago de Compostela (see page 28). By the 12th century, tourist trade in the town was beginning to flourish, and the devout pilgrims had named the small town after the martyr, St Sebastián. In 1180, the town received its charter and the king swore the *fueros* that would guarantee its status.

With the vast majority of pilgrims choosing to use the southern route however, they did not have nearly as great an impact here as on towns such as Burgos, and much of San Sebastián's early prosperity came from whaling and deep sea fishing, particularly for cod. From the 14th century onwards, trade also began to play an increasingly important part in the local economy, as the harbour expanded into a major export centre, handling oil and wine on their way to France, England and Flanders. By the 18th century, it had become the main port for Navarra, a major shipbuilding industry had grown up and it was the headquarters of the Royal Caracas Sailing Company, which was one of Europe's largest importers of spices from the New World.

The town grew and prospered, but its progress was not easy. Strategically close to France, it was an inevitable target in any war and it came under attack many times, although it was rarely captured. The one exception came in 1808, when it was seized by Napoleon, whose troops stayed there until defeated by an Anglo-Portuguese army in 1813.

Lucky in war, natural disasters had more success and no less than twelve serious fires swept through the town over the centuries, each causing widespread damage. The last, in the wake of the Napoleonic conquest, was in 1813. Some say it was the French who torched the town before they left, but most blame it on the victorious and vengeful English and Portuguese troops! Virtually the entire city was destroyed, with only 35 houses and a couple of churches still standing, but the townspeople held a public meeting and decided to rebuild. The project was placed in the hands of architect Pedro Manuel de Ugartemendia, who began by rebuilding the old town, roughly along the lines of the existing roads, but with a superb neo-classical uniformity.

The effects of the tourist trade once more came into play in 1845 with the arrival of Queen Isabela II. Thoroughly convinced of the beneficial effect of seabathing in her constant search for a cure for herpes, she so liked the town that she came back year after year, trailing after her most of the Spanish Court, much of the government, and a large proportion of the aristocracy. There was a short hiatus a few years later when a cholera scare in France made the nervous nobles look elsewhere and they all moved along the coast to Santander, safely out of harm's way. Having created a similar boom in that city, they returned once the scare was over and development at San Sebastián continued apace. In 1854, the city became the capital of Guipúzcoa province and by 1863, the city was growing so rapidly that the town walls were pulled down to make way for further development.

King Alfonso XII, his wife Maria Christina, and his son, Alfonso XIII all kept up the tradition of seaside holidays and under their patronage, San Sebastián flourished. Of all the resorts in Spain, this became the most sophisticated and glamorous, a leader in civil technology as well as fashion. It was the first city in Spain to develop a tram service, telephone lines and street lighting, while the new developments were laid out with wide boulevards and paseos, shady parks and graceful apartment blocks and hotels. It was placed firmly on the European map as one of the places to see and be seen, and while Nice and Monte Carlo suffered during the First World War, San Sebastián escaped almost unscathed as the beau monde flocked south to sit out the horrors of war in neutral Spain.

Today, the city continues to grow and now has a permanent population of about 182,000, with a summer population many times higher. The social balance of the visitors has shifted to some extent, but the city still has the power to draw the chic, and for every pair of jeans you see on the streets, you can find a pair of diamond earrings or Gucci shoes.

The eastern edge of the city is marked by the bulky headland of **Monte Ulía**, as yet still a green retreat, although modern housing developments are beginning to creep up its slopes. There are several sports facilities here, including trap-shooting, along with picnic sites and tea rooms. At the top is the Peña del Ballanero (Whalers' Rock), from where the whalers kept a look-out thoughout the season. When a whale was sighted out to sea, a huge bonfire was lit to call the fishermen down to the boats. Needless to say, the view is excellent. At the western foot of the hill, on largely reclaimed land is the smallest of the three beaches, the Playa de Gros. This is also the least attractive of the beaches, mainly surrounded by post-1950s development, and strong undercurrents can make swimming dangerous.

The imposing Urumea River marks the boundary of the old town and the 19th-century extensions. The further away from the coast you head, the scruffier the river and the surrounding development becomes, but the area towards the sea is marked by three wide and graceful bridges, the María Christina, the Santa Catalina and the Zurriola (Kursaal). Beside them stretches a broadwalk popular with local fishermen, some of it transformed into a leafy boulevard. Behind this stand some of the city's most gracious buildings, yet they almost pale into insignifance behind the tiny detail of the streets furnishings, such as the ornate lights and patterned railings that provide the perfect, frivolous trimmings for the clean, austere lines of the streets and walks themselves.

A couple of blocks west from the Maria Christina Bridge stands the huge neo-Gothic Cathedral del Buen Pastor, designed by Manuel Echave. Work began in 1889, using local stone from the Igueldo quarries, and the church was consecrated in 1897, with several members of the royal family, including the Queen Regent, Maria Christina, present. Its chief claim to fame, the 75m high spire, was finished in 1899, and in 1953, it was given cathedral status as head of the new diocese of Guipúzcoa.

Walk north through the grid of streets to the Avenida de la Libertad, which crosses the peninsula from the Santa Catalina Bridge to the Plaza de Cervantes. This is the city's main shopping street. Staying within the town, two blocks north of this is the **Plaza de Guipúzcoa**, an enchanting garden square, laid out on the English plan, but containing a great many lushly tropical plants. On one side of the square stands the headquarters of the regional government, the Diputación Regional de Guipúzcoa. Built originally in 1855 by José Giocoa, it was burnt down within a year of its completion, but rebuilt to the same design by Luis Aladrén in 1856.

Turn left (east) from here, and you come out into the huge formal gardens of the Alderi Eder where processional rows of ferociously trained tamerisk trees provide shade for those who wish to sit or stroll. The **City Hall**, at the north end of the gardens, was built by Aladrés and Morales de los Ros in 1887. This was the city's original casino, the focus of all the excitement of the Belle Epoque, visited by such contrasting guests as Leon Trotsky, Sarah Bernhardt and King Leopold of Belgium. Gambling was banned in 1924, and for the next 20 years the building stood empty, until it was adapted into the new seat of local government in 1947.

Standing at the sea wall beside the town hall, you can, for the first time, get the full impact of the city, with a sweeping panorama of the whole horse-shoe shaped bay laid out before you. To your right are the old town, the fishing harbour and marina, and Monte Urgull. To your left is the long curve of the Playa de la Concha. At the far end of this, on a tiny headland stands the Palacio de Miramar, and beyond that the smaller Playa de Ondarreta. At the far end of the bay stands the peak of Monte Igueldo, while smack in the middle of the bay is the little rocky Isla de Santa Clara.

Head first into the old town, turning right behind the Town Hall on the Alameda del Boulevard, which marks the barrier between the two areas. From here, there are good views up the Calle Mayor to the Basilica of Santa María del Coro and down the Calle de Hernani to the Cathedral, while a few blocks over you come to the huge, vividly colourful indoor Market.

Calle San Jeronimo and Calle Narrica both lead up to the neo-classical **Plaza de la Constitución** which is the central focus of the old city. It is an elegant square, with an arcaded walkway at ground level and wrought iron balconies above. At one end stands the former Town Hall, built after the 1813 fire by Silvestre Perez and completed in 1832. It is now the Municipal Cultural Centre and Public Library.

Plaza de la Constitución, San Sebastián

The numbers painted beneath the balconies date back to the time when the square was used as a bull ring, with the balconies as stands. These days, you are also likely to find plenty of graffiti extolling the virtues of the Basque Nationalist Party, Herri Betasuna, or lamenting the horrors of the Guardia Civil. Under the arcades and in the surrounding streets are numerous small bars, cafés and restaurants which are alive with noise and the smell of seafood every evening.

Two blocks north is the Gothic **Church of San Vicente**. There is thought to have been a church on this site since the 12th century, but the existing one dates from the late 15th. Nevertheless it is widely recognised as the oldest building in the city, its fortress-like exterior perhaps a clue to its persistent survival.

A block north of here, at the foot of Monte Urgull, is the **Museum of San Telmo** housed in a Dominican Convent designed by Fray Martín de Santiago and built between 1544 and 1562. The building alone is worth a visit, with both Gothic and Renaissance elements in the design and a particularly fine two storey cloister. In 1836, the Dominicans were expelled and the convent became an artillery barracks until the council decided to buy it to convert into a museum in 1928. In 1931, it was declared a National Monument. There are several different collections here, including archaeology, Basque ethnography, and a wide-range of paintings from the Gothic through to the 20th century. Of the modern artists, particular attention is given to A. Ortiz Echagüe and Ignacio Zuloaga, while pride of place goes to a series of oils painted by Catalan artist, José Maria Sert, in 1931, telling the story of the Basque people. When commissioned, they were destined to be installed in the old convent church.

One block west of this is the city's architectural jewel, the fine Baroque **Basilica of Santa María del Coro** which is generally regarded as the most important of the city's churches, in spite of the presence of the much larger cathedral. This is the third church on the site, with Romanesque and Gothic forbears. This one was paid for by the Royal Caracas Society with American gold and consecrated in 1764. Its best feature is the wonderful Baroque façade. In a niche high up above the main door stands a tortured statue of San Sebastián, bristling with arrows. The saint who gave his name to the city was a Roman soldier and a member of the personal bodyguard of Emperor Diocletian. In 288, it was discovered that he was a secret Christian and was martyred, by being shot full of arrows. Artworks depicting him rank among the goriest in Christian iconography. A large 19th-century painting of him by Luis Bocia inside the church is no exception. There are numerous other works inside, but those worth looking for include a statue of Christ, called Peace and Patience, which used to stand beside one of the town gates, the Puerta de Tierra until its destruction, and the organ, built in Paris in the mid-19th century by Cavallie Coll.

Beside the church, you find yourself once again on the edge of the old town, looking down on the fishing harbour, where rows of rickety fish restaurants and darkened wine bars line the quay. It is from here that the small ferries run through the summer season to the Isla de Santa Clara, a popular spot for daytrippers.

Walk along to the far end of the quay and you come to the **Aquarium and Oceanographic Museum**. Founded in 1928, pride of place is given to the enormous skeleton of a whale captured in the bay in 1828. Around it on the ground floor is

The church of Santa María, San Sebastián

the aquarium, with a range of species found along the Basque coast. Upstairs the Oceanographic collection has a complete mix of natural history of the coast, from shellfish to climate and coral. On the second floor is the Sea Museum, giving a history of local seafaring with scale models of ships and boats as well as displays on the sailors' lifestyles. The building is also the headquarters of the Guipúzcoa Oceanographic Society.

From here, the Paseo Nuevo is a walkway leading right around the head of the peninsula, just above sea level. The better option however is to backtrack a little way along the quay and take the narrow footpath that winds its way steeply up to the top of **Monte Urgull**. Crowning the summit are the walls of the **Castillo de la Mota**, the city's fortress, rebuilt many times over the centuries. The first castle was built here by Sancho the Elder of Navarra in the 12th century and reinforced a few years later by Sancho VII el Fuerte (the Strong). In 1476, Ferdinand and Isabela (the Catholic Monarchs) reinforced it, encircling the foot of the mountain by strong walls that were joined to the city walls. French king, François I, was held prisoner here after his defeat at the battle of Pavia.

The existing citadel was built in the 17th century, while the batteries were added in the 18th. The last fortifications known variously as Napoleon's Battery or Wellington's Battery were added during the Peninsula Wars in the early 19th century. In 1863, the encircling walls were destroyed along with the city walls, but the citadel was kept intact and remained in the hands of the War Ministry until 1921, when it was sold to the City Council and the surrounding area was land-scaped as a park. Inside the castle itself there is now a small Arms Museum. Walk through this and continue up to the vast Statue of Christo del Sogrado Corazón. Built in 1950 by sculptor Frederic Coullant, to a design by Pedro de Muguruza, it is 28.8m tall, a spectacular monument that has become the city's most recognisable landmark. On a clear day, the view from the pedestal is superb.

Heading back down the hill, make your way back to the Alderi Eder, and walk along the seafront, either on the walkway above, the Paseo de la Concha, or on the beach itself, if you can manage to pick your way across the press of bodies. On the small headland at the far end stand the **Palacio y Parque de Miramar**. The palace was built in 1892 by Queen Mara Christina, as her summer residence. Designed by English architect, Selden Wornum, along the lines of a Queen Anne English country house (of which it is a rather angular pastiche), the actual work was overseen by a local architect, José Goicoa. The grounds were landscaped by Pierre Ducasse. On the queen's death in 1929, the house was abandoned and left to rot until it was bought by the Council in 1971. It is now used as a venue for art and cultural events and the gardens are open to the public.

Beyond the gardens, you come to the third of the city beaches, the Playa de Ondarreta, which leads across to **Monte Igueldo**, the mountain that marks the western edge of the bay. From the Plaza de Tenis at the far end of the beach, a walk leads along the headland to the dramatic clifftop sculpture, the Peine de los Vientos (Comb of the Winds) by Eduardo Chillida. From the back of the plaza, a funicular railway winds up the hill to the small funfair and amusement park at the top.

There is very little worth seeing away from this coastal strip. The one exception is the **Palacio y Parque de Ayete**. An elegant neo-classical building, completed in 1878, this was originally the home of the Duque de Bailen. In 1883, however, King Alfonso XII moved in and in 1887, it was given to the royal family who used it until they built the Miramar Palace in 1892. Since 1940, it has belonged to the City Council and is used to house any visiting dignitaries. The park is open to the public.

With a city based on enjoyment, it is perhaps inevitable that there are numerous festivals scattered throughout the year, some religious, some celebrating Basque tradition, and some devoted to the arts. The best of all for visitors is the week of

15 August (the Feast of San Sebastián), known locally as the Semana Grande (Big Week). This combines all the different elements, and, for good measure, throws in the International Fireworks Competition. If you can't make it then, try the pre-Lentern Mardi Gras carnival. Other major events include two horse-racing seasons a year and international film, classical music and jazz festivals.

The Coast Road East – San Sebastián to Irún

This short route covers the last 20km of the Basque coast to the French border.

Leave the centre of San Sebastián, heading east towards Irún. The road runs through the suburbs to the village of Pasaia Antxo (Pasajes Ancho), now a continuation of the city in all but name. This has become far distanced from its roots as a pretty little fishing village, and the houses now look out over the vast and business-like modern port of San Sebastián, situated in an inland basin on the Bidasoa River. A small road to the left leads through the smaller and more traditional village of Pasajes San Pedro. At the far end of the road, there is a seawall, from where you can walk round the headland to the open coast. Although there are no official paths, it is also easy to climb up onto the hill behind, from where there are lovely views and, in season, a host of wild flowers.

On the opposite bank of the river is the tiny and enchantingly pretty village of **Pasaia Donibane** (Pasajes San Juan). There is a ferry for foot passengers, but the easiest way to get here is to continue on along the main road and turn left on the opposite side of the river. A little medieval village strung out along the river bank, it was founded in the 11th century on the fishing and whaling industries. It was from here that Lafayette embarked on his journey to America in 1776, Victor Hugo lived here for a short while in 1843, and in the final months of the Peninsula War, it became Wellington's main supply depot. Today, you can visit the ruined fort built in 1621 and a minor 16th-century church, or walk along the river bank and round the corner to a small, but pretty beach. The village is chiefly popular with both tourists and locals because there are several very good fish restaurants here.

Follow the small road round the curve of the coast up to **Mount Jaizkibel**, where it crosses a 448m pass, almost within feet of the sea. The resultant views along the coast, the Bidasoa estuary and as far as Bayonne in France are spectacular. As you twist down the far side, you come to the little Church of Nuestra Señora de Guadalupe, patron saint of Fuenterrabía, who is said to have miraculously saved the town after a two-month siege in 1638. Her feastday on 8 September is always an occasion for great festivities.

Standing at the estuary of the Bidasoa River, staring across the water at France, **Hondarribía** (Fuenterrabía) has always been in a strategically important position and the site of numerous armed clashes across the centuries. It came into existence however not as a military outpost, but as a crossing point for pilgrims on the road to Santiago de Compostela (see page 28). Today, it is still a busy fishing port, but it is also one of the most popular coastal resorts on the Atlantic coast, fizzing with life and colour throughout the summer.

Market stalls in the streets of Hondarribía

The town has two very distinct areas. The flat, marshy area around the fishing port and fishermen's quarter is known as La Marina. The narrow streets here are a riot of colour, the houses brightly painted with ornate balconies heavy with flowers. At street level, open air market stalls rich with fruit add to the general sense of gaiety. Modern development, much of it unfortunately ugly, is rapidly filling the gap between this district, and the old walled town, built up onto a defensive mound.

The entrance to the old town is through the Puerta de Santa María, an imposing gate through the 15th-century ramparts decorated with the town's coat of arms. Dominating this area is the formidable square Fortress, known as the Palacio de Carlos V. Built on the 10th-century foundations of the original fortress of King Sancho of Navarra, the existing castle was erected in the 16th century by Carlos V. The walls still show the marks of cannons used during the many battles it has seen. The town was captured by the French under Francois I in 1521, besieged by the French under the Duc de Condé in 1638, by the English under the command of the Duke of Berwick in 1719, and by Wellington's army in 1813. Today, the castle has been converted for use as a parador. There are several fine mansions in the maze of streets surrounding the castle and plaza, particularly in the Calle Mayor and Calle Obispo. The 11th-century Church of Nuestra Señora de la Asunción and the 15th-century Church of Santa María were both heavily remodelled in the Baroque style in the mid-17th century.

A small road on the left leads from the town up to the lighthouse at the tip of Cape Higuer, from where there is an excellent view back across the town and the mouth of the river to Hendaye.

Heading south along the riverbank, you will find yourself almost immediately entering the outskirts of **Irún**, a bustling modern town largely rebuilt since its almost total destruction during the Civil War. This is the main French frontier in the west, and is also the line of both motorway and railway across the border. There are relatively few old buildings of any note left. The Town Hall in the Plaza de San Juan was officially opened in 1763 to celebrate the town's independence from Fuenterrabía. A monument to San Juan de Arri in the square in front of it celebrates an earlier, symbolic independence. The Renaissance Church of Nuestra Señora del Juncal, built in 1508, houses the oldest Romanesque carving in the province. Other interesting buildings can be found in the Calle Mayor and the Plaza de Urdanibia.

The rather boring little island in the middle of the river is known both as the Ile des Faisans or the Ile des Conferences. Over the centuries it has provided a convenient piece of no man's land for a series of crucial conferences between France and Spain. Louis XI and Enrique IV of Castile met here in 1468. In 1615, two princesses met en route to royal marriages. Isabelle, the daughter of Henry IV was on her way south to marry Felipe IV, while Felipe's sister, Ana of Austria, was heading north to marry Louis XIII. In 1659, Louis XIV and Felipe IV met here to sign the Treaty of the Pyrenees which ended hostilities between them during the Thirty Years' War. Part of the agreement was for Felipe's daughter, the Infanta Maria Louisa, to marry Louis. A proxy wedding was held at the Church of Santa María in Fuenterrabía before she was allowed to travel.

Nearby, on the riverbank near Mount Ibaieta, the Hermitage of Santa Elena began life as a Roman crematorium before the site was converted to Christian use. A small museum is now housed within the hermitage, displaying archaeological finds from this site, as well as from the underwater excavations at Cape Higuer, and the digs at el Juncal and the Arditurri mines.

Two km south of the city centre, along a small side road, is the Hermitage of San Marcial, set on the summit of a 225m hill that is said to have been the site of two great victories (assisted by the saint) against the French, in 1521 and 1813. The view from the top is lovely.

For the route from Irún to Pamplona, see page 220.

Durango to Vitoria

This route heads south across the mountains of the Sierra de Gorbea, offering an extraordinary range of dramatic scenery within a very short drive. (*To join this route from Bilbao or San Sebastián, follow the Inland route see pages 82–90. A description of Durango is on page 84*).

Leave Durango on the C6211, heading south towards Vitoria. Just on the edge of town, you come to the tiny village of **Izurtza** (Izurza). Here, set against a mountain backdrop and surrounded by humble cottages, there are three powerful medieval tower houses, the Torre de Etxaburu, the Torre de Lexartza and the Torre de Beko.

A little way south, **Mañaria** is chiefly famous for its eight quarries, four of them marble. It was also the birthplace of Basque writer, Evaristo Bustinza Kirikiño, and a modern monument to him stands in the square beside the church.

The road climbs steeply to highest point of the route at the 700m **Puerto de Urkiola** (Urquiola), from where there are wonderful views across the mountain peaks of Urkiolamendi and Saibi, famous as the site of three bloody battles during the Civil War. Beside the road at the pass, surrounded by oak and beech woodland, is the Sanctuary de los Santos Antonios, a truncated Romanesque church that is a popular pilgrimage site. The surrounding area is protected as a natural park.

As the road winds back down the southern slopes, you come to the village of **Otxandio** (Ochandiano) which has a fine Town Hall and Church of Santa Marina. The town has been famous as an ironworking centre for centuries, specialising in making chains and huge iron nails for boats, and in the centre of the square stands a statue of Vulcan, the pagan god of iron, set up as a tribute to the town's smiths.

About 1km south of the village, the road crosses the provincial border into Araba (Alava). Almost immediately, you find yourself travelling along the shore of the ribbon-like northern arm of the Lago de Santa Engracio (Lago de Urrunaga), one of three large reservoirs huddled together in this area. The other two, the Embalse de Albiña and the Embalse de Zadorra (Ullivarri) are to the east (left) of the road. All three offer a variety of watersports and picnic sites and are popular with daytrippers from Vitoria.

As you meet the main body of the lake, you turn onto the main road from Bilbao, the N240. Shortly afterwards, this becomes a dual carriageway. At the village of **Miñano Mayor**, the 13th-century Church of San Vicente belongs to the late Romanesque, early Gothic period. There are also attractive early churches in the nearby villages of Miñano Menor and Durana, just off the main road.

Vitoria-Gasteiz

Of the three main cities in the Basque Country, Vitoria is the least visited, in spite of the fact that it is not only capital of Araba (Alava) province, but since, 1980, has been the capital of the whole Basque Automonous Community. Set on a small hill in the middle of the huge Llanada plateau, geographically and historically, the city's ties are far closer to the Castilian plains than to the mountainous regions of the north. There is a large Basque community in the northern part of the province, but in and around Vitoria-Gasteiz itself, the Basques are in the minority, although the presence of the legislature makes them highly visible.

It is thought that the first settlement on this hill near the Zadorra River was a Visigothic village called Gasteiz, but the modern city dates from the 11th century when the site was repopulated following the Reconquista. The origin of the name Vitoria is still disputed. Some say that it was King Sancho el Sabio (the Wise) who renamed it Nueva Vitoria in 1181 when he gave the town its charter and swore the local *fueros*, while others say that the name is actually a derivation of the Basque word *beturia*, which means height. Whichever the correct version, the Basques know it as Gasteiz, and the two names are usually seen hyphenated.

From the word go, the town made its money as a trading and manufacturing centre, assisted, at first, by a large Jewish community. There were three main products – iron, wool and wine. The Rioja-Alavesa, just to the south, is still a main wine-producing area, incorporated as part of the Rioja appellation (see page 245). The newly chartered town at the beginning of the 13th century consisted of little more than three streets, two churches and an encircling wall, most of which were destroyed by fire in 1202. King Alfonso VIII rebuilt, taking a larger area inside the line of the walls and in 1256, yet another, larger ring of fortifications was created by Alfonso X. There things remained for several centuries until the city finally grew too big in the 18th century, and the southern section of the walls was knocked down to create a new area for expansion around the Plaza Nueva.

Perhaps inevitably, the city has seen its fair share of death and destruction. Several famous battles have been fought on the surrounding plain. The last, in 1813, is the one officially known as the Battle of Vitoria. Eight thousand French and 5000 Allied troops died in a single day that resulted in a severe defeat for Napoleon, who was forced to withdraw back into France, ending the Peninsula War.

Since then the city has continued to grow, spreading out across the plain. Today its population of 192,000 is still rising, industry is still coming in and there is a wide range of manufacturing. Amongst its other claims to fame are its supremacy in playing cards and its wonderful chocolate truffles.

Most of the sights of interest are clustered together in the remarkably small city centre, with the near perfect medieval hill town surrounded by the elegance of the neo-classical extensions of the 17th and 18th centuries.

Start your sightseeing in the **Parque de Florida**, a small but very pretty park just to the south of the city centre. Laid out in 1820, it has a number of sculptures and monuments, including one to the city's most famous son, the 19th-century explorer, Manuel Iradier y Bulfy, who discovered the Muni River in Spanish New Guinea. Band concerts are held here every Sunday morning. The tourist office is on one side of the park, while just to its left is the huge neo-Gothic **Cathedral of María Immaculada**. Designed by Julián de Apraiz and Javier Luque, work on its construction began in 1907, but was abandoned in 1914. It was 1946 before they started again and the cathedral was eventually consecrated only in 1960. Built in the shape of a Latin cross with five aisles, it has some fine stained glass windows depicting the resurrection and a series of sculpted figures by Enrique Monjó on the walls behind the presbytery. The stone-masons all carved their self-portraits amongst the gargoyles.

Turn right from here along the Calle de El Prado towards the old city. On your right, you will see simple neo-classical building that is the home of the Basque Parliament. Built in 1851 as a school to a design by Pantaleón Iradier, it has previously housed various academic bodies including the Literary University, the Vitoria Atheneum, the Academy of Scientific Observation and the Explorers' Society.

At the top of the road, you enter the triangular **Plaza de la Virgen Blanca**, the official centre of the city, named after its patron saint. At the centre, surrounded by formal walkways and fine 19th-century houses with glassed-in balconies, is an ornate monument erected in 1917 to commemorate Napoleon's defeat at the Battle of Vitoria.

Up the hill at the top of the square is the **Church of San Miguel**. There was already a church here by the late 12th century when it was specifically mentioned in the *fueros* sworn by King Sancho. The existing church however dates from the

Plaza de la Virgen Blanca, in Vitoria

103

late 14th century and was enlarged in the 18th. The fine portal under the entrance porch contains relief carvings of the legend of St Michael, as well as a depiction of the Trinity standing between the Virgin and St John. Inside, there is a beautiful 17th-century altarpiece by Gregorio Fernandéz, also showing scenes from the life of St Michael, the Immaculate Conception and the Crucifixion, together with various saints, apostles, angels, evangelists and doctors. In one of the side chapels stands the highly venerated late Gothic sculpture of the Virgen Blanca, showing the Virgin with Christ on one arm and holding a flower in the other hand. She is housed in an elaborate jasper niche carved in 1761.

Following the edge of the old town round to the left of the church, you come to the Church of San Pedro, built originally in the early 13th century on the orders of King Alfonso VIII and rebuilt in the 14th. It has a fine, deep portal containing statues of the Virgin and twelve apostles, while inside are several beautiful late Gothic and Renaissance tombs.

Behind the church is the solid mass of the late 15th-century **Torre de Doña Ochanda**, a medieval tower house that once formed part of the city's defenses and which now houses the Natural Science Museum of Araba, with public displays of geology, botany and zoology as well as research collections and laboratories.

Turn from here into the old town and walk north along the Calle Fray Zacarias. This area at the top of the hill, known as **El Campillo**, is the original walled city. The best thing to do here is to take your time and just wander, as the narrow dark streets, many of them stepped, fairly ooze with atmosphere. Magnificent mansions huddle against rickety cottages while deep wine vaults shrink back into the shadows between. Even the street names hark back to the early trading areas. There are far too many wonderful buildings to list more than the few outstanding ones. On Calle Fray Zacarias, look out for the 16th-century Plateresque Palacio de Aguirre (also known as the Montehermoso Palace), now the episcopal palace, and the Palacio de Escoriaza-Esquibel, built in 1536 and sporting a magnificent doorway by Juan de Alava, with the shield of the founders supported by wild animals.

At the northern end of the old town are grouped several particularly fine buildings. The first you will come to is, confusingly, the **Cathedral of Santa María**. This was founded in the 12th century on the site of a small Visigothic church, was rebuilt in the 14th century and remained as the city cathedral until the eventual completion of the new one in 1960. The tower is a 17th-century addition. The doorways of the main entrance, dating to about 1400, are superb, with intricately detailed carvings depicting the lives of Spain's most popular saints – the Virgin and Saints Lawrence, Ildefonsus, James, Nicholas and Peter. Inside are numerous artistic treasures including a 14th-century statue of the Slave Virgin, a series of murals of the descent of the Cross by Craier, a sculpture of the birth of Jesus by Valdiviesco and several Gothic and Plateresque tombs.

Just behind the cathedral are a medieval tower house, the Anda Fortress, and a large wood-framed house with brick infill, El Portalón. This was built in the 16th century and is one of the finest surviving examples of a type of architecture common at that period. It is now a restaurant with a small private museum of art, sculpture and heraldry.

Beyond here, you reach the 15th-century Monumental Gate that marked the edge of the city and the **Araba Museum of Archaeology**, housed in another fine wood and brick mansion, the Casa de Guevara-Gorbeo-San Juan. Exhibits have been gathered in from archaeological sites all over Araba, with a heavy concentration on pre-historic and Roman finds.

Turning back to the south, walk through the Plaza de La Brulleria and round the cathedral into the Calle de la Cuchilleria. Any of the surrounding streets have treasures, but this is positively packed with them. Off to the left is the 16th-century Convent of Santa Cruz, while partway along is the Bendaña Palace, also 16th-century. This will eventually become the home of the Fournier Card Museum, now housed in an annexe of the art museum.

At the southern end of the street, you come out into the **Plaza del Machete**, named after the ceremonial Axe of Vitoria, used by all officials to swear formal oaths. The reply ran to the effect that if they didn't keep their oath, that same axe would have their head! It was kept in a niche in the wall of San Miguel until *fueros* were abolished in 1841 and is now kept in the municipal archives. In the plaza are several fine buildings, including the 16th-century Renaissance Palacio de Villa-suso and the 14th-century Gothic Church of San Vicente, with a tower added in 1865. Inside this, there are several fine artworks including a Baroque altarpiece, and a Plateresque choir.

From here a carefully constructed arcade known as **Los Arcillos** (the Arches) curves round to the lower level of the city. It was designed in the late 18th century, after the destruction of the walls, to provide a link between the old and new sections of the city. At the lower end, it leads round into the magnificent neo-classical **Plaza de España** (also known as the Plaza Nueva), a huge and wonderfully harmonious square built between 1781 and 1791 by Vitorian architect Justo Antonio de Olabui-gel. The whole north side of the plaza is taken up by the City Hall. The west side leads back into the Plaza de la Virgen Blanca, from where you should retrace your steps to the Parque de Florida.

At the southern end of the park, walk down along the **Paseo de la Senda**, the first stretch of a 3km long, tree-lined promenade with several different names that leads eventually to the Basilica of Armentia on a hill at the edge of the city. There are numerous sights along the way.

The second stretch of the paseo, the Paseo de Fray Francisco de Vitoria is probably the most interesting, containing a couple of museums and a great many beautiful houses. The first stop, on your left in an elegant, ivy-clad mansion, is the small **Arms Museum**, with exhibits of arms across the ages from prehistoric times, via the Roman and Visigothic eras, right up to the 20th century. The highpoints of the museum are a fine collection of 16th-century Renaissance armour from Italy, Germany and Spain, and a display dedicated to the Battle of Vitoria. Next door to this, armed guards stand at the entrance of the Ajuria Enea Palace. Built in 1918 in typically Basque style, this is now the official home of the President of the Basque Community.

On the opposite side of the paseo, the **Araba Art Museum** is housed in the neo-baroque Palacio de Augusti, designed by Javier Luque and Julián Apraiz in 1912. Founded in 1941 as a general museum, various different collections have been hived off to other buildings, finally leaving only the fine art in residence.

Works have been gathered from across Spain, including some from the Prado in Madrid, while active buying is still increasing the number of modern works. There are fine collections of 14th-century religious art, 16th-century Flemish triptychs and Spanish paintings from the Baroque period. Best of all however are the modern collections, with early 20th-century works by Spanish masters such as Picasso, Miró, José Maria Sert and Manuel Angeles Ortiz, and a wide ranging selection of post-1950s painting and sculpture.

In the same building as the art museum is the **Fournier Card Museum**, dedicated to the history and art of the playing card, one of the Vitoria-Gasteiz's main industries. One of the major collections of playing cards in the world, it has the earliest known surviving card, from the late 14th century, together with 66 from the 15th and 16th centuries. It also has good collections of tarot cards, and engravings used in the printing process.

Continuing along the Paseo de Fray Francisco, look out for the ornately decorated mansion nicknamed locally 'Headache House', because of the weight of the balconies pressing down on the heads of their supporting statues. At the far end, beside the Parque de Prado, there is a monument to Fray Francisco, a 16th-century Dominican monk who was one of the creators of modern international law.

The next stretch, the Paseo de Cervantes, leads through the city's main, vast sports complex with several stadiums including a professional *pelota* court (see

---

Pelota

In Basque, the word simply means 'ball'. More than any other game, pelota is the Basque national sport, and there is no village without its *cancha* or *frontón* (court), even if it is little more than a patch of dusty land with a wavy line painted on the side of a house. Under the name of *jai alai* (literally 'merry festival'), the popularity of the game has spread across the Iberian peninsula over the centuries and, with many of the early sailors coming from the Cantabrian coast, it also made its way across to the New World becoming a traditional sport throughout Latin America. The massive Hispanic immigration of recent years is also beginning to make it a popular sport in certain parts of the United States.

Similar to squash, pelota appears to date back as far as the 3rd century AD, when it was played by up to ten people, wearing gloves. Today, there are several versions, played with the hand, a small paddle, a bat

similar to a baseball bat or with a *txistera* (long, sickle-like basket) that is strapped to the wrist and is used to scoop the ball from the air, and hurl it against the wall. This is by far the most dramatic version to watch, and is claimed to be the fastest game in the world.

Although football is also as popular here as elsewhere in Spain, other Basque sports tend to be based on feats of strength that are necessary in the farming life of the country. *Aizkolaris* involves splitting massive logs with an axe, the *soka-tira* is a good, old-fashioned tug-of-war, while other events include tossing the caber, lifting rocks and dragging weights, either by hand or with a team of oxen, and even grass-cutting contests. From the maritime tradition come trawler regattas, in which the teams row heavy old fishing boats over a three mile course in the open sea. There are still numerous contests in all these events at the village fiestas held throughout the summer.

box). A short way beyond this, the last leg, the Paseo de San Prudencio leads into a woody area, known as el Mineral, after a sulphurous spring discovered here in 1819. Finally you come to the village of **Armentia**, from where there is a good view across the city. At the top stands a monument of San Prudencio, the patron saint of Araba, sculpted by local artists Marn and Goicoelea and erected in 1937. Beside it is a neo-classical building called the 'House of San Prudencio' because it was said to have been built on the same spot as the saint's own house. The **Basilica de San Prudencio** is a beautiful late 12th-century Romanesque church, altered to some extent in the 18th century, but still retaining much of its original grace and simplicity. There are some lovely capitals and a finely sculpted portal. It is the centre of local festivities on the saint's feast-day of 28 April.

EXCURSION EAST FROM VITORIA
Head east from the city along the C132. signposted to Estella. At **Estíbaliz** are a cave sanctuary and Romanesque chapel dedicated to Nuestra Señora de Estíbaliz, the patronness of Araba. Turn north from here to join the N1, signposted to Alsasua and Pamplona. The other sights are all close together, between 15 and 25 km from the city. In **Gaceo**, the church is decorated by a wonderful series of late Romanesque frescoes. **Salvatierra**, a little further on is an attractive old town with a number of imposing mansions. A short way further and you reach the huge dolmen at **Eguilaz**.

EXCURSION WEST FROM VITORIA
Just on the western side of the airport and new ringroad are three more fascinating sights. At **Mendoza**, a formidable if much restored 14th-century castle now houses the Heraldry Museum of Araba. Just to the south of this, at **Trespuentes**, there is a wonderful Roman bridge, with 13 arches, across the Zadorra River. On the far side, near Nanclares, is the Roman city of **Iruña**, where you can tour the partially excavated site and a small explanatory musuem that also houses most of the finds.

From Vitoria-Gasteiz, the N1 south-west connects up, via Miranda de Ebro, with Pancorbo and the route from Burgos to Reinosa (see page 150); and with the N232 to Haro. For details on Haro, and the route from Haro to Logroño via Laguardia (which is technically inside the Basque Country), see page 244.

Basque Country: General Information

Regional tourist office

Gobierno Vasco, Departamento de Política Territorial, Transporte y Turismo, c/ Duque de Wellington 2, 01011 Vitoria (Alava) (tel. (945) 246 000).

The Basque Coast

BERMEO
Where to stay:
Txaraca, Almike Anzoa 5, 48370 (tel. (946) 885 558). Small comfortable hotel in a quiet location. Bed and breakfast only. Moderate.
Where to eat:
Restaurante Jokin, Eupeme Deuna 13, 48370 (tel. (946) 884 089). Seafood and Basque traditional dishes, with a wonderful view out over the fishing harbour. Moderate-expensive.

BILBAO
Tourist Office, Alameda Mazarredo, 12-A, 8009 (tel. (944) 244 819).
This is a huge city in an already expensive part of Spain, and it is also one of Europe's major ports. As a result, the bottom end of the market is of flea-pit standard, and to get reasonable quality, it is necessary to pay more. It is also impossible to list all the good hotels and restaurants, so I have concentrated on a very few of the really special ones.
Where to stay:
Gran Hotel Ercilla, Ercilla 37, 48011 (tel. (944) 438 800; fax (944) 439 335). Huge and extremely sumptuous modern hotel right in the city centre, catering mainly to the international business trade. No gardens, but every other luxury on offer. Expensive.
Villa de Bilbao, Gran Via Don Diego López de Haro 87, 48011 (tel. (944) 416 000; fax (944) 416 529). Half the size of the Ercilla, but still a big modern business hotel, just across the road from a park. Expensive.
Vista Alegre, Pablo Picasso 13, 48012 (tel. (944) 431 450; fax (944) 437 398). Bed and breakfast only. Cheap-moderate.

Zabálburu, Pedro Martinez Artola 8, 48012 (tel. (944 437 100). Medium-sized, basic but comfortable bed and breakfast. Cheap.
Where to eat:
Zortziko, Alameda de Mazarredo 17, 48001 (tel. (944) 239 743). This old private house scatters its dining rooms through the building, each decorated in a different style. The food is as imaginative, and this is one of the finest restaurants in the Basque Country. Expensive.
Goizeko-Kabi, Particular de Estraunza 4, 48011 (tel. (944) 415 004). This is not as attractive, but it is the other restaurant that is vying for top position in the province, with a menu based on traditional Basque cuisine. Local guides virtually write poems to it. Expensive.
Restaurante Bermeo, Hotel Ercilla (see above). Another extremely good restaurant that is a common gathering place for the local politicians and intelligentsia. Expensive.

GETARIA (GUETARIA)
Where to eat:
Astillero, Puerto (tel. (943) 832 413). Simple fish restaurant on the second floor of a boat workshop, with wonderful harbour views. Cheap-moderate.

HONDARRIBÍA (FUENTERRABÍA)
Where to stay:
Parador el Emperador, Plaza de Armas del Castillo, 20280 (tel. (943) 642 140; fax (943) 642 153). Closed for renovations at the time of writing, but due to re-open some time in 1993. A splendidly dour 10th-century fortress overlooking the river estuary and French border, still showing the marks of the cannons, from when it was sacked during the reign of Charles V. Moderate.
Hotel San Nikolás, Plaza de Armas 6, 20280 (tel. (943) 644 278). Looking out over the fortress, river and French coast, this is a small modern hotel disguised by a 16th-century façade. Bed and breakfast only. Cheap-moderate.
Where to eat:
Ramón Roteta, c/ Irún (tel. (943) 641 693). A small, cosy restaurant with a clutch of awards. Expensive.

IRÚN
Tourist Office, Behobia. (Complejo Comercial), 20300 (tel. (943) 622 627).
Where to stay: Hondarribía or San Sebastián.

MUNDAKA
Where to stay:
Hotel El Puerto, Portu Kalea 1, 48306 tel. (946 876 725; fax (946 177 064. Small, pretty family-run hotel with good views over the fishing harbour and coast. Bed and breakfast only. Moderate-expensive.

PASAI DONIBANE (PASAJES DE SAN JUAN)
Where to eat:
Casa Camara, c/ San Juan 79 (tel. (943) 517 874). Probably the best of the many fish restaurants in this tiny pretty village just beyond the dock area of San Sebastián. It is right on the water's edge with a jetty for a terrace. Moderate.

SAN SEBASTIÁN (DONOSTIA)

Tourist Office, Fueros, 1, 20004 (tel. (943) 426 282.

Where to stay:

Hotel Maria Cristina, Paseo República Argentina 4, 20004 (tel. (943) 424 900; fax (943) 423 914). The most elegant hotel in the most elegant resort of the region. Built during the *belle époque*, it has been recently renovated. Managed by the Ciga group. Very expensive.

Hotel de Londres y de Inglaterra, Zubieta 2, 20007 (tel. (943) 426 989; fax (943) 420 031). Something of a local landmark, this is right on the beach in the city centre. It is very luxurious after its recent renovations, but has lost something of its former charm in the process. Expensive.

Monte Igueldo, 20008 (tel. (943) 210 211; fax (943) 215 028). A good, large hotel but relatively uninteresting if it was't for one thing – its superb views right across the city and bay. It has its own garden and swimming pool. Moderate-expensive.

There are a number of purpose-built holiday hotels, which are all much of a muchness, along the beach, all at moderate prices. The cheap fondas are away from the shore, back towards the railway station in what can be a fairly rough area.

Where to eat:

Restaurante Arzak, Alto de Miracruz 21 (tel. (943) 278 465). The setting is not one of the best around, but this is the undisputed king of restaurants, with every possible award and honour. Eating here is a serious business, but the food warrants the attention. Booking essential. Expensive.

Akelarre, Paseo del Padre Orcolaga 56, 20008 (tel. (943) 212 052). The other really top-notch restaurant in San Sebastián, out near the Barrio de Igueldo, with fine sea views and excellent food. Expensive.

Casa Nicolasa, Aldamar 4, 20003 (tel. (943) 421 762). Right in the city centre. The food is good, classic Basque cuisine. Expensive.

Casino Gran Kursaal, Hotel Londres (see above). The food in the hotel restaurant is good, but nowhere near the standard of those listed above. The casino however, is good fun.

Black tie is not necessary, but a tie is, and no jeans or trainers. Expensive.

Restaurante Itzalian, Muelle 12 (tel. (943) 431 266). Basic, cheerful family-run fish restaurant overlooking the beach down in the old port. Outdoors in good weather. Cheap.

For other good, cheap and cheerful fish restaurants, go out to Pasai Donibane (Pasajes San Juan).

Inland Basque Country

VITORIA-GASTEIZ

Tourist Office, Parque de la Florida, s/n (tel. (945) 131 321).

Where to stay:

Parador de Argomaniz, 01192 Argomaniz tel and fax: (945) 282 200). This former palace is actually 12km from Vitoria, right out in the country, near an abandoned village.

Nevertheless, for those with a car, it is probably the most interesting place to stay while visiting the city. Moderate.

Gasteiz, Av. Gasteiz 45, 01009 (tel. (945) 228 100; fax (945) 226 258). The most comfortable of the city's large business hotels, this is on a main road beside the modern city and business district. Moderate-expensive.

Hotel Dato, c/ Eduardo Dato 28, 01005 (tel. (945) 232 320; fax (945) 242 322). Charming turn of the century town house, decorated in Art Nouveau style. Bed and breakfast only. Cheap.

The cheapest hotels and fondas are in two separate clusters around the bus and train stations. The better area is in the old city, near the train station.

Where to eat:

El Portalón, Correria 151 (tel. (945) 142 755). 15th-century coaching inn, decorated with Basque art and antiques and specialising in simple, regional cuisine. Moderate-expensive.

For those who prefer to live more simply and get to know the people better, there is a government-sponsored network of rural homes and farmhouses offering self-catering or bed and breakfast accommodation. For information or central booking, phone 010-34-946 201 188; fax 010-34-946 201 163.

The Trans-Cantabrico Train

This luxury tourist train is used to provide upmarket packages, covering the length of the Costa Verde, along the line of the pilgrim route from San Sebastián to Santiago de Compostela. For more details, contact the Madrid office (tel. 010-34-1-553 7656; fax 010-34-1-553 7904).

Cantabria

The Cantabres tribe might have donated their name both to the Cantabrian Sea and the massive mountain range of the Cordillera Cantábrica, but their Spanish homeland became known as Cantabria only after the 1978 constitution. Before that, the land, simply a minor province of Castille, was known either as Santander or La Montaña. Covering 5300 square kilometres, it is one of the smaller provinces in modern Spain. The total population is around 500,000, over a third of whom live in Santander, while most of the rest live in the small fishing ports along the coast.

Scenically, Cantabria forms a microcosm of the whole north-west region, at the border between the more gentle, heavily populated coast of the Basque Country and the rugged cliffs of Asturias and Galicia. Like the other provinces in the region, it has a narrow, fertile coastal strip backed by a sheer mountain wall that proved virtually impenetrable until the 'Royal Road' to Reinosa and Burgos was built in 1748 on the orders of King Felipe V, to carry wool north from the Castillian meseta to the port at Santander. Today, the Cantabrian mountains are home to two of the largest mountain resorts in the region, Fuente Dé in the Picos de Europa and the Alto Campóo ski resort.

Ethnically, too, Cantabria is an Iberian melting pot. Numerous cave dwellings near the coast show signs of human habitation as far back as 30,000 BC. The Cantabres arrived in the Iron Age, to inhabit the borderlands between the eastern Basque Country and the Celtic west. To these, over the centuries have been added the Romans, Visigoths, and, in recent times, large numbers of Spaniards drawn in by the prospect of work in the industrialised north.

Most foreign tourists to north-west Spain will inevitably spend at least some of their time in Cantabria with Bilbao airport, the Santander ferry port and the French border all within easy reach. It would be a shame not to stray further, but for those who prefer a gentle stroll over short distances, there is plenty of interest, with fascinating architecture, fabulous scenery and, for those with more energy, plenty of outdoor activity from fishing and swimming to hiking, climbing, riding and, in winter, skiing.

Santander

To the British, the name Santander is synonymous with the ferry port and, people tend to regard all port towns as necessary evils — convenient but ugly, and worth leaving as fast as possible. Santander has been a major port since long before the arrival of Brittany Ferries, but the city has a great deal more than that to offer. It is also the capital of Cantabria and a major seaside resort, which is regarded by the Spaniards as one of their more elegant and popular holiday destinations. Parts of the city are a little rough, but much of it is remarkably beautiful and well worth more than a cursory glance. Hotel rooms can be very hard to find, however, especially in high summer, so book before you go, even if just passing through.

The city stands on a peninsula which curls over the western edge of a large bay, creating a large, calm natural harbour, a particularly fine haven from the infamous Bay of Biscay, welcoming a procession of great ships coming in to dock, against a background of high mountains. All the shoreline within the city itself faces across the bay to the south or east, rather than to the open sea to the north.

The first known settlement here was the Roman town of Portus Victoriae, which stood roughly on the site of the modern fishing and ferry port. It was fortified in the 4th century by Emperor Aurelianus, but was virtually abandoned in 409 when the Gothic attack led to the collapse of the western empire. The town remained dormant for nearly four centuries, until the start of the Reconquista in the early 9th century led to the repopulation of this entire coastal strip. It was really kicked into life only in the early 11th century, however, when some monks from Calahorra fled north ahead of the Moorish attack, bringing with them the relics of the saintly martyrs, Emeterio and Celedonio. They founded a small chapel and abbey on a hill in the Roman city, and dedicated it to Santo Emeterio. The martyrs' pilgrimage trade came too, and a small, but thriving town grew up once more. The name Santander is simply a corruption of Santo Emeterio. The town was first given a charter in 1068 by Sancho II, while in 1187, it received a second from Alfonso VIII, making it directly responsible to the crown, and free from the authority of either the feudal lords or the church.

Throughout the middle ages, the city flourished as one of the major ports on the north coast, the centre of the wool trade, as well as a main exporter of wine, olive oil, fish and a host of other products. It was also the port preferred by royalty and regularly hosted magnificent feasts, which could take several years to pay off, as various kings passed through on their way to or from other countries. It was with the arrival of Margaret of Austria in 1497, on her way to marry Ferdinand and Isabela's son, Prince Juan, that disaster struck the city. Her ship carried the plague which, once ashore, swept through the crowded streets, killing three-quarters of the population over the next eight years.

For the next two centuries, it seemed that nothing could go right. The plague lingered and there were regular outbreaks that kept the city from regaining its former strength. Bilbao began to rise as a major port, taking much of Santander's former revenue, and as relations with France and England deteriorated, the city was forced into building and paying for expensive fortifications. Many of the sailors

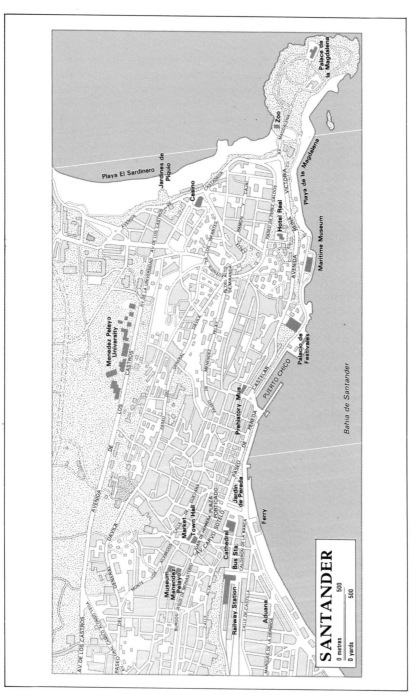

SANTANDER

on the ill-fated Armadas also came from the area. Large numbers of them died, and many others returned sick, or maimed and unable to work.

By the mid-18th century, the situation began to improve again, thanks to the new Bourbon king, Felipe V, who pumped money into the decaying region to rebuild it as a centre for the wool trade. In 1754, Santander became the centre of a new diocese; in 1755, it was given city status; and in 1779, it was at last given official status as capital of Cantabria, a position it had held unofficially for some 150 years. By the end of the century, it began to receive a share of the enormous wealth created by the Spanish empire in the Americas. Gradually, Santander became a major port for trade with the New World, and the city regained its former glory. Part of the old city had been destroyed by fire in 1763, but in the early 19th century, a new town rose from the ashes. By the middle of the century, it was a major centre for the new steamships, including the trans-Atlantic mail ships. Like other ports along this coast, it benefited from the rapid growth of the coal and iron industries inland, and it added ship-building and later, chemical and other heavy industries to its other sources of income. In 1866, the railway arrived and ensured the city's position as a centre of both freight and passenger traffic.

Meanwhile, in 1849, an outbreak of cholera in France forced Spanish high society to look elsewhere for fashionable seaside resorts, and its gaze fell on Santander. Eager businessmen rushed to build suitably elegant hotels on the Sardinero peninsula, to the east of the existing city. In 1861, a doctor suggested that bathing in the Cantabrian sea would cure Queen Isabela II of herpes. The queen duly arrived, followed by a huge train of interested aristocracy. The summer was spent in a round of riotous gaiety and Santander was placed firmly on the social map. It retained this status up until the Civil War. It was taken by the Nationalists in 1937 and 60,000 Republicans were arrested, but the city itself survived relatively unscathed.

In February 1941, however, disaster struck once again with the arrival of a tornado which also caused fire to break out in the old town. By morning, some 400 houses, in 40 streets, had been destroyed, and many others were damaged. Rebuilding started immediately, but there was no attempt to recreate the old town. Instead, this too was laid out in the grid system used in the 19th century, and those left homeless were moved into massive high-rise blocks on the edge of the city.

Modern Santander has a population of only about 180,000, but it sprawls out across a wide area, and its few specific sights of interest are equally scattered. For all but the most energetic, distances are too far to walk. If you don't wish to drive from area to area and risk fighting for parking spaces, the city does have a number of huge underground car parks and an excellent local bus service.

There are several very distinct districts, each with a totally different atmosphere. The first is the site of the Roman and medieval city, although virtually nothing survives of its ancient past. Right at its heart is the ferry port, bordered by a charming garden square and boulevard, the **Paseo de Pereda**. The tourist office is in the square, only a couple of hundred yards from the terminal, while the road behind is lined by cafés that are not only convenient for waiting travellers but are a popular stopping-place during the evening paseo. Just inland from this are the wide streets of the city's commercial and shopping centre.

A couple of blocks to the left (west) of the square is a hill on which stand the somewhat decayed remnants of the old town. The **Cathedral** at the top of the hill was originally built in about 1400, on the site of the original Chapel of Santo Emeterio. This was itself built on top of a Roman villa, the hypercaust of which was discovered under the north aisle in 1983. The cathedral was heavily altered in the 16th and 18th centuries and almost entirely rebuilt in 1955, after the great fire, and is worth little more than a passing glance. The Gothic cloister is also heavily restored, but retains a little more of its original character than the main church. Beneath the cathedral, however, a vaulted passage leads to the earlier crypt, now the parish Church of El Santísimo Cristo. Built in about 1300, this miraculously survived the various disasters to befall the area and remains a charming early Gothic church that is the oldest building in Santander.

Continue west and you come almost immediately to both railway stations and the bus station. To the south of the railway lines an increasingly sleazy district of ugly high-rise blocks leads down to the modern fishing port, really only worth visiting if you want to sample the catch at one of its cheap and cheerful fish restaurants. Further west still, you reach the massive new port, with all its attendant warehouses and factories.

Just to the north of the cathedral, the Avenida Calvo Sotelo marks the southern edge of a much more pleasant area of modern city. Leading directly off the avenue is the galleried Plaza Porticado, surrounded by numerous small shops, restaurants and cafés, created as an official new city centre after the 1941 fire. Take the Calle Juan de Herrera to the left off the plaza and you emerge a few blocks later into the little Plaza de Generalísimo, still complete with its statue of Franco. On the north side of the plaza is the flamboyant main façade of the Town Hall, erected in 1907. A block behind this you come to Santander's splendid **market**, with a huge, two-storey hall, the Esperanza, surrounded by a small army of outdoor stalls that have spilled over into every available nook and cranny. Even if you don't want to buy, take the time to wander around this wonderful, noisy, crowded and colourful area. The massive fish market is particularly impressive, selling every sort of fish you could dream of and a lot more besides.

Keep going to the left from here and you will reach a complex of museums, centred on the home of Marcelino Menéndez y Pelayo (1856–1912), who was probably the city's most famous son. A writer, critic and philosopher himself, he made his reputation as the curator of the National Library in Madrid, a post he held for the last 14 years of his life. He is buried in Santander cathedral. His personal library of some 50,000 books was left to the city of Santander. The building which once held his library now houses the **Museum of Fine Art**, with an excellent collection of 17th- and 18th-century Spanish, Italian and Flemish paintings, including several by Goya, as well as a wonderful collection of Spanish modern art. Next door, Pelayo's family home is also a small museum, dedicated to his life and work. Behind this, an ornate neo-classical building designed by Leonardo Rucabalo in 1951 now houses the library itself, which is still being added to and ranks as one of Spain's greatest literary collections.

A bay in the La Magdalena park, El Sardinero, near Santander

Back in the Paseo de Pereda, now head east (right) along the paseo. At the far end, you come to the **Puerto Chico**, built in 1910 as a fishing port, but now used as a marina, which is permanently stuffed with a wonderful array of pleasure boats including racing yachts and gin palaces. A block inland, in the basement of the Diputación General, is the city's **Prehistory Museum**, with a small but rich collection found in the many inhabited caves nearby. At the far end of the marina is the Nautical School, the latest home of a teaching institution first founded in 1785. The road along the coast from here leads past Santander's new Festival Hall to the **Maritime Museum**, which is still gathering together its collections of marine biology, which will include a small aquarium, nautical history and traditional shipping, including a few renovated ships and boats.

As you continue along the shore, the whole atmosphere changes again to one of slender summer houses and leafy streets. This is **El Sardinero**, the ridged peninsula that represents the beau monde of the late 19th and early 20th century at its very best. On top of the ridge above you, you will see the bulk of the Hotel Real, built by González de Riancho in 1917, and still the best of the city's hotels, with superb views in every direction. Next to it, the small neo-Gothic castle, also built by Riancho, is a private residence, belonging to the family who own the Banco de Santander. Just beyond this, you meet the edge of the long, curving Playa de la Magdalena. Nearly 1.5km long, it is still the smaller of the city's two main beaches and although crowded is also the less built-up and more beautiful.

The last third of the beach is backed by the massive public **gardens of the Palace de la Magdalena**, which cover the whole tip of the peninsula. Stunningly beautiful,

La Magdalena Palace, El Sardinero, near Santander

with sweeping lawns, conifer woods and sculpture gardens that lead down to superb cliff views, the gardens are today the most popular picnic site in the city. The palace itself, a neo-Tudor affair designed by the ever-adaptable González de Riancho and completed in 1912, is said to have been modelled on Balmoral. It was paid for by the city and donated as a gift to Alfonso XII. On the abdication of Alfonso XIII in 1931, it reverted to the city and is now used as part of the International University, a summer school for both Spanish and foreign students.

On the north cliffs of the gardens, there are a couple of restored boats and a small zoo, more attractive in design than in its creature comforts, with some relatively happy, if hot, seals and penguins, and some decidedly miserable polar bears. From here, there is a superb view over the vast sweep of the 3km long El Sardinero beach, lined for much of the way by shady parks and gardens, interspersed by grand hotels, mansions, and restaurants, of which the finest is, without doubt, the magnificent Casino.

The best time to visit Santander, hotel space permitting, is surprisingly in August, when the city is humming with all the exuberance of the summer holidaymakers. This is also when the city holds its month-long International Festival, which begins on the Feast of Santiago, 25 July. Founded in 1952, it has grown continuously in recent years into a major cultural event, with theatre, music and dance groups from across the world, as well as more traditional Spanish pastimes such as bullfighting, and an exciting parade of street entertainment.

For the coast road east to Unquera, see page 122; for the route south to Aguilar de Campóo, see page 132.

The Coast Road East – Santander to Bilbao

This route heads east from busy Santander to massive Bilbao, just across the border in the Basque Country. For much of its distance it follows the main N634 coast road, which has recently been upgraded to near motorway status. It is a busy road, through a very convenient area, and most of the once small fishing ports have been growing rapidly and virtually without check into resorts towns filled with high-rise hotels that are overcrowded in high summer and virtually deserted for the rest of the year. If you like noisy crowds, this is the place to be. If you want to stay beside the sea and get a real feel for northern Spain, head west from Santander.

Leave Santander on the S443, signposted to the airport and El Astillero. This first stretch of road leads south along the edge of the bay, past the modern port and airport, and through the industrial district of the city. The main road bypasses El Astillero, a major shipbuilding centre since the 16th century. About 5km beyond the town, a small, steep road off to the right leads up to the 569m **Peña Cabarga**. At the summit, there is a monument to the Conquerors of America and the Seamen Adventurers of Castille, and beside this is a tall observation platform which offers superb views, both of the Santander Bay and across the mountains to the south.

Return to the main road and turn right. At Hera, 3km on, turn left onto the small road, signposted to Rubayo. Just before you reach the village, turn left at the

T-junction onto the S430 to **Pedreña**. On the east shore of the Santander Bay, this is the first of the growing summer resorts. Once a small fishing village, it achieved recent fame as the birthplace of golfer, Severiano Ballasteros, and it is also rapidly becoming a dormitory town for Santander commuters. A long bridge crosses the river estuary just north of the village, connecting it to **Somo**, another somewhat soulless resort with a long spit of sand, El Puntal Beach, which stretches out into the bay, offering excellent views of Santander's Magdalena seafront. In spite of a total lack of shade, this is highly popular with day-trippers from the city, and ferries run regularly across the bay.

The road roughly follows the line of the coast through Galizano, with some attractive views, both out to sea and of the mountains, and comes to **Bareyo**, a once attractive old village on the Ría de Ajo (Garlic) gradually being overwhelmed by concrete blocks. Stop off for a look at the Romanesque Chapel of Santa María, which was altered to some extent in the Gothic era, but still retains a marvellous collection of carved capitals. To the north of the village, a road leads to the beach and the Cabo de Ajo, the most northerly cape on this route, crowned with a lighthouse.

From here, the road leads directly west to Santona, but there are turnings to the coast to the small resorts of Isla, which has a 17th-century Baroque church, a medieval tower and a fine mansion, the Palacio de los Condes de Isla, Quejo, Playa de Ris and Noja. All of them have attractive beaches which get very crowded in high season.

Santoña is one of the more attractive towns on this route, although once again, the charm of its old harbour and fine setting, beside the 400m Monte Buciero, are threatened by the tidal wave of development. Traditionally one of the larger ports on the Cantabrian coast, it was once the centre of a large ship-building industry, and it is said that both Columbus's ship, the Santa María, and the Invincible, flagship of the Armada, were built here. Certainly the town was the birthplace of Juan de la Cosa, who was the navigator and cartographer on Columbus's expedition. There is a statue of him in the Paseo Marítima, and a ceramic mural of him in one of the nearby side streets. The Church of Santa María del Puerto dates originally from the 12th century, although only the capitals now remain of the Romanesque church. The nave is now Gothic and the west front dates from an 18th-century rebuilding. Inside there is a 12th-century statue of the Virgin which locals claim travelled on the ship during the Santa María's first voyage to the West Indies. The town has also always had strategic importance and two fortresses were built here in the late 17th century. The one still standing today, the Fuerte de Napoleón, was built by the French during the Peninsula Wars in the early 19th century.

Take the causeway from Santoña signposted to Cicero. Crossing several small inlets, it runs across an area of salty marshland that has recently been given protected status as a nature reserve, while several walking trails have been set up for visitors.

At Cicero, turn left onto the main N634 and follow it through the industrial town of Colindres to **Laredo**, the largest of all the resorts, with a winter population of about 10,000 and a summer population ten times larger. It has an attractive, long curving beach completely ruined by a continuous line of 1960s style hotels – a horror aggravated by the fact that many were built far more recently at a time when people should have known better. The town has an illustrious past, having been granted its charter in 1200 by Alfonso XIII. For the next few centuries, it thrived as one of the main trading and fishing ports in the area. In the heart of the old town, around the fishing harbour and the steep narrow streets leading to the church, you can still see sections of the 14th-century town walls as well as several fine mansions belonging to the late Middle Ages. The Renaissance Town Hall was designed by Simón de Bueras in 1557. The 13th-century Church of La Asunción was heavily altered in the 16th and 18th centuries but is still worth a visit, with a fine Baroque high relief altarpiece, and a small museum in the 18th-century Sacristy. Nearby the church of the Convent of San Francisco contains a small museum, a 17th-century altarpiece and the tombs of many of the local noble families.

At the end of August each year, the highlights of the local festival include donkey and horse races on the beach and a battle of flowers.

From here, keep following the road east along the coast to **Castro-Urdiales**, the other main town on this stretch of coast, and by far the most interesting and attractive of them all. With a population of around 12,000, it has, so far, escaped the worst excesses of the tourist development, although it is becoming increasingly popular as a wealthier commuter suburb of Bilbao. There has been a continuous settlement here since the Romans built the town of Flaviobriga in the early 1st century AD. The town received its charter from Alfonso VIII in 1163, and reached its first heights of prosperity in the 13th and 14th centuries as a fishing and trading port. A slump followed for several centuries until the 19th, when it became a popular resort at much the same time iron-mining started in the hills behind the port.

Today, the town has two distinct centres, one medieval, one 19th-century, linked by a seafront of elegant houses with glassed-in balconies. The Upper district, or old town, centred on the colourful fishing port, is dominated by two buildings. On top of the hill is the huge parish Church of Santa María de la Asunción. Work began on the early Gothic church in 1208, but some 50 years later, there was a change of plan on its design, which left it with two distinct sections, divided by arches. The Chapel of Santa Catalina, which now houses the parish museum, was added in the 15th century, and the neo-classical south portal, the Puerta de los Hombres, in the 18th. There are a ruined Templar house and 12th-century Church of San Pedro nearby. At the end of the quay squats the powerful, pentagonal Castillo de Santa Ana, an originally 13th-century fortress that has been shored up and reinforced at various periods since. It now houses the town lighthouse.

In the Lower district, there are also several buildings of note, including the 18th-century Town Hall, the 20th-century Casa de Los Chelines, by Leonardo Rucabado, in the arcaded plaza beside the town hall, and the Toki-Eder Mansion in Paseo Menéndez Pelayo, built by Eladio Laredo in 1914.

From here, the route continues east, crossing the border into the Basque Country just after Onton and plunging almost immediately into the outer suburbs and industrial areas of Bilbao.

For a description of Bilbao, see page 73, and for the continuing coastal journey east to San Sebastián, see page 78.

The Coast Road West – Santander to Unquera

This route runs along small coast roads in the beautiful western half of Cantabria. The area is popular with tourists and there is some development, but as yet it has been more carefully thought through and kept under control and most of the towns en route are still charming.

Leave Santander via the El Sardinero and head up to **Cabo Mayor**, where a monument to Santander residents killed in the Civil War stands beside the 19th-century lighthouse that marks the entrance to the Santander bay. As you follow the same road back inland, you reach a small turning to the right, signposted to San Román. Keep going straight through until you reach **Liencres**. The village itself is not worthy of note, but just to the west of it is an area of particularly beautiful dunes, some reaching over 30m in height, fringed by forests of pine and euforbia. A rich nesting ground for a variety of sea birds, this is now protected as a 194.5 hectare Natural Park.

From here, follow the road round as it heads inland, joining the N611, just before Arce. Turn right and follow the main road through to Barredo, where you turn right onto the C6316, signposted to Santillana del Mar and Suances. You can go straight through to Santillana, but alternatively, turn right onto the S472 to **Suances**, a fishing port and resort on the mouth of the Bareyo River. The existing town came into being during the Middle Ages as a whaling, fishing and trading port, built on the site of the Roman port of Blendium. In the 19th century, it became a popular resort area, a status it still claims today. Unfortunately, however, the river runs straight through from Torrelavega, which has Cantabria's largest concentration of heavy industry, and the water in both beach and harbour is a beautiful and utterly unnatural indigo blue, with a thick skin of polluted foam. The fishermen are up in arms and everyone is agreed that it must be cleaned up, but they are still arguing about who is going to do it.

Take the pretty S474 through Tagle and past the Mirador de Ubiarco, to **Santillana del Mar**, a town which has to be a highlight of any trip to northern Spain. In spite of its name, the town now stands about 6km inland, gradually stranded as the nearby coastline advanced northwards.

Santillana del Mar

There is plentiful evidence of humans living in this area for at least 30,000 years, although it is not known whether they lived on the exact site of the town. This owes its early existence to the repopulation of the coast in the 9th century after the first Asturian victories in the Reconquista. By the 10th century, a monastery was founded here to house the relics of Santa Juliana, a saint from Asia Minor who was martyred in 308 AD by the Emperor Diocletian. Santillana is a corruption of Santa Juliana.

The monastery grew in stature and power, becoming a major local landowner, while a town grew up around its walls. In 1209, its religious owners were granted a city charter that placed it on an equal footing with Santander. Shortly after that, it became the capital of an autonomous region, Asturias de Santillana, which covered most of western Cantabria and parts of eastern Asturias. The 14th and 15th centuries were dominated by a major power struggle between the all-powerful abbey and the local aristocracy, and finally, in 1445, Juan II revoked the existing charter and gave the town to the nobles' leader, Don Iñigo Lopéz de Mendoza, together with the title of Marquis.

In spite of the change of ownership, the town remained popular with other aristocratic families, many of whom built mansions here. In 1575, a by-law was passed forcing everyone who wished to build here to get permission from the Marquis. In effect, this acted as a type of rudimentary planning permission, and ensured that any new development met the already high aesthetic standard of the community.

The final impetus for construction came with the return of gold and silver rich 'Indianos' in the 17th and 18th centuries, back from the Americas with their fortunes, who built yet more grand houses in the little town. And as their influence began to wane in the 19th century, the poets and artists moved in, waxing lyrical about the place, and forcing the authorities to realise that they had something special – and worth preserving – on their hands.

The net result is that today, the town is indeed one of the prettiest in Spain, with none of the ugly development that has marred so many places nearby. Unfortunately, it has been so carefully preserved that it feels at times as though it lives in aspic and is balanced precariously on the border of becoming twee. Every house is covered with flowers, and while the cows are still herded home through the narrow streets, and their milk is sold to passing tourists, they give the appearance of being a carefully groomed, token herd, kept around to provide local colour. More and more of the charming old mansions are being turned into charming small hotels, while those between have become artists' studios and upmarket souvenir shops.

It is possible but difficult – and heavily discouraged by the authorities – to squeeze a car through most of the narrow streets. Unless you can't walk, leave it in the huge free car park just on the edge of the village. Directly opposite this is a large park, the Campo de Revolgo, now a shady haven from the mid-day heat, but in the Middle Ages the site of jousts and tournaments, while at a later date it became the local duelling ground. Beside this stands the first of many great mansions, the 15th-century Palacio de los Tagles. The coat of arms shows a knight killing a dragon and rescuing a maiden, whom he later married – a somewhat familiar figure claimed by the family to be a Tagle.

As you walk into the village along the cobbled Calle Santo Domingo, you will find on your right the Convent of Regina Coeli, founded in 1593 as a Dominican house. Since 1835, however, it has been the home of an enclosed order of Poor Clare nuns, while the Dominicans now live in the 17th-century San Ildefonso Monastery next door. In the 1960s, the Regina Coeli nuns were persuaded to part with one section of the building, around the remarkably peaceful double-storey

A view through the narrow village streets of Santillana del Mar

cloisters, and this now houses the Diocesan Archives, a restoration workshop, and the Diocesan Museum. The museum's founder, a local priest, Antonio Niceas, searched far and wide for exhibits, rescuing them from abandoned or damaged churches throughout Cantabria. An immense amount of effort then went into their restoration, and the result is a stunningly powerful collection of beautifully displayed church art, including some 200 polychrome wooden statues, created over a spread of several hundred years. Other mansions to look out for along this road are the 17th-century Casa de Villas, now a restaurant/bar, with semi-circular balcony arches and a motto that translates as 'A fine death honours one's whole life', and the Palacio de Peredo, an 18th-century mansion now owned by the

124

Marquesses of Benemejis de Sistallo. It has a wonderful art collection and an important library founded in the 19th century by Blas de Berreda.

Shortly after this, the road forks. The left hand fork, the Calle Juan Infante, is a narrow street overhung by balconies, which leads towards the triangular Plaza de Ramón Pelayo, the main centre of the town. There are numerous grand and extremely beautiful buildings crammed into the plaza, which also doubles as marketplace. The 18th-century, balconied Town Hall stands next to the 14th-century Torre de Merino, built as the home of the Governor of Asturias de Santillana. This is now owned by the Marchioness of Toralba and is used as an art gallery in season. The 15th-16th-century Torre de Don Borja is now the headquarters of the Cultural Association, the Fundación Santillana. The Parador Gil Blas is the former palace of the the Barreda-Bracho family. Opened as a hotel in 1927, it takes its name from a fictional hero created by writer, Alain René Lesage, in 1715. Also in the square are the Tourist Office and the adjoining Casas del Aguilar y de la Parra which house a small Ethnographic Museum, with exhibits of rural life collected from across Cantabria.

You can cut round the back streets to join the right fork towards the church, but it is better to retrace your steps back up to the end of the Calle Juan Infante and turn right. This long road is a delight from end to end, lined by multitudes of grand mansions, interspersed by more humble, but still entrancing cottages, while the final section down a steep hill offers a lovely view over the Collegiate Church. The first section, along the Calle Santo Domingo, is almost uniformly 18th-century. Houses to look for include the homes of the Barreda, Gómez Estrada, De la Cueva, Peredo and Bustamente families. At the end of this section, you reach the Torre de los Velardes, a 15th-century tower house. This marks the spot where the road changes its name to the Calle del Cantón. Continuing on, you will see, on the left, the 18th-century Palacio de los Valdeviesco, which has now become the Hotel Altamira. On the right are a string of houses including the home of a local sculptor, Jesús Otero; the 15th-century Palacio de Leonor de la Vega, home of the mother of Iñigo Lopez de la Vega, the first marquis; the Casa de las Vegas; and the 15th-16th-century Casa de los Villas, with a massive baroque high-relief coat of arms, flanked by knights in armour – the so-called 'shield of hefty men'.

As you reach the bottom of the hill, the road changes its name again, to the Calle del Río, then opens out into a plaza facing the church. Here too, there are several mansions, including the Casa de Cosso, the Casa de Quevedo, and the late 16th-, early 17th-century Casa de los Archiduques de Austria, formerly the home of the abbots.

Here, however, the houses pale into insignificance against the magnificent Collegiate Church of Santa Juliana, one of the finest Romanesque buildings in Spain. This is the site of the 10th-century monastery that provided the focal pivot for the growth of the town. As a major pilgrimage centre as well as an administrative one, the abbey grew in stature and wealth, and in the 12th century, became an ecclesiastical college. At roughly the same time, the authorities decided that they needed a new, grander church more befitting their station, and work on the current church began.

Before you go inside, take the time to walk around the back of the church, to

125

see the superb east end, with its three pure Romanesque apsidal chapels. In the tiny Plaza de Las Arenas behind the church, stands the last of the grand mansions, the 16th-century Palacio de Velarde.

Unusually, the main entrance is in the south wall, facing the plaza, reached by a shallow flight of steps flanked by sculpted lions. In the 18th century, the Romanesque south façade was remodelled. The portal, with its bas-relief figures of 'bishops, apostles and monks, many of them without heads, owing to time and carelessness' (according to one local guidebook), was topped by a surprisingly harmonious, neo-classical pediment, containing a statue of Santa Juliana. Above this, tucked under the eaves, an open arched gallery was created, to run the length of the building, connecting the lantern tower above the transept cross with the belfry. The belfry was itself a 13th-century addition which resulted in the destruction of the original, superlative west door. Several of the polychrome figures from the door have survived and are now displayed within the church. The decorative sculptures removed from the south façade during the 18th-century remodelling were discovered in the vaults in 1966 and are now on display in the cloister.

Inside, the rather dark church is of classic Romanesque design, a rectangular building, with three aisles and three apses. The vaulting in the apses and transepts is original, while that of the nave is 13th-century. The wonderful capitals in the nave are all Romanesque, and the choir is 17th-century Baroque. In one side chapel, there stands a beautiful 12th-century font depicting Daniel in the Lion's Den, while the Chapel of El Santísimo contains a wonderful 17th-century crucifix. In the centre of the nave stands the tomb of Santa Juliana herself, with a 15th-century sculpture of the saint trampling on the devil, surrounded by a wrought iron railing.

The eye is drawn inevitably however to the high altar and vast altarpiece behind it. The altar itself is a Baroque 17th-century work of beaten Mexican silver, inset with the 12th-century figures of the apostles, rescued from the original west door. Behind it, the altarpiece as a whole dates from the 17th century, but contains a 15th-century Calvary, while the painted panels of the lives of Christ and Santa Juliana, and the sculptures of the Evangelists are all 16th-century.

A door in the north transept leads through to the cloister, a graceful, single storey building with an open-arched gallery and several side chapels containing the tombs of local noble families. Of greatest interest are the superb capitals, some of strapwork or floral decoration, others depicting stories from both old and new testaments, local legends, and 12th-century social scenes. Also displayed here are various stone figures that formed part of the Romanesque south façade, together with several polychrome figures rescued from the original west door, including the central Pantocrator, a panel showing St Anne holding the Virgin, and Santa Juliana subduing the devil.

A door in the south transept leads into the 18th-century Sacristy, now used as the church's treasury and archives. A number of gold and silver pieces are on show here, including a magnificent Gothic silver processional cross, and a silver reliquary bust of Santa Juliana, together with a number of sculptures dating from the 15th to 18th centuries.

About 1km from the town, well signposted from the centre, is the Santillana

The portal of the Collegiate Church of Santa Juliana, in Santillana del Mar

El Capricho, a house designed by Gaudí, now a restaurant, in Comillas

Zoo, the largest in the region with some 130 species of animals, birds and reptiles, including all the large cats, apes and European brown bears.

Two km south of the town, also on a well signed small road, are the **Altamira Caves**, which contain one of the most important collections of pre-historic cave paintings in Europe, matched only by those of Lascaux in southern France. The caves were discovered in 1868 by a local hunter, Modesto Cubillas, whose dog chased a hare through the opening, but although he found some of the sketches in the long opening tunnel, it was 1879 before local archaeologist, Marcelino Sanz de Sautola, penetrated further to reveal the full glory of the painted caves. He published a pamphlet about the paintings only to find himself vilified by numerous 'experts', one of whom virtually accused him of painting them himself. By the time he died in 1888, they were almost forgotten, and interest was only revived when the red-faced sceptics discovered a whole series of similar caves in and around Les Eyzies in France.

There is a total of nine painted tunnels and caves in the Altamira complex, but only the 300m long entrance corridor, the 'Horse's Tail', and the main vault, dubbed by one French writer as the 'Sistine Chapel of Quaternary Art' are ever opened to the public. It is here, however, that you can see the most magnificent of all the paintings, including a 16m long frieze of bison on the ceiling.

Sadly, however, as an attempt to preserve the caves for the future, only 30 people a day are allowed into them. It is virtually impossible to get onto the list, as bookings are made literally years in advance. Beside the entrance however, there is a small but fascinating museum, giving a wealth of detail about the paintings and the other archaeological finds made within the caves. Just next door, there is also another small cave, with unlimited entry, which is hung by a beautiful collection of stalactites and stalagmites.

Leaving the caves, return to Santillana and rejoin the coast road, heading west to **Comillas**. The village first came into being in 1483, when a major fire destroyed part of nearby San Vicente de la Barquera, and the homeless fishermen decided to decamp and build a new hamlet further along the coast. So far, so good. Unfortunately, in doing so, they alienated those who stayed behind, clutching a charter allowing them sole fishing rights to this stretch of coast. A major feud ensued, which lasted for nearly 200 years, during which time, they raided each others' warehouses, stole equipment, and fought on land and at sea. Only after two more fires in the luckless San Vicente, in 1563 and 1636, after each of which more people moved out to Comillas, did they eventually call it a draw.

In the late 19th century, Comillas gained popularity as a resort among the smart folk from Madrid and Barcelona, and for some years, they rushed to build themselves elegant summer houses here. For a short while it seemed as if it could rival Santander's El Sardinero district, but gradually the city overhauled the little town, leaving it once more small but with a legacy of some extraordinary architecture. On the hill above the town centre stand the large neo-Gothic Palacio de Sobrellano and an adjacent chapel, built between 1881 and 1890 by Catalan architect, Joan Martell. Just beside it is the utterly extraordinary El Capricho, a fantasy house of turrets and towers, all covered with ceramic flowers and tiles. Built by Catalan

Prehistoric art

About 12–15,000 years ago, in late Paleolithic Europe, there was a sudden flowering of artistic talent, as people began to decorate the deepest recesses of dark caves. They used a wide range of mineral dyes from yellow, brown and red ochre to iron oxide and even charcoal, which they bound together with anything from animal fat to blood to make a durable paint. Some of their paintings were abstract, some purely decorative or ritual, from friezes of palm prints to representations of the vagina, the ultimate fertility symbol. A very few were of men out hunting. Most however were of the animals on which they depended for their food – bison, deer, boars, horses and even mammoths, which they depicted in a flowing, lifelike fashion, galloping freely across the walls and ceilings of the caves. Some even have a distinctly cartoon-like twinkle in their eye.

The artists worked in near darkness, in tiny, cramped conditions, often hunched over double or flat on their back á la Michelangelo to reach the perfect site. The natural form of the rock was used to flesh out the contours of the body. Around these, the outlines of the body were etched into the rock or drawn in black, and some were filled in by rich pigments that must have glimmered into sharp life in the dim light provided by their fires.

So impressive are the paintings that the whole age was named the Magdalenian after the site of La Madeleine, near the Dordogne Valley in the south of France. The very best of the paintings can be found at two sites, Lascaux in France, and Altamira in Spain. There are many more caves however, sweeping across the continent in a broad band between these two points. Other sites in northern Spain include the Tito Bustillo Caves near Ribadasella, the El Buxu Caves near Cangas de Onís, and the Pindal Cave near Ribadadeva.

Sadly, the enormous interest shown in these paintings since their discovery at the turn of the century has led to untold damage, as the delicate micro-climate which preserved the paintings has been disturbed. Large quantities of people have crowded into the caves, their bodies raising the temperature, their breath increasing the humidity, and their bacteria escaping to attack the fragile pigments. After millenia of perfect preservation, many of the paintings have deteriorated sharply and now, in an effort to halt their destruction, some caves have been completely closed, while others limit entry to a few people a day. Waiting lists can be years long, while everyone else has to make do with modern copies that go some way at least towards revealing the full impact of the originals.

architect, Antoní Gaudí, it was commissioned by Máximo Díaz de Quijano as a present for his daughter, but she never lived here, and it had become almost derelict before its recent transformation into an extremely upmarket and expensive restaurant. As a final twist, amongst the tourists sunning themselves on the bench outside sits the pensive bronze figure of the architect, gazing up to the sky in search of inspiration.

On the hill opposite stands an enormous, largely deserted building, built in 1883 as a Pontifical Seminary, a place in which to give under-privileged children a free education while training them for the priesthood. Financed by Claudio López as a memorial to his wealthy 'Indiano' father, the course lasted 12 years, during which time the children had no holidays and were not permitted to leave the grounds. The first group of 54 completed their training in 1904, and Pope Pius X granted the university the right to award degrees in philosophy, theology and canon law. Over the next 60 years, it turned out some 40 bishops and 200 priests, but in 1966, the institution was transferred to Madrid, where it survives as the University of Comillas in Madrid, now teaching secular as well as religious courses. The building remained, a crumbling white elephant that is used only for a few courses run by the Santander International University (an upmarket summer school).

The final stop in Comillas should be in the cemetery, to see the huge white statue of an angel by sculptor, J. Llimona. This was originally designed for the entrance hall of the Papal University but was too big to get through the door, so had to take up residence here instead.

For the route south from Comillas into the mountains, see page 132.

Just beyond Comillas, on the road west, you come to the enormous curve of the **Playa de Oyambre**, one of the longest beaches along the Cantabrian coast. At the far end, you rejoin the main N634, which leads down to **San Vicente de la Barquera**, a tiny fishing port and resort town in a wonderful setting. With one of the longest beaches in Cantabria, this is a popular holiday resort, its shops festooned with beach balls, buckets and spades, and heaving with people in midsummer. For just a few weeks before and after high season however, it calms down into a charmingly pretty town made better by the presence of several tiny, but good fish restaurants. An impressively long, low bridge with 28 arches, the 16th-century Puente de la Maza, stretches across the wide ría to the arcaded plaza which forms the centre of town.

Humans have lived here since the Bronze Age, and there was also a Roman settlement here. The existing town dates back to the early stages of the Christian resettlement in the 9th century, at which time a Jewish community was also encouraged to settle and stimulate trade. The first castle was built shortly afterwards, although the existing one dates from the 13th-15th centuries. The town received its charter from Alfonso VII in 1210, and like the others along the coast went on to flourish on a mixture of fishing and whaling. Its luck didn't continue however and three times, in 1483, 1563 and 1636, the town was almost demolished by fire. In between, plague swept through and by the mid-17th century, it had lost almost everything.

From the plaza, walk up the narrow stepped street to the Puerta del Preboste, the gate which marks the edge of the medieval town. The nearby Town Hall was originally built in the 16th century as the home of the famous Inquisitor, Antonio del Corro. The massive Church of Santa María de los Angeles was originally built in the 12th century, but its Romanesque form has gradually been lost over the years in a mish-mash of design, as succeeding generations altered and rebuilt it to their taste. Down on the far side, in the fishermen's quarter beside the Brazo Mayor, there is a small sanctuary which has become the centre for a popular pilgrimage cult and local fiesta, La Folía, held on the first Sunday after Easter. Tradition has it that a disabled sailing ship was washed ashore in the 12th century, completely empty except for a statue of the Virgin, for which the locals promptly built the little chapel.

The road climbs steeply as it leaves San Vicente, still heading west towards the Asturian border. As you reach the top of the hill, stop and look back for a wonderful view over the town. The border is reached at Unquera, 12km further on.

Unquera is one of the main access points for the Picos de Europa route, see page 231. For the continuation of the coastal route west to Ribadesella, see page 50.

Santander to Aguilar de Campóo

The first part of this route follows the coast before turning inland to climb into the dramatic heights of the Cordillera Cantábrica, visiting the high mountain ski resort of the Alto Campóo before connecting up with routes south to Burgos and Carrión de los Condes, on the Camino de Santiago.

For the first section of the route, follow the coastal route west as far as Comillas, then turn south on the S484, signposted to Cabezón de la Sal. With so much to see along this stretch of coast, this is effectively a day's journey on its own. The second stage of the route, through the mountains, offers some stunning scenery, but relatively little actual sightseeing and is a far more leisurely affair for everyone but the driver.

About 8km south of Comillas, you reach a crossroads, where a turning to the right signposted to Pumalverde leads up into a range of low limestone hills and the opencast zinc mines of Udías. From the top, there is an excellent view back down to the coast. Return to the S484, which continues through to **Cabezón de la Sal**, an area famous for salt mines, first exploited by the Romans. Production only ceased within the last century. The town centre has a number of 17th- and 18th-century mansions emblazoned with coats of arms, as well as a beautiful park.

From here, follow the C625 south along the line of the Saja River Valley, through the charming little village of **Carrejo**, and across the Puente de Santa Lucía, beside which stands a monument to the Foramontanos, Christian pioneers of the 8th and 9th centuries who acted as the vanguard for resettlement while the area was still under Moorish rule.

A little way south of here, you come to the village of **Ruente**, where you can see an old, eight-arched stone bridge and several fine mansions dating from the 15th to 18th centuries. Chief amongst them is the Casa del Rey, a 15th-century house that was once the home of Charles V. A footpath from the village leads to La Fuentona, the source of a stream which gushes from a cave.

With the road climbing fairly steadily now along a beautiful route of bubbling river and rich woodland, you pass through the villages of Cabuérniga and Renedo before turning off to the left up the recently improved road to **Barcena Mayor**, a village to rival Santillana del Mar in sheer beauty – with one major exception. This wonderful huddle of charming old houses has not, as yet, been severely attacked by tourism. Needless to say, the new road was designed expressly to remedy that fact, and visitors over the next few years will find its decaying streets becoming ever smarter, as houses become hotels and every balcony sprouts geraniums.

Back-track down to the junction and turn left (south), back onto the C625. About 1km on, the Mirador del Pico del Castron offers a wonderful view across the Argoza Valley to the east and the 1272m Pico del Castron, to the south. As the road continues south, climbing all the while, you pass through the village of Saja itself, into the Saja Valley Hunting Reserve, a huge preserve created in 1948 and rich in wildlife including some of the larger species such as deer, boar, wolves and even bears (see also page 66). Three kilometres south of the village, the road crosses the Puerto de Palombera, a dramatic bridge across a deep gorge carved out by the small, but turbulent Saja River. Another mirador, at the Balcón de la Cardosa, marks the best view back to the north just before the road crosses the Puerto de Palombera, a 1260m high pass that marks the boundary between the north and south faces of the Sierra del Cordel.

At Espinilla, 5km south, turn right onto the C628, leading up to the resort area of the **Alto Campóo**. Just off to the right, in the little village of Proano, the 16th-century mansion of the Rios family is attached to the square 12th-century Torre de los Rios Mier. A little further on, beside the church in Hoz de Abiada, there is a giant walnut tree, christened 'el Abuelo' (the Grandfather), with a trunk over 6m in diameter. The Parish church beside it has a beautiful Baroque altarpiece and a Gothic statue of the Madonna.

From now on, the villages all have a number of small guest houses and hotels geared to catering for the ski trade. Chief amongst them is Braña Vieja, from where the chairlifts run to the tops of the ski slopes. The best of the chairlifts for sightseers is the one to the top of the 2175m **Picos de Tres Mares**, the highest peak in the eastern Cordillera. The mountain gets its name from an extraordinary fact – three rivers come to life here, eventually arriving at three different seas. The Hijar joins the Ebro on its journey to the Mediterranean, the Pisuerga flows into the Douro, which eventually comes out into the Atlantic, and the Nansa heads north to the Cantabrian Sea. The view from the top is superb in every direction. At the far end of the road, the Mirador de la Fuente del Chivo offers a fine view across the fledgling Nansa Valley.

To reach Reinosa, you have to backtrack the whole way down to Espinilla, then continue straight across, heading east on the C628. On your left, just beyond Espinilla, the ruined Castle of Argueso, with 12th-century towers linked by a 15th-century manor, is currently undergoing an extensive programme of rebuilding and restoration. Just beyond this, Fontibre was a spa of some renown in Roman times when many people, including Pliny, flocked here for treatment of jaundice and hepatitis. At the centre of the attention is the source of the massive Ebro River.

Reinosa is the main town in the area, set in a wide, flat depression has long been a major grain growing area. The permanent population is only about 13,500, but thousands more use the town as a resort base for winter sports and summer exploration of the surrounding mountains, giving it a lively, cosmopolitan air at odds with its real size and status. The town first grew to prominence in the Middle Ages as a milling centre, strategically placed on one of the main routes north to the coast. Its viability was assured when the railway arrived in the mid-19th century and today it is increasingly attracting heavy industry as well as the ski set.

Just to the east of the town is the end of the vast **Embalse del Ebro** (Ebro Reservoir), built in the 1940s as an irrigation supply for the surrounding agricultural lands. It is the largest man-made lake in Spain, covering an area of 6200 hectares and with a shoreline about 125km long. Today, the reservoir has itself become a holiday attraction, with watersports, fishing, hunting and a varied population of migrant and water birds.

For the route south from Reinosa to Burgos via Briviesca and Frías, see page 150.

This route now joins the N611 heading south towards Aguilar de Campóo in neighbouring Castilla-y-León. About 3km south of Reinosa, the village of **Retortillo**, set dramatically on the edge of the Reinosa basin, overlooking the Picos de Tres Mares and the Ebro Reservoir, is the site of the Roman town of Julióbriga. This was a civil administrative centre that was partially destroyed by a Cantabre uprising in 224, although it was later rebuilt and eventually survived until the collapse of the western empire in the 5th century. The remains are all clustered around the small Romanesque church, part of which was built using stones from the Roman walls and which, in summer, houses a small exhibition of finds from the site. Excavations have been ongoing sporadically since the 1880s, and gradually more and more of the town is being uncovered, including the foundations of a large villa, a group of smaller villas surrounding a courtyard, part of a colonnaded street and the corner of a large public building that is possibly the forum.

Another 3km on, at **Cervatos**, there is a fine Collegiate Church, built between 1129 and 1199 as part of the Abbey of San Pedro. Considered by many to be the finest Romanesque church in Cantabria, it is remarkably untouched by succeeding generations and richly decorated with a recurring theme of lions as well as the more normal strapwork and floral motifs on its superb capitals and portal. As the road heads south from here, it crosses the 987m Puerto Pozazal a few kilometres before the border with Castilla-y-León.

From here, follow the N611 south to Aguilar de Campóo, where the road links up with the route north from Carrión de los Condes described on page 157. For the Cantabrian Picos de Europa, see page 231.

Cantabria: General Information

Regional tourist office:
Diputación Regional de Cantabria, Consejeria de Industria, Transportes, Comunicaciones y Turismo, Palacio de la Diputación Regional, c/ Casimiro Sáinz 4, 39003 Santander (tel: (942) 312 761).

The Cantabrian Coast

This is a holiday resort coast, and although it is utterly unlike the concrete jungles of the Mediterranean coasts, there are numerous small hotels and restaurants in all the villages along the shore. I have listed only a very few of the best.

CASTRO URDIALES
Where to stay:
Hotel Miramar, 39700 (tel. (942) 860 200). Uninspired but comfortable beach-front hotel with a terrace and good views. Cheap-moderate.
Where to eat:
Mesón Marinero, Correria 23 (tel. (942) 860 005). Bright and cheerful seafood restaurant looking out over the fishing harbour. Moderate.

COMILLAS
Where to eat:
El Capricho de Gaudí. (tel. (942) 720 365). One of the finest restaurants on the Cantabrian coast, in one of its most extraordinary buildings, a part Moorish, part fairy tale extravaganza built by Antoní Gaudí. Visit the building even if you can't afford the prices. Expensive.

QUIJAS
Where to stay and eat:
Hosteria de Quijas. (tel. (942) 820 833). A delightfully converted 18th-century manor house, with a vine-covered terrace, garden and swimming pool. 4km from Santander on the main Oviedo road (N611), it is convenient for Santander, Santillana del Mar and for exploring the Cantabrian mountains and coast. Moderate.

SANTANDER
Tourist Office, Plaza de Velarde, 1-bajo (Plaza de Porticada), 39001 (tel. (942) 310 708).
Where to stay:
Santander is not only the ferry port, but also a large freight port and a major holiday destination in its own right. Finding a room can be extremely difficult, and advance booking is essential. The modern holiday hotels are mainly near the beach, and leading up to the top of the ridge. Most of the cheap hotels and fondas are clustered in the old town near the railway and bus stations. Prices here are higher than average, and the quality of the cheap places is lower, so be prepared to spend a little more. Better still, stay outside the town.
Hotel Real, 28, 39005 (tel. (942) 272 550; fax (942) 274 573). Wonderfully grand resort hotel on the ridge with views over both beaches. Now one of the most luxurious hotels in Spain. Very expensive.
Hotel Roma, Avenida de los Hoteles 5, 39005 (tel. (942) 272 700; fax (942) 272 751). Elegant turn-of-the-century hotel with many of its original furnishings and all its original flavour. In a quiet position, with its own gardens. Moderate-expensive.
Maria Isabel, Avda de Garcia Lago, s/n (tel. (942) 271 850). Comfortable but unpretentious modern high-rise holiday hotel on the beach, with fine views over the bay. It has its own gardens, with a terrace bar and swimming pool. Moderate.
Hotel Las Brisas, Trav de los Castros 14, 39005 (tel. (942) 270 991; fax (942) 281

173). Small, friendly country house-style hotel across from El Sardinero beach. Bed and breakfast only. Moderate.

Where to eat:

El Molino, Carretera N-611, Puente Arce (tel (942) 574 052). Actually 12km out of Santander, this is the place for the city's serious eaters. An elegant restaurant in a beautifully restored old mill, the food is an imaginative variation on traditional regional dishes. Expensive.

Gran Casino del Sardinero, Plaza de Italia, 39005 (tel. (942) 276 054). Elegant restaurant serving Spanish-style haute cuisine, next to the casino. Black tie not required, but you must be reasonably smart. Take your passport as ID if you wish to play. Expensive.

La Sardina, Dr Fleming 3, 39005 (tel. (942) 271 035). Lively seafood restaurant decorated as a fishing boat. Expensive.

Bodega Cigaleña, Daoiz y Velarde 19, 39003 (tel. (942) 213 062). The food is average, but the ambience is great, with rustic decor, and a small wine museum attached. Moderate.

Los Peñucos, Barrio Pesquero (tel. (942) 229 445). Extremely popular spit-and-sawdust style fish restaurant in the commercial port. Cheap.

Bodega La Conveniente, c/ Gomez Oreña 9, 39005 (tel. (942) 212 887). Turn-of-the-century bodega with its original trimmings, a good range of wines and tapas and a piano player. Cheap.

The Paseo de Pereda, opposite the port, is lined with cafés that serve dubious food, but are a very pleasant place to sit and watch the world. There are also several pleasant cafés on the other side of the peninsula overlooking the beach.

SANTILLANA DEL MAR

Tourist Office, Plaza Mayor, s/n, 39330 (tel. (942) 818 251).

Where to stay and eat:

This is usually either the first or last stop on any tour of the region, as well as being one of its main tourist centres. There are quite a few hotels, but advance booking is still essential.

Parador Gil Blas, Plaza Ramón Pelayo 8, 39330 (tel. (942) 818 000; fax (942) 818 391). A 15th- to 16th-century country house, this is now one of the most charming of the region's paradors, named after a local fictional hero. The front rooms look out over Santillana's main square, the back ones over a delightful courtyard garden. Moderate-expensive.

Hotel Altamira, Cantón 1, 39330 (tel. (942) 818 025). A large old house decorated in the rustic style, right in the heart of the old village, with an attractive walled courtyard that doubles as bar and restaurant in good weather. Moderate.

Hotel Los Infantes, Avenida Le Dorat, 1, 39330 (tel. (942) 818 100). An 18th-century house outside the old village, but still within easy walking distance. Still pleasant, this is a bit too 'done-up', and even has a disco in high season. Cheap-moderate.

Hotel Santillana, El Cruce, 39330 (tel. (942) 818 011). Another largish, stone-built hotel, right on the main crossroads, so it can be a bit noisy, this is similar in style and price to Los Infantes. Cheap-moderate.

SAN VICENTE DE LA BARQUERA
Where to stay:
Hostal Luzón, Av Miramar 1, 39540 (tel. (942) 710 050). An old house right on the main square which provides bed and breakfast in an atmosphere of decaying grandeur. Cheap-moderate.
Where to eat:
Hotel Miramar, 39540 (tel. (942) 710 075). You can stay at this hotel on the west bank of the river, with fine views of the town, but the rooms don't match the restaurant, which specialises in local seafood, and is one of the best nearby. Cheap-moderate.

REINOSA
Where to stay and eat:
Corza Blanca, 39200 (tel. (942) 779 511; fax (942) 779 576). About 25km from Reinosa, this is a comfortable hotel with 69 rooms high up on the Alto Campóo, miles away from anywhere. In winter, it is a skiing centre, in summer, its calm atmosphere and lovely views turn it into a wonderful retreat. Moderate.

Castilla-y-León

Almost from its conception, the kingdom of Castille not only covered at least half of Spain geographically, but was the real power broker on the Iberian peninsula. While the mountains of Cantabria and Asturias might have been the only places never conquered by the Moors, the real drama of the Christian Reconquista was played out on the plains of northern Castille. This became – and still is – the home of the court and central government, preserving its supremacy as one kingdom after another merged into the main block that eventually became Spain. Although regional languages and dialects are accepted today, Castillian Spanish is still the official language of the country, while the finest accent, equivalent to BBC English, is said to be that of Burgos – at least by the citizens of that region!

Today this vast region of Castille is divided into two separate Autonomous Communities, Castilla-La Mancha (including Madrid) in the south, and Castilla-y-León in the north. Even divided, they are still two of the largest states in Spain and Castilla-y-León is further sub-divided into no less than nine provinces. Because of the geography of this book, we are concerned here with only the northern section of the three northernmost provinces, Burgos, Palencia and León. This long, thin strip runs east-west across the southern edge of Green Spain. In the north section of the state, the land climbs to the cool green mountains and lakes of the Cordillera Cantábrica, while to the far west, the Montes de León block the way to Atlantic Galicia. To the south of this is the northern edge of the *meseta*, the massive central plateau, a prairie land of wheat production, with a harsh, continental climate, bitter in winter and burning in summer. Different in the extreme, physically and temperamentally, from the damp mountainous north, the scenery is dull to those who crave trees and hills, stunningly and dramatically beautiful to others. Villages built of golden stone rise from the dune-like gold of the wheat, and the golden shimmer of the bare earth, while dim and distant on the horizon, a shallow rim of mountains edge the platter with a gleaming royal purple.

Of the three provinces, León, to the west, is the largest, and the seventh largest province in Spain, with an area of nearly 16,000 square kilometres, and a population of about 530,000. Palencia, in the centre, covers 8,029 square kilometres and has a population of around 186,000. Burgos, to the east, covers an area of 14,328 square kilometres, and has around 360,000 inhabitants, about a third of whom live in the city of Burgos itself.

Ferdinand and Isabela

Fernando and Isabel are probably one of the most famous royal partnerships of European history. Second-cousins, he was king of Aragón and Catalunya, she was queen of Castille. They married in 1469 and combined their kingdoms in 1472, effectively creating modern Spain. Both came to their thrones after long civil wars and needed both to distract attention from their internal difficulties and to replenish their finances. Leaping on the Catholic bandwagon of discontent against the Jews, they set up the infamous Spanish Inquisition in 1478 and, in 1482, marched against Moorish Granada. It took them ten years, but the city state finally surrendered in 1492. In the same year, they expelled all Jews who refused conversion. Most of the Muslims left the country, but two years later, there were still over quarter of a million left. These were now offered the same choice

as they had given the Jews – convert or go! Most of them chose to stay as they could not afford to leave, so converted to Christianity, were given the name of *moriscos* and were sent to live in mountain reservations.

In 1492, also, the royal couple met Cristóbal Colón (Christopher Columbus) and, on his assurance that he wanted gold, but also wanted to convert the heathen, agreed to finance his first expedition. In 1494, the Pope granted them the title of the 'Catholic Monarchs' in deference to their zeal, leading them on to even greater efforts on behalf of the Catholic Church. Isabel died in 1504, leaving the throne to their daughter, Juana, until Juana's son, Carlos, came of age, with a proviso that Fernando should remain as regent. This he did, in spite of a great deal of Castillian opposition, until his own death in 1516.

Like Navarra (see page 215), this region has suffered from constant invasion and conquest over the centuries, starting (in known history) with tribes like the Celts and Cantabres, each of which was driven up into the mountains by the next wave of attackers. The Romans had such a secure hold on the region that they had special Spanish legions, who were, unusually, given full citizenship of Rome. There are still a number of Roman sites in existence. With the collapse of the Roman Empire in the 5th century, the Suebis, Vandals and Visigoths arrived. After another short break of relative stability came a new threat, this time from the south, with the arrival of the Moors, who swept across the plains swallowing all before them.

La Reconquista officially began in 718 when the Moors were defeated at Covadonga (see page 238). By the early 9th century, sufficient land had been secured for the 'new peoples' or Christians to begin to leave the mountains and settle on the plains, although they were not totally secure against Moorish attack for another couple of centuries. Castille gained its name from the many powerful castles which were thrown up across the region to cope with the threat. The situation in the south continued to be precarious for much longer, and it was natural for Burgos and León to become the two great centres of Christian Spain. In 1037, Burgos, León and Asturias were united as one kingdom by Ferdinand I with Burgos as capital. It remained as capital of Spain until 1492 when Valladolid became the capital, followed by Madrid in 1561. Valladolid is still the capital of the Autonomous Community.

The area later saw a great deal of military action during the Peninsula Wars of the early 19th century, and again during the Civil War, when Burgos briefly regained its status as Franco's capital until the fall of Madrid in 1939.

The single most important reason why people visit this region is the Camino de Santiago, which runs through here, entering Castille a few miles east of Burgos, and leaving León just west of Villafranca del Bierzo. Along, or near the route are not only the cities of Burgos and León, some of the most fascinating in Spain, but several other stupendous architectural achievements, such as the Church of San Martín at Fromistá.

The northern mountains are a wonderful retreat from the heat of the plains, an outdoor playground for fishing, hiking or hunting. The southern slopes of the Picos de Europa are actually in León, but are covered in the separate chapter on the Picos (see page 231).

Burgos

For those who have been roaming the remote hills and small villages of this northern region, Burgos comes as a shock to the system. Not only is it a large and busy city in its own right, but it is one of the great historic cities of Spain, lying moreover on a direct route between the coast and Madrid. The place is waist-deep in tourists and there are so many churches that even the most committed groupie would go weak at the knees. Luckily, there are only a few that are truly spectacular, and the others pale into insignificance beside them. Instead of trying to crawl your way around everything, allow these highlights the time they deserve.

The real history of the city dates back to 884 AD, when Count Diego Porcelos, on the orders of King Alfonso III, built the first castle on the banks of the Arlanzón River. Rebuilt and extended in later years, the ruins of the castle still survive on the hill above the city. The walk up is steep, and while the ruins themselves are not terribly exciting, the view from the walls is wonderful.

The city and province took their name from the bourgeois traders who settled at the foot of the castle. For the next 500 years, Burgos was one of the most important crossroads of the medieval trade routes, and the main centre on the Iberian peninsula for the export of wool, particularly to Flanders. The city was under the rule of León until 926 when the burgers broke away and elected two judges as their rulers. A brief period of war with León and Asturias followed until the region became established as an independent County in 950, under Fernán González. It was his great-grandson who transformed it into a kingdom in 1037, taking the title of King Fernando I. He went on to marry the Infanta Sancha of León and reunited the two kingdoms, with himself as ruler.

As the capital of Christian Spain, a rich trading centre and one of the most important stops on the pilgrim route to Compostela, Burgos flourished throughout the Middle Ages, and its wealth is still visible in the quantity and grandeur of its architectural monuments. Its most famous inhabitant was the 11th-century hero, Rodrigo Díaz de Vivar, better known as El Cid, who was born a few miles from the city, spent much of his life here, and is buried in the cathedral (see page 142).

The city had a relatively peaceful time over the following centuries, and didn't

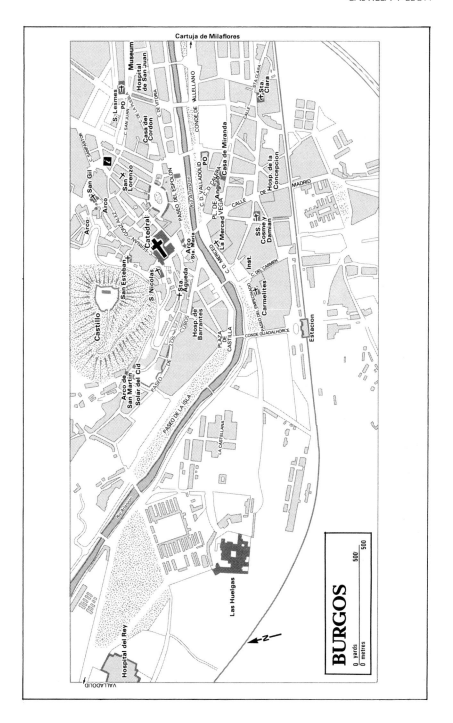

Cartuja de Milaflores

Museum
Hospital de San Juan
S. Lesmes
Sta. Clara
VALLELLANO
CONDE DE
Casa del Cordón
C. DE VITORIA
C. SAN JUAN
Casa de Miranda
San Gil
Arco
San Lorenzo
Hosp. de la Concepción
MADRID
Catedral
C. D. VALLADOLID
PL. DE
La Merced VEGA Anguix
SS. Cosme y Damian
San Esteban
Arco Sta. María
Inst.
C. DE CARMEN
Castillo
S. Nicolás
Sta. Águeda
Carmelites
Estacion
Hosp. de Barrantes
CONDE GUADALHORCE
Arco de San Martín
Solar del Cid
PLAZA DE CASTILLA
PASEO DE LA ISLA
LA CASTELLANA
Las Huelgas
Hospital del Rey
VALLADOLID

BURGOS

0 yards   500
0 metres   500

El Cid

El Cid, known to most of us as Charlton Heston, was in fact a Spanish mercenary named Rodrigo Díaz who was born in around 1043 in the village of Vivar, about 9km from Burgos. A captain in the Castillian army, he first served Sancho II, winning numerous battles including a famous victory against the Moors in 1081. On Sancho's mysterious death, he forced Alfonso VI, whose cousin, Ximena, he had recently married, to proclaim publicly, if reluctantly, that he had had no part in the affair. Shortly afterwards, Alfonso, jealous of his reputation and resentful of his influence, sent him into exile.

Díaz went south to fight for the Muslim Emir of Zaragoza, and from then on, hired himself out impartially, fighting for both Christians and Muslims with equal stunning success. He won a victory against the Christians in Rioja, destroying Logroño in the process, then, in 1094, led a Christian army of 7000 men in a nine-month siege which captured Valencia from the Moors.

He remained as ruler of Valencia until 1099 when he was eventually defeated at Cuenca, dying shortly afterwards. Ximena continued to rule the city until 1102 when she set fire to it before returning to Castilla. His body was buried at the Monastery of San Pedro de Cardeña, 10km east of Burgos, until 1921, when it was moved, with that of Ximena, to Burgos Cathedral.

A redoubtable man, Díaz was equally admired by both sides, being named *el campeador*, or 'the champion' by the Christians and *el cid*, 'the lord' by the Muslims within his lifetime. After his death, his stature continued to grow until he became a legend. By 1180, an epic poem, *El Cantor de mio Cid* had turned him into the perfect chivalrous knight, a true champion of the Christian cause. Different versions of the story have continued to be told ever since, including *Las Mocedades del Cid* by Guillén de Castro, written in 1618, *Le Cid* by Corneille, written in 1636, and, of course, *El Cid* – the movie!

see battle again until the Peninsula Wars, when Wellington's disastrous siege of Burgos in 1812 was one of the bloodiest of the war, and one of the Iron Duke's few defeats. In 1813, the French blew up the castle during their retreat from Vitoria.

During the Civil War, the city was strongly Nationalist, and in 1936 became the Nationalist Headquarters. It was here, in October 1937, that Franco formed his Falangist government. It remained as his capital until the fall of Madrid in 1939, and it was from here that he declared the ceasefire, on 1st April, 1939, that eventually brought the Civil War to a close.

Perhaps as a reward for this loyalty, in 1964, Franco used the city as the headquarters of his Industrial Promotion and Development Plan, creating a huge manufacturing base and doubling the population of the city almost overnight. Burgos, capital of the Catholic Monarchs, is also still one of the most deeply Catholic cities in Spain, with a number of still active seminaries, convents and monasteries as well as the normal sprinkling of churches.

Of all the sights in the city, the **CATHEDRAL** is, without a doubt, the most outstanding. In her book, *Spain*, Jan Morris says that Burgos Cathedral is 'a gnarled, dour, idiosyncratic building . . . (that) remains in your memory not as a joy, nor even an inspiration, but as an iron glower in the mind.' Teófilo Gautier, however, described it as 'gigantic as a pyramid and delicate as a lady's jewel'. For me, the

A view of the cathedral of Burgos from the castle

lasting impression was of the sheer opulence of the dark interior, glittering with gold and silver like a dragon's lair, an ostentatious display of the vast wealth and power of the Catholic church, laid out for all to see in wonder and fear.

The diocese, said to have been founded by St James himself, is thought to have been centred originally on Oca, 40km away, until this city was completely razed during a Moorish attack in 714. In 1074, the sisters of King Alfonso VI, the Infantas Urraca and Elvira, moved the See to Gamonal, 2 km from Burgos. The first cathedral on the present site was built by Alfonso in 1081. In 1219, King Fernando III was married here to the German princess, Beatrice de Suabia, but the cathedral was not large enough to hold all the guests. The embarrassed king and bishop both agreed that a larger and far more magnificent cathedral was needed for a city as powerful as Burgos. They started by knocking the old one so flat that only a few fragmentary pieces have survived, and those were discovered in the foundations. The first stone of the new creation was laid in 1221, the first mass was celebrated in 1230, and it was finally consecrated in 1260. Work continued for the next 400 years, and the final product is the third largest cathedral in Spain (after Toledo and Seville).

At first glance, the cathedral appears remarkably un-Spanish. This is because, at the time of its foundation, the Bishop was an Englishman, Maurice, who brought with him plans drawn up in France, and one of the earliest architects was the Frenchman, Enrique, responsible also for León Cathedral. So many different architects and artists took a hand over the centuries however that it is difficult to attribute the cathedral to any one of them. This has also resulted in the graceful, soaring architecture of the English and French Gothic receiving a typically Spanish twist that adds a solidity to the whole while piling on ornamentation to an overwhelming degree.

Before you set foot inside, walk right around the outside of the cathedral to see all its amazing twists and turns, buttresses and decorative friezes. Go at least partway up the hill to get a view over the incredibly complex roofline with its fretwork spires, turrets and towers. If you are staying overnight, go back and do it all again once the floodlights are on, because the entire mood of the building changes. There are four main doors. The lower half of the West Front was lost during an 18th-century renovation, but the upper half still exists in all its glory, its rose window flanked by 90m high open spires created by Johan of Cologne between 1442 and 1458. In the north wall (to the right), a flight of steps leads up to the Puerta del Sarmental, an elaborate Gothic rendition of Christ in heaven, dictating to the four apostles. This dates from the 13th century and is thought to have been the work of the master architect, Enrique, although it has been restored recently. In the south wall (to the left) is the Puerta Alta de la Coronería, a more delicate affair, but of the same period, completed in 1257. Tucked just round the corner beside this is the smaller Plateresque Puerta de la Pellejería (Skinners' or Leatherworkers' Door), created in the 16th century by Francisco de Colonia.

As you enter the main (west) door, the massive length (109m) of the 13th-century, rib-vaulted nave is spread before you, although the effect is somewhat spoiled by the choir, which blocks the apse and high altar from view. The medieval windows were tragically destroyed in 1813 by the blast which blew up the castle, so the current windows all date from the 19th and early 20th centuries. The cathedral has 19 chapels and 38 altars altogether. This description is designed to lead around the cathedral in a clockwise direction.

Just on the left near the door is one of the cathedral's great talking points, the Papamosca or Flycatcher Clock, a 15th-century clock topped by the carved figure of a man whose mouth opens as it strikes the hour. Next to this is the Chapel of San Tecla, the very last to be created within the cathedral, in 1734. Founded by Archbishop D. Manuel Samaniego, the immensely ornate work, including the heavy, gilded altarpiece, was carried out by Alberto Churriguera, who gave his name to the Chirrugueresque style, the overblown Baroque successor to the Plateresque. A little further on, also on the left is the Chapel of Santa Ana, which has a superb, vast gilded altarpiece, created in the 15th century by Gil de Siloe and Diego de la Cruz. At the centre are St Anne and St Joachim. At the bottom, Jesse lies asleep, while above him stretch the branches of the Jesse Tree, showing the dynastic lineage of the Virgin, who sits at the top. In front of the altar is the alabaster tomb of Bishop Luis de Acuña, founder of the chapel, sculpted by Diego de Siloe (son of Gil).

In the centre of the nave is the massive and quite splendid choir, carved by Felipe de Vigarni between 1507 and 1512. It has 103 stalls, all carved in walnut inlaid with box, depicting scenes from the Bible, mythology and local folk tales. The tomb at the centre, carved in wood and plated with gilt and embossed copper, is that of the founder of the cathedral, Bishop Maurice, who died in 1238. The screen at the entrance of the choir is the work of Juan Bautista in 1602, while the paintings around the outside were done by Juan Rizi between 1654 and 1659.

Walk round behind the choir and you eventually come to the transepts and high altar. The transept vault, an immense 54m high, has a superb Mudéjar star dome. Two simple stone slabs directly underneath mark the tomb of El Cid and his wife, Ximena. Originally buried in the Monastery of San Pedro de Cardeña, some miles away, his tomb was ransacked and his bones stolen during the Peninsula Wars. Once retrieved, they were brought to the cathedral for safety and finally buried here in 1921.

The high altar, directly ahead, was sculpted between 1562 and 1580 by local artists, Rodrigo and Martín de la Haya. Although gilded and painted, it is actually made of solid silver, is classic Renaissance in style and depicts scenes from both Old and New Testaments.

At the far end of the north transept is the Escalera Dorada, the Golden Staircase created by Diego de Siloe in 1523. A grandiose double stairway of Carrera marble and gold, it is now used only during Holy Week, but climb it for the best possible view of the fine rose window in the south transept, the only window in the cathedral to keep its late Gothic glass. An apsidal walk leads round the back of the high altar, decorated by a series of five high-relief medallions depicting stations of the cross. The three in the centre are the 16th-century work of Felipe de Vigarni, the two at either end were carved in the 17th century by Alonso de los Ríos. Of the many chapels surrounding the apse, the finest by some way, and one of the most beautiful in the cathedral, is the one at the top, the Chapel del Condestable. This was built in 1494 by Simon of Cologne for Don Pedro Hernández de Velasco and his wife, Dona Mencía de Mendoza, the hereditary Constables of Castille, whose tombs stand in the chapel. Its finest feature must be the beautiful octagonal cupola, with decorative lacework, star vaulting and a central lantern, but in this one chapel, you can find the work of all the greatest sculptors to work on the cathedral through the centuries. Amongst other treasures are a grand 16th-century entrance screen designed by Cristóbal de Andino, the gilded Renaissance central retable created by Felipe de Vigarni and Diego de Siloe in 1532, a Gothic retable (on the right), the work of Gil de Siloe, and a Plateresque one (on the left), the work of Diego de Silo. A Plateresque doorway on the right leads into the Sacristy, in which there is a portrait of Mary Magdalene, probably School of Leonardo da Vinci, although some attribute it to the master himself.

Continuing round, the entrance to the cloister leads from the east wall of the north transept. Built in the early 14th century, with an open arcaded walkway, the rooms and chapels off here house the amazingly sumptuous Diocesan Museum. In the gallery itself there is a fine collection of Gothic religious sculpture in poly-chrome wood, stone and terracotta, as well as an ornate silver processional chariot. At the entrance to the main sacristy stands a small brazier, used for lighting incense, that has been lit every day without exception since the 17th century. The most valuable treasures are housed in the various chapels, the chapterhouse and sacristy. Look out in particular for the four collections of tapestries, three of them Flemish from the 16th century, the fourth Goblin; for a collection of 15th-century robes and 13th-century Moorish cape in the Chapel of San Juan Bautista; the 1927 Guardian of Granada, a solid gold chalice weighing 14kg, inlaid with ivory and enamel, with a monstrance of platinum and jewelled cross, the 16th-century

145

Metropolitan Cross by Juan de Arfe, and several Byzantine and Romanesque Crosses in the Chapel of Santa Catalina; and for the various books and documents, the earliest recording a donation to the church of Valpuesta in 774. The marriage certificate of El Cid and Ximena is also here.

Physically the least valuable, but perhaps most interesting exhibit in the whole museum is a tatty leather chest, the Cofre de el Cid, in the Capitular Hall. This is not, as their English translation states, his coffin, but is the subject of an enjoyable legend. In 1081, El Cid was exiled and in desperate need of money. He took this sealed chest to the Jewish moneylenders and used it as security to borrow 600 gold marks, on the strict understanding that it was not to be opened for a year. He went off, conquered Valencia, and before the year was up, returned to repay the loan and retrieve the chest. When opened, it proved to have nothing more inside it than sand and stones, but he explained it away by saying that what had been inside was the word of El Cid, a prize more valuable by far than gold.

Back in the main church, the first chapel of interest in the south wall of the nave is the Chapel de la Presentación, built in 1520 by Felipe de Vigarni. It has a beautifully delicate star vault, almost like a lotus blossom, and contains the alabaster tomb of the founder, Don Gonzalo de Lerma, also sculpted by de Vigarni in 1524. The altar painting is by Sebastian de Piombo, and the screen is by Cristóbal Andino.

Finally, nearest the door, is the Chapel of the Santísimo Cristo, with a horribly realistic crucifix. Said to have been found floating at sea by a local merchant and donated to the cathedral in the 13th century, the body is made of buffalo hide, with human hair, beard and finger nails. The head moves from side to side, and the arms, if released from the nails, drop to its sides. At its feet are five ostrich eggs, donated by another merchant on his return from Africa. The image is the centre of a pilgrimage cult, and its feast is celebrated on 14 September.

Leaving the cathedral by the west door, turn right, go up the steps and through the plaza to the small **Church of San Nicolás**, begun in 1408, which has a magnificent retable created by Simon of Cologne in 1505: 465 figures are grouped in scenes from the life of the Virgin, St Nicholas and the Last Supper. To the right of this is the Gothic Church of San Esteban, which has a fine west front, while further along to the right is the 14th-century Arch of San Esteban, one of the old gates through the city walls. Just behind these churches lies the path up to the castle (see page 140).

Turn left beside San Nicolás, along the road which skirts the foot of the hill and you enter the old Jewish Quarter. Little now remains of this, but in the Middle Ages there was a flourishing Jewish community in the city, which only came to an abrupt end when the Jews were all expelled by Ferdinand and Isabella at the end of the 15th century (see page 142).

At the far end of this road, past the 14th-century Moorish Arch of San Martín. there is a monument to El Cid, erected in 1791 on the site of his family home, which had been destroyed in 1771. The vast building behind is a seminary. Head down the hill and you reach the line of bastions which are one of the few remaining portions of the city walls, built in 1276. Follow these, along the Paseo de los

Cubos, back into the town centre. The road passes the Archbishop's Palace on the right, and the Church of Santa Agueda on the left. It was on the steps of this early Gothic church that El Cid forced King Alfonso VI to swear three times and in public that he had not killed his brother, Sancho II. The king was livid, but had to comply, but he never forgot his humiliation and got rid of El Cid as soon as he could.

The Arch of Santa María, Burgos

The road comes out beside the river next to the **Arch of Santa María**, originally a fortified 14th-century gateway guarding both the bridge and town walls. In 1536 however, it was altered and decorated as a tribute to Charles V, with statues of the great names of the city's history. Amongst them are Diego Porcelos, the founder

147

of Burgos, the two judges who were appointed to rule in the 10th century, Count Fernan González, El Cid and of course, Charles himself.

Follow the pleasant walk along the Paseo del Espelón beside the river and turn left back into the old city through the Plaza del General Primo de Rivera, at the end, which has an equestrian statue of – El Cid! Just to your right, next to the small Plaza de Calvo Sotelo, is the **Casa de Cordon**, the 15th-century palace of the constables of Castille. It got its name from the two stone ropes, modelled on the rope belts of the Franciscan Friars, which flank the main door. After Christopher Columbus returned from his second, triumphant voyage to the New World in 1496, he came here to make his report to Ferdinand and Isabella. Heading back towards the cathedral, you come to the circular, arcaded Plaza José Antonio, the city's main square, with the town hall on the south side.

The Marceliano Santa María Museum, dedicated to the work of this Impressionist painter, one of the most famous in Castille, is housed in the old Monastery of San Juan, some distance east of the city centre. Some 150 of his canvases are hung around the Plateresque cloister, itself a thing of beauty. The **Provincial Museum** is to the south of the river in the Casa de Miranda. The house, built in 1545, is a beautiful example of secular Plateresque architecture. The Museum was originally founded in 1871, although both it and the house have recently been renovated, and it is now one of the best museums in Spain and a National Monument. The section on prehistory, Roman and early medieval (including Visigothic) archaeology includes some fine Roman mosaics from Clunia, Roman and Visigothic sarcophagi and other funerary monuments. There is also a collection of Gothic and Renaissance tombs, a collection of Moorish and Mudéjar art and ivories, Limoges enamels, ceramics, and a wide range of religious art and artefacts. Of these, probably the most interesting is the 12th-century font from Santo Domingo de Silos, made of enamelled copper and covered in the figures of saints. There is also a collection of 16th- and 17th-century furniture and a small collection of fine art, mainly by local artists.

The two remaining sights of real interest in Burgos are away from the city centre, out of walking distance. The **Cartuja de Miraflores** is 4km east, along the Paseo de la Quinta. Enrique III began to build a palace here, but in 1441, his son, King Juan II, changed his mind and turned the site into a Carthusian monastery, to be used as a royal pantheon. The church was designed in 1454 by Johan of Cologne, and later taken over by his son, Simon. It was eventually completed in 1488 under the reign of Isabela I (the Catholic). The decorative parapet was added only in 1539, and the exterior is generally somewhat austere. Inside, it is a different matter, a profusion of rich decoration in what has come to be known as the Isabelline style. This is the halfway point between the Gothic and the Plateresque, with a profusion of light and appealing ornament and lacy stonework, and a great treasury of art.

The church is divided into three sections, for the public, the lay brothers and the monks. The magnificent wooden retable on the high altar, created by Gil de Siloe and Diego de la Cruz between 1496 and 1499, is said to have been gilded with the very first gold to have been brought back from the New World. In front of the high altar stands the tomb of King Juan II (d.1454) and his wife, Isabel (d.1496). The tomb, also by Gil de Siloe, was completed in 1493. The monarchs lie within a flamboyantly decorated, eight-pointed star, surrounded by 16 lions bearing the royal coat of arms and scenes from the New Testament. The tomb in the left (north) wall is that of their son, Infante Don Alfonso, who died in 1468, aged 13, leaving his sister, Isabella, to inherit the throne. The tomb was completed in 1492, when his body was moved here from Arévalo, and was also the work of Gil de Siloe. At the bottom, to the left, is a sculpted figure of a man in glasses, said to be a self-portrait by de Siloe. There are two sets of choirstalls, both of which are marvellous work. The monks' stalls, beside the mausoleum, were created in 1488 by Martín Sánchez, the lay brothers' stalls in the centre, were by Simón de Bueras in 1558.

On the other side of town, 1.5km west of the centre is the **Convent of Las Huelgas Reales**. From the outside, this is imposing, but not particularly beautiful. Inside however, it is a fascinating and enchanting treasure trove. Built originally as a summer palace for the Kings of Castille, in 1180, Alfonso VIII and his wife, Eleanor (daughter of Henry II of England and sister of Richard Lionheart) handed it over to the Cistercians as a convent. Only the daughters of the nobility were accepted here, and all of them brought with them large dowries and immense power. By the 13th century, it was the royal pantheon, and one of the most powerful religious houses in Spain, in direct control of some 50 towns, and with great influence elsewhere. The abbess held the title of princess-palatine, second in authority only to the Queen. It is still a working convent today, although its influence is not as strong.

The church was built between 1180 and 1230 in the English Gothic style. A gilded screen separates the transepts and high altar from the nave. Beside it stands a revolving pulpit (erected in 1560) allowing the preacher to be seen from both sides. Sculptures of the founders, Alfonso and Eleanor, kneel at either side of the high altar, while the central apse is lined by 17th-century tapestries from Beauvais. The porch and nave are lined by numerous richly decorated tombs, some of them belonging to abbesses and ladies of the court, but many of them members of the royal family. The tomb of Alfonso and Eleanor, who both died in 1214, is the fairly plain one in the Nuns' choir. The monastery was sacked by the French in 1809 and the only tomb to escape their attentions was that of Fernando de la Cerda, the son of Alfonso X, who died in 1275.

The Gothic Cloister, to the south of the church, was begun in the mid-13th century, although work carried on into the 15th. A peaceful, arcaded courtyard, its best feature is the delicate Mudéjar stucco ceiling, unfortunately badly damaged, which would have been equally at home in a Moorish palace. A few last traces of paint give the faintest idea of how it would have appeared in its glory days. The vaulted Chapterhouse, off the cloister, contains a number of flags taken from the ships of Don Juan of Austria at Lepanto, a tent flap of the Moorish king brought back after Las Navas, and several 15th-century Flemish paintings. The more recent historic significance of this room however is that this is where General Franco formed his first Nationalist Government in 1937.

The Textile Museum is a unique treasure house of early materials, robes and arms, all taken from the various royal tombs, particularly from that of Fernando de la Cerda. Dating back to the 12th to 14th centuries, the fabrics include Christian and Moorish designs, as well as more luxurious imports from the east.

From here, the tour leads into the elegant, round-arched early Romanesque cloister and garden, dating back to 1187. In one corner stands the tiny Chapel of St James, with an extraordinary statue of the saint, seated and holding a sword. Worked by a pulley system, the sword arm can be raised and lowered. It is said that the statue was created in 1219 for the knighting of King Ferdinand III, who was so grand that he could not be knighted by any inferior – and that meant any human. This way, he could receive the honour direct from the saint himself!

Excursion south from Burgos

This is officially outside the area covered by this book, but covers some sights of great interest, so I have briefly included details which would make up a day tour. Leave town on the N1 heading south. The first stop is at **Lerma**, an attractive old town with a palace and collegiate church.

From here, turn left for **Santo Domingo de los Silos**, a still active Benedictine Monastery with a School of Gregorian Chant and a superb two-storey, 12th-century cloister. Leave in the direction from which you came, then turn right to **Covarrubias**, a village that has been a little too prettified, but is nevertheless one of the most beautiful in the region, with a collegiate church, palace, Mozarabic tower and numerous fine stone mansions. Go right here, and at Hortiguela turn left onto the N234. Seven km on is the Visigothic church at **Quintanilla de las Viñas**. Keep going on the N234 back to Burgos.

For the next section of the Camino de Santiago going west to León, see page 153; for the next section going east to Logroño, see page 247.

Burgos to Reinosa and the Coast

This route winds north through the mountains from Burgos to Reinosa, in the Cordillera Cantábrica. Although the region is surrounded by main thoroughfares, most of this is along small roads, designed to make the most of the scenery and link the best of the sights. Through routes to Vitoria, Bilbao and Santander are highlighted at the turn-off point.

Leave Burgos on the N1 (E3) heading east. For the first third of the route as far as Pancorbo, this follows the same route as the A1 motorway, which you can use instead if you prefer. If you have not already seen it, your first stop should be at the Cartuja de Miraflores, 4km out of town and a little way off the route proper (see page 148 for a description). The road begins to climb gently as soon as you leave the suburbs behind, reaching the top of the 981m Puerto de la Brújula about 23km from the city. A steeper drop on the far side leads back onto the plains. A few kilometres on, on the left, is the Monastery of Rodilla, a Benedictine monastery built around the charming Romanesque Church of Santa María del Valle, which began life as a hermitage.

From here, keep going through to **Briviesca**. In 1388, in this small, rather uninspiring town on the Oca River, now famous mainly for producing pralines, King Juan I created the title of Prince of Asturias for his eldest son, Enrique (later Enrique III), in honour of his marriage to Catherine of Lancaster. The title, similar to that of Britain's Prince of Wales, has belonged to the heir to the throne ever since. The town has an old bridge, several attractive mansions and a pleasant square, bordered on one side by the Town Hall. Its most interesting sight however is the Church of Santa Clara, built between 1525 and 1565. Basically octagonal with side bays, it has a Gothic star vault, and a flamboyant Baroque retable, carved in wood in 1568.

Keep going along the N1 to **Pancorbo**, about 20km further on. The village itself is pretty, but its setting is wonderful, perched on a 635m cliff above the Pancorbo Ravine. The two main roads and the railway all converge along the bottom of this great rocky gorge which was the site of a battle between Wellington and the French in 1813. Some say that this is the real gateway between Green Spain and 'Spain proper' for this marks the abrupt end of the Castillian plateau. There are a ruined Moorish castle and 18th-century fort on the cliff top.

To continue on to Vitoria, keep on the N1. For Bilbao, either turn left onto the N625 on the far side of the defile, or continue on to Miranda de Ebro and take the A68 motorway north.

This route turns back a little way along the N1. About 5km on, near Cubo de Bureba, turn right and follow the N232 round the edge of the mountains to **Oña**. Take time to walk round this small medieval town tucked under the hills beside the Oca River. In the area around Calle Barruso is one of the most complete *Juderías* in northern Spain (see page 152). One of the houses in the street is thought to have been the synagogue. Look out also for the Arch of the Star. A flight of steps leads up to the Church of San Salvador, originally part of a Benedictine Abbey, founded in 1011 by Count Sancho of Castile as his family pantheon. There are several 11th-century royal tombs inside. The nave and choirstalls are 13th-century Gothic, while the murals are late 13th- to early 14th-century, and little remains of the Romanesque church. The cloister belongs to the Isabelline period of the late 15th century. The unusual and pretty town square is on three different levels.

Turn right along the smaller road to Pancorbo, then, after about 15km, turn left and drive through the hills to **Frías**, an enchantingly pretty town that climbs its way up the limestone cliffs above the Ebro River. At the top, like a beacon, the crumbling tower of the castle, one of the earliest to be built in Castille, caps an extraordinary chunk of rock known locally as La Muela (the Molar). From the top, there are amazing views along the length of the river valley to the Embalse de Sobron, the dam on the Ebro which created the long thin lake which winds its way back some 5km to Frías and beyond. There are no great monuments here, and not even a single church that you have to look at. Instead take time to wander through the cobbled streets, past pretty half-timbered cottages, and round-tiled roofs, past small

Jewish Spain

Although it is possible that there was a Jewish community on the Iberian Peninsula long before, the first real evidence of their being here dates back to the 3rd century AD. During the Reconquista, the royal family of Castille, needing people, money and trading expertise, encouraged the Jews to settle here. Many made their living as weavers, tailors, dyers and jewellers, while a few formed small farming communities, but above all they took over most of the banking, official and unofficial. Many rose to senior positions in government as tax collectors, royal advisers and even judges.

Never overtly popular amongst the Christians because of their success and financial power, the Jews suffered from the first from the official prejudice of the Catholic Church. The kings, who needed both their expertise and their taxes, offered a sort of informal protection, but tended simply to turn a blind eye to the various Papal decrees and leave the Jews to sink or swim. Each city had a distinct Jewish Quarter or *Judería*, often huddled between the walls of the castle and the city. At its centre was the Synagogue, which had to be limited in size so that it could not be seen from the Christian areas. Private houses tended, at least from the outside, to be relatively humble and indistinguishable from other local dwellings, although inside they were often as luxurious as palaces. The Jews soon learnt not to parade their money too openly. Within the Jewish Quarter, they could dress as they liked, but once outside, courtesy of a Papal Bull, they had to cover their finery by a coarsely woven robe displaying a red or yellow mark known as the 'Jewish Insignia'.

Trouble first began towards the end of the 13th century with religious disputes, many of the monastic orders openly preaching anti-semitism. The plague of 1348 hit the huddled Jewish Quarters particularly badly and was promptly interpreted as the punishment of God. Anti-Jewish violence broke out, and many of the Jews, faced by death or exile, asked to be baptised. This only inflamed things further however, particularly when it came out that for many, it was baptism in form only, and they were still following their old religion in secret.

The end did not come for another century however, until 1492, when Ferdinand and Isabella, finally free of the Moors and no longer so desperately in need of Jewish money, embraced Catholicism at its most fanatical, set up the Inquisition and expelled the Jews, making sure they left all their wealth behind. Today, only a few architectural fragments remain to mark the passing of this once great culture.

vegetable gardens and down to the lake to see the old bridge, a mellow, multi-arched stone affair, with a rare surviving guard tower halfway across.

The onward route crosses the river and turns left towards Trespaderne. Keep going along this road for 28km to **Medina de Pomar**. Now a small and insignificant town, this was once a far grander place whose most famous son, Juan de Salazar, voyaged to the Americas with Mendoza and, in 1537, founded the city of Asunción in Paraguay. Only the shell and two great square towers now remain of the once powerful 15th-century castle. Inside you can see the last few fragments of Mudéjar stuccowork with which it was decorated. Nearby is the 14th-century Convent of Santa Clara, which has fine star vaulting and a 15th-century altarpiece by Felipe de Vigarni and Diego de Siloe. Look out also for the renaissance tomb of Don Iñigo Fernández de Velasco, Duke of Frías and Constable of Castille. There is a small museum beside the church.

Keep going along the same road to Villarcayo, then turn left onto the C629 and right onto the N232. This runs along the north bank of the Embalse de Ebro across the Cantabrian border to Reinosa.

Turn right onto the N623 for Santander. This route can connect up with the route from Carrión de los Condes to Reinosa (see page 157) to make a circular tour back to Burgos.

The Camino de Santiago – Burgos to León

This section of the pilgrim route is one of the most beautiful in its whole length, wandering across the open *meseta*, on virtually empty back roads for at least half of the time. Running across the golden plains through endless tiny villages, with views that stretch forever, there is plenty to see and do, although most of the sights are small pilgrim churches and it is perfectly possible to leave some out if it's all too much. Those places absolutely not to be missed are Fromistá and Carrión de los Condes. There are plenty of signposts along the way pointing out the direction of the route.

Leave Burgos on the N620, signposted towards Valladolid. If you have not already seen it, you can visit the Convent of Las Huelgas Reales as your first stop of the day (for description see page 149). Six km from the city, turn right onto the N120. Follow this for about 30km until you reach Olmillos de Sasamón, where you take

Castrojeríz, on the Camino de Santiago

153

the small road on the right for 2km to **Sasamón** and the small Gothic Church of Santa María la Real.

Although this was a bishopric in the 11th century, the existing Gothic church dates from the 13th to 15th centuries. The cloister is rather badly damaged, but the main portal, which shows the gospellers taking dictation from Christ, is charming. The town's history dates back much further still to the Roman town of Segisamo, founded by Augustus and Agrippa during the Cantabrian Wars.

From here, head back onto the N120 and follow it through to Villasandino, where you turn left. This small road winds up a valley past the two small villages of Villasilos and Villaveta, both of which have attractive churches. Stop and look back for a lovely, if gentle view. Just after you top the brow of the hill, the road runs literally through the middle of the ruined 14th-century Convent of St Anthony. Shortly after this, the view opens right out and in the distance you will see the almost perfect pyramid of **Castrojeríz**, topped by its ruined castle, rising from the fields. The village itself is huddled at the foot of the hill, now rather shabby and neglected. In its heyday however, this was a major stopping point on the pilgrim route, and in the 16th century it was the seat of government of the Council of Castille. The earliest of the *fueros* (Acts of Common Law) still in existence is the Fuero de la Caballería Villana, given to the town by García Fernández in 974 AD. The tourist information board at the edge of the village, which lists all its many monuments, is daunting to say the least, but while the town is worth a stop, it is not really worth lingering over. Have a quick walk around the old medieval streets, past the many former pilgrim hostels and keep an eye open for the 16th-century Church of San Juan, built onto a 12th-century tower with fish scale tiles. It also has a 12th-century cloister. Also look out for the Collegiate Church with a simple but elegant façade, the Church of Santo Domingo, which has a collection of 16th-century tapestries inside, the Monastery of the Clarisas, and the Paroquial Museum.

Turn right here, and left a few kilometres on and follow the road which runs down to **Fitero**, on the Pisuerga River. This is the border between Burgos and Palencia provinces. It is also the site of a splendid old stone bridge with 11 arches.

Cross the river and carry on through **Boadilla del Camino**, which has a fine 16th-century church with a Plateresque retable, and a 15th-century Gothic column in the plaza. A short while later, turn right at the T-junction for **Frómista**. This seemingly rather non-descript town is one of the essential stops en route, for stuck in the middle of a crossroads, and idiotically draped in cables that ensure it is impossible to take a good photo, is the enchanting Church of San Martín. This has to be one of the most beautiful churches in the whole of Spain, small, remarkably simple, perfectly proportioned, with an elegance of decoration, inside and out. It has remained unaltered over the centuries, and breathes an air of tranquillity which is surely what Romanesque architecture is all about. The church was founded in 1056 as part of a Benedictine monastery (now disappeared) on the order of Doña Mayor, Countess of Castilla. In 1188, it came under the control of the Cluniac monastery at Carrión de los Condes. Built of a rich golden stone, with two small circular turrets flanking the west door and an octagonal cupola above the altar, it has a triple barrel-vaulted nave, separated by columns with a wealth of beautifully

The Romanesque church of San Martín at Frómista, on the Camino de Santiago

carved and imaginative capitals. The three oven-vaulted apsidal chapels add a flowing grace.

There are several other churches and hostels in the town, which was one of the official stops on the pilgrim route according to the Codex Calixtus, but they cannot compare with San Martín. They are the Gothic Hermitage of Cristo del Otero, the transitional Gothic Church of San Pedro, with a 15th-century retable, and the 16th-century Church of Santa María del Castillo, which has a fine Gothic retable with 29 painted panels.

155

For a direct route back to the coast, turn right here onto the N611 and follow it north the whole way to Santander.

Leave Frómista on the small road leading to Carrión de los Condes. At **Villacazar de Sirga** is the vast Templar Church of Santa María la Blanca, famous along the pilgrim route for the many miracles performed by its seated Romanesque statue of the Virgin. Built in the early 13th century, this grand, rather sombre church has a fine façade, with a double frieze, and a massive painted retable on the high altar. In the south transept are the splendid royal tombs of the Infante Don Felipe y Caballero del Temple (d. 1274) and his second wife, Doña Leonor Ruiz de Castro, sculpted by Antón Peréz in the late 13th century. The Infante is said to have been murdered by his brother, King Alfonso X.

You will reach **Carrión de los Condes** 6km on. On the banks of the Carrión River, this town, which has now grown into a lively market centre for the surrounding farmlands, is roughly halfway along the Spanish section of the Camino de Santiago. It is an attractive place, with numerous old mansions as well as the expected plethora of churches.

The legend of El Cid (see page 142) rears its head again here. The wicked Counts of Los Condes heard on the grapevine about the hero's wealth and the fabulous dowries being offered with his daughters. They set off to Valencia to meet and marry the girls, but on the way home, the dowries safely in their pockets, they beat up their wives and left them beside the road. El Cid was, needless to say, a little upset, and gathering his forces, he swept into town, and killed the Counts. He found new husbands for the girls in the royal families of Navarra and Aragón.

Of the various churches, the best is probably the 12th-century, Romanesque Church of Santiago, which has a beautiful west front, with a finely carved high relief frieze of Christ in Majesty, surrounded by the Apostles. The portal arch below is a precious record of the everyday life of the period, showing various craftsmen such as the potter, cobbler, sheep shearer and architect at work. The Church of Santa María del Camino, also 12th-century Romanesque, has a fine south portal, with a series of three friezes. Inside it is divided in classic Romanesque style into three aisles, with three apsidal chapels.

The Benedictine Monastery of San Zoilo was originally founded in the 11th century to house the relics of San Zoilo, given as tribute to the Count of Carrión by the Emir of Córdoba in 1047. It was almost completely rebuilt in the Renaissance style in the 16th century. It has a highly decorative cloister originally designed by Juan de Badajoz in 1537, but only completed in 1604 by Pedro Torres, who was responsible for adding the second storey. The 16th-century church has a Baroque portal, attributed to Felipe de Berrojo. Other churches include the 15th-century Sanctuary de Belén, the classic hall Church of San Andrés, and the 13th-century Convent of Santa Clara.

A route north along the Carrión Valley and through the Montes de Palentina to Reinosa leaves from here (see page 157). If you wish, you can do the first part of this route, to the Roman villa at Pedrosa de la Vega and Saldaña as a detour, rejoining the pilgrim route near Calzadilla de la Cueza.

From Carrión de los Condes, the pilgrim route turns back onto the N120, signposted to León. A few kilometres on, near **Quintanilla de la Cueza**, a small lane leads off to a Roman villa of the 3rd to 4th centuries AD, that stands in the middle of a field, now safely housed beneath a vast barn-like building. It has a series of beautiful mosaics, with a number of human figures, animals and geometric designs. Some areas of the hypocausts are also visible from the well-designed walkways, and the museum has a display of pottery and other small finds from the site. The Church of the Ascension in Quintanilla de la Cueza itself, has some fine examples of Mudéjar decoration in the porch and presbytery, together with a 16th-century painted retable. Shortly after this, the road crosses the border into León province.

Sahagún was, in its prime, a great town, Picaud's seventh stop of the pilgrim route and one of the main centres of Mudéjar and Mozarabic art. It was also home to the Benedictine Abbey of San Lorenzo, one of the largest and most powerful in all Spain. Today, only the abbey church survives, and that is in ruins, with the rest of the town crumbling round it. The most interesting sight here is the heavily restored Romanesque Church of San Tirmo. Unusually built of brick, its typically rounded apse is topped anachronistically by a square, open arched, Mudéjar tower. Most of the many other churches and chapels in the town also contain fragments of Mudéjar and Mozarabic work, including stucco decoration and horseshoe arches, for those who care to seek them out.

The last section into León follows the N120 and the LE911 to rejoin the N601. This follows the Roman Via Trajana through the small troglodytic village of Calzadilla de los Hermanillos to **Mansilla de las Mulas**, a small town with an attractive arcaded plaza and the last few remnants of its medieval city walls. A road off to the right here leads off on a final detour of 13km to the Mozarabic **Monastery of San Miguel de Escalada**, built in 913 by monks who had fled from persecution in Córdoba. Standing on a remote terrace in the hills, this is probably the best surviving example of Mozarabic architecture in Spain, with horseshoe arches everywhere, an external gallery and an 11th-century tower. Return to the main road for the easiest route into León.

For a description of the city of León, see page 159.

North from Carrión de los Condes to Reinosa

This route heads north along the Carrión River and through the Montes de Palentina, offering an alternative and more interesting way of reaching Reinosa and the coast, along the back roads. *(For a description of Carrión de los Condes and the Camino de Santiago, west to León and east to Burgos, see pages 153–157).*

Leave Carrión de los Condes on the C615 heading north towards Saldana. The road follows the west bank of the Carrión River for 10km to **Renedo de la Vega**, where the Church of San Martín has a 17th-century retable and fine 16th-century cross. Nearby are the ruins of the Monastery of Santa María de la Vega, founded in 1215, whose Mudéjar architecture is most clearly visible in the surviving apse.

Seven km further on, at the village of Lobera, turn left on a 1.5 km detour to **Pedrosa de la Vega**, where you will find the superb Roman Villa of Olmeda, discovered in 1968. Built at the end of the 3rd century AD, at the height of Rome's glory in Spain, it has a superlative collection of mosaic pavements, in excellent condition. Some are geometric designs, but there are several vividly lifelike and richly coloured pictures of people and action-packed hunting scenes. Small finds from the on-going excavations are in the museum in Saldaña.

Back on the C615, the next stop is at **Saldaña**, a small, attractive medieval town with a ruined 11th-century castle. Several fine 15th- and 16th-century mansions emblazoned with coats of arms line the streets and there is a beautiful old stone bridge with 23 arches across the river. The 16th- to 18th-century Church of San Miguel has both Plateresque and Baroque retables, while the tiny Hermitage of Nostra Señora del Valle has an 8th-century Byzantine statue of the Virgin that is at the centre of a significant pilgrimage cult. The small archaeological Museo de Cortes concentrates mainly on the smaller, movable finds from the Roman Olmeda villa (see above).

The road crosses the river here, and continues north along the east bank to Guardo, a rather dull industrial town. Keep going straight through here to **Velilla del Río Carrión**, a pretty village whose pedigree is thought to stretch back through the Romans to the Cantabres. There are several attractive old mansions, the 16th-century Church of San Salvador, and an 18th-century Baroque palace. Take the right fork here past the Embalse de Camporrendendo. This road (the P210) runs along the lake shore and through the Montes de Palentina to Cervera de la Pisuerga. The area is littered with tiny, pretty Romanesque churches, none of which is particularly worth stopping for. Stroll your way along the road gently and enjoy your surroundings, for this is remarkably pretty countryside, lush, green, rolling and well watered. It is a favourite area for walking in summer, hunting in season and skiing in winter.

Cervera de Pisuerga was a major centre and frontier town during the Reconquista, but it shows little sign of this important role. Its one monument of any importance is the heavily restored 16th-century Renaissance Church of Santa María del Castillo, which has, amongst other fine works of art, a retable created in 1513 by Felipe de Vigarni.

A small road leads north from Cervera. From this you can either turn left to reach the Picos de Europa at Potes (see page 233) or go straight on, across the mountains, to come out on the coast at San Vicente de la Barquera (see page 131).

This route now follows the P212 east to **Aguilar de Campóo**. The last section runs along the side of the Aguilar Reservoir, an attractive lake whose beach and watersports centre are popular with locals. The town itself is charming, built between the shady green Pisuerga river and a towering limestone outcrop on which still brood the ruins of the formidable 11th-century castle, with its five circular towers. Tucked at the foot of the cliff on one side is the Hermitage of Santa

Cecilia, built originally in 1041, and virtually rebuilt in the 12th century. It has a Byzantine-style tower and some superb capitals.

Aguilar de Campóo was founded in the 9th century as part of the repopulation of Castille during the Reconquista, and was proclaimed a Marquisate by Ferdinand and Isabela in the late 15th century. It is still surrounded by the remnants of the city walls, erected in the 14th century, and several of its six original gates are also still standing. Of these, the finest is the Puerta y Torre de Reinosa in the north-east corner of the town, built between 1331 and 1360. Its inscription, in both Castillian and Hebrew, is the last surviving memorial of the significant Jewish population who helped to build the town from the 11th to 15th centuries.

The oldest quarter of the town is just within this gate, a maze of streets lined with 15th-century buildings, many of them sporting grand coats of arms. Some of the finest, including the 16th-century Palacio de los Marqueses, the Casa del Cura and the Palacio de Villatorre are in the arcaded Plaza de España, still the centre of the town today. At one end of the plaza is the Collegiate Church of San Miguel, built in the late 13th and early 14th centuries. This vast Gothic building has a number of fine retables, sculptures and other works of art, together with some beautiful tombs. The best are the 16th-century Mausoleum of the Marquesses of Aguilar, and the kneeling figure of the priest, García González in the north apsidal chapel. In one of the side chapels to the right of the nave is a supposedly miraculous figure of Christ, said to have been found by a soldier in the 9th century. Such was its popularity as an object of pilgrimage that in 1609, a new monastery in Madrid, in search of relics, led a midnight raid to steal it. They got as far as Burgos before irate locals caught up and forced them to give it back.

A little way to the west is the Monastery of Santa María la Real, built by the Cistercians between 1180 and 1213. Recently restored, it is a fine example of Cistercian building, with a Romanesque cloister and chapterhouse, and some magnificent capitals.

Turn left from here along the N611 which heads north across the Cantabrian border to Reinosa and Santander.

For the scenic route from Reinosa to the coast, see page 132. For the route from Reinosa to Burgos, if you wish to complete the circular journey, see page 150.

León

Tucked into the confluence of the Bernsega and Torio Rivers, and surrounded on all sides by the rolling *meseta*, **LEÓN** was first founded by the Romans in 68 AD when Emperor Galba built a fort here to house the Iberian 7th Legion, as a base from which to defend the empire against the Asturians and Cantabres. León, like other cities in this region, has had a somewhat chequered past. Captured by the Visigoths under Leovigild in 586, and by the Moors in the early 8th century, it was retaken by the Christians, under Ortoño I, in 850, and declared the capital of the Christian Reconquista. All sorts of people, from the mountain Christians to Jews

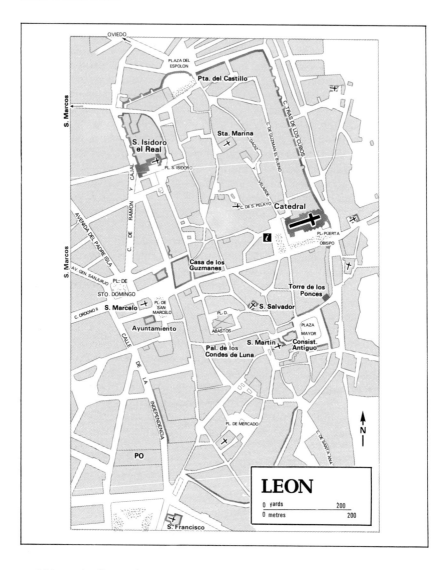

and Mozarabs fleeing from the Moorish kingdoms of Córdoba and Todelo, were encouraged to settle within the line of the old Roman walls and build up the city's prosperity and strength. As it grew, it also became one of the main halts on the pilgrim route to Santiago, marked as the eigth official stop by Picaud's Codex Calixtus.

In the early 10th century, Ortoño II (913–923) created the kingdom of León, with the city as his capital. In 996, a lengthy and bloody siege, during which the city was almost completely destroyed, led to its capture by the Moorish Almanzor. It was eventually recovered by the Christians after the battle of Calatañazor in 1002,

160

and King Alfonso V promptly set to work to rebuild the stricken city, putting up new and extensive fortifications as a protection against further attack. In 1037, the kingdoms of León and Castille were combined under Fernando I, who was crowned in León Cathedral. In 1188, Alfonso IX summoned his first Cortes, or parliament, here, said to be one of the earliest democratic governments in Europe. In 1230, however, the court moved away permanently, leaving León as a trading post without real power or influence.

The town's history then followed an uneventful course until the 20th century, when huge iron and coal deposits were discovered in the region to the north and the city began to grow rapidly, from 22,000 in 1920, to nearly 140,000 today. Still also an agricultural centre, since the reorganisation of the country in 1978, it has once more been given a role in government, as capital of the province of León.

Today the city is thriving. The old city still exists, but without the great division between narrow alleys and grand boulevards that is the mark of so many of the large cities in the region. It is an attractive town of wide streets and shady plazas, but for the tourist the real attraction is a relatively few outstanding monuments, all within easy walking distance of each other.

Of these, the largest and most spectacular, from the outside at least, is the **Hospital de San Marcos**, a vast, superbly decorated pilgrim hospital that stands on its own, a little way from the old city, on the banks of Bernsega River. Beautifully restored and used today as a hotel (one of the finest in Spain), this was founded originally in 1173 as the headquarters of the Military Order of the Knights of Santiago, established to protect pilgrims to the holy city. Nothing remains of the original building however, and the present one dates from 1513 to 1549, designed as a pilgrim hospital by Pedro Larrea on the orders of Ferdinand and Isabella. The superb, two storey façade was created between 1533 and 1541 by Juan de Badajoz. It is around 100m long and is covered in delicate, elegant decoration, with a frieze of busts by Juan de Juni depicting historic, biblical and mythical figures from Augustus Caesar to Isabela the Catholic herself. The pediment above the main door, which shows St James killing Moors, is an 18th-century Baroque addition, but the building must still be one of the finest examples of Plateresque work in the country. The main door leads into the hotel, which you should visit at least for a drink, if you cannot afford to stay there, as the communal areas are as beautiful and finely furnished as any museum. The formal gardens beside the river are also lovely. To the left, a separate door leads into the church, its façade emblazoned by scallop shells, which now houses an archaeological museum. Consecrated in 1541, it has some star vaulting, fine, if poorly restored Renaissance choir-stalls, carved by Guillermo Doncel between 1537 and 1543, and a highly ornate sacristy created by Juan de Badajoz in 1549. Although the museum is small, it has a fascinating collection, from memorials of the Roman 7th Legion, to medieval robes and arms, and a wide range of religious art. Look out in particular for the small ivory 11th-century Carrizo Crucifix, and the 10th-century Mozarabic Cross from Santiago de Peñalba.

From here, take the large Avenida de Suero Quinones which leads off to the left,

The Plateresque façade of the Hospital of San Marcos, now a five-star hotel, in León

away from the river. This runs past the railway station to the old city. This is still bounded by fragments of the city walls, constructed by Alfonso XI in 1324, on the line of the Roman and early medieval fortifications. Altogether, 31 of the original 80 bastions are still standing, forming a small and tight-knit square around the area of the Cathedral.

On the right, along the line of the walls, you will reach the **Royal Basilica of San Isidoro**, which was founded by King Fernando I and his wife, Doña Sancha, to house the relics of the 7th-century saint, Isidoro of Seville, whose body had been rescued ahead of the Moorish conquest. Built on the remains of a pre-Romanesque church destroyed by Almanzor, it was consecrated in 1063. Only the narthex, built as a royal pantheon, now remains of this church, which is entered by a separate door to the west of the main basilica.

The pantheon is by far the most interesting section of the building and should not be missed. Heavy marble pillars support a barrel-vaulted roof covered by magnificent frescoes dating from the late 12th century, considered by many to be the finest surviving Romanesque frescoes in Spain. Richly coloured and with a wealth of detail, the many scenes include a frieze depicting the farmer's tasks through the seasons, hunting scenes, the signs of the zodiac and tales from the New Testament. The capitals are also superb, some of the earliest to use human figures as well as geometric and floral decoration, telling stories such as the raising of Lazarus, the sacrifice of Abraham and Daniel in the lion's den. Amongst the many tombs are those of Alfonso V (d. 1028), Fernando I (d. 1065) and his daughter, Doña Urraca de Zamora. The treasury next door has a rich collection of religious art, including several caskets, one of which is decorated in the 11th-century Mozarabic style with ivory plaques, while another, dating from the 12th century, is covered by Limoges enamels. Possibly the greatest of the treasures is a chalice, donated by Doña Urraca in the 11th century, made from two Roman agate cups set in gold and ornamented with jewels. Much of the basilica's library was destroyed by the French in the 19th century, during the Peninsula Wars, but the surviving remnants still form a priceless collection, whose star is an illuminated bible of 960.

The existing basilica was actually built as an extension to the earlier church by Alfonso VII in 1149 but was heavily altered in the early 16th century. The massive capitals and the chapel in the north transept date from the 12th century. Much of the rest of the church, such as the Capella Mayor, was the work of Juan de Badajoz in 1513. Outside, the Puerta del Cordero, is basically Romanesque, but a Renaissance cornice, pediment and statue of San Isidoro were added in the 16th century. The Puerta del Perdón is thought to be the work of Maestro Esteban, who also created the Las Platerías façade on the cathedral of Santiago de Compostela itself.

A short walk through the streets of the old city brings you to the Plaza de Regla and the west front of the **Cathedral of Santa María de Regla**. There have been three previous cathedrals on this same site, but the present one was built mainly between 1258 and 1303, to the design of Maestro Enrique, also responsible for Burgos cathedral, and Juan Pérez. Partly because it was built over a relatively short period, partly because a major restoration at the end of the 19th century stripped it of many later additions, this is a much simpler, less fussy and more harmonious affair than Burgos, although some similarities can be seen. The overwhelming impression however, inside and out, is that this is not Spanish. Closely modelled on the great French cathedrals of the period, such as Chartres, Amiens and Reims, it has a grace, a soaring elegance and use of light utterly unlike the sombre power and heavy ornamentation of most Spanish churches.

Built of the local rich golden stone, the west front has a vast rose window and three sculpted porticos, flanked by asymetric towers, the shorter El Reloj (the Clock) on the left and the tall Las Campanas (the Bells) on the right, which date from the

13th to 15th centuries. The central portal shows Christ presiding over the Last Judgement. To the left are a copy of a statue of Santa María la Blanca (the original is now inside the cathedral) and a statue of St James, its base worn down over the centuries by the touch of pilgrims. The left portal shows the childhood of Christ, the right, the life of the Virgin. Traces of the original paintwork remain throughout the carvings of these arches. The richly carved south portal, and openwork south tower were the work of Jooksen van Utrecht in the mid-15th century. Elegantly thin flying buttresses surround the apse at the east end.

Inside, the impression is of light and space and the overwhelming glory of the stained glass windows. In all, the cathedral has around 1800 square metres of glass, in 125 windows, often separated only by a slim column. This huge expanse of glass, together with the delicacy of the stonework, is actually a threat to the fabric of the building, which needs constant renovation, but the effect is superb and the windows, which owe their influence more to the Sainte Chapelle or Chartres than to Spain are, without doubt, the finest on the Iberian peninsula. The oldest glass, dating back to the 13th century, is that in the west front rose window and the three apsidal chapels. The rose window in the north transept and the glass in some of the chapels at the west end of the nave date from the late 15th century, while the rest of the windows in the nave and chancel belong to every period since, including the 20th century.

A beautiful gilded Renaissance trascoro, created by Juan de Badajoz between 1570 and 1587, separates the main body of the nave from the choir. It has four alabaster high reliefs around the main arch, with painted figures by Esteban Jordán. The beautifully carved, two-tier choirstalls were the work of Juan de Milanas and Diego Copín de Holanda between 1467 and 1481.

Behind the choir is the Capella Mayor, the high altar decorated by a triptych containing a powerful, late 15th-century painting of the Burial of Christ by Nicolás Francés. The silver urn on the altar contains the relics of San Froilán, the patron saint of León, while a pietá by Roger van der Veyden stands beside it. Amongst the many Gothic tombs in the chapels, look out for the 14th-century tomb in the East Chapel of the Condesa Sancha de León who was murdered by her nephew. The frieze around the base depicts him undergoing his grisly punishment of being torn apart by wild horses.

The Plateresque Puerta del Dado leads from the cathedral to the cloister. This dates originally to the 13th and 14th centuries, although the ornate vaulting is a 16th-century addition. There are some faded 15th-century frescoes by Nicolás Francés in the galleries and a Plateresque staircase, built by Juan de Badajoz in 1534 leads up to the Chapterhouse. This is now the home of the Diocesan Museum, a fine but rather motley collection of religious art, including some 50 Romanesque statues of the virgin, a Visigothic illuminated bible, an 11th-century Mozarabic Antiphoner, a 16th-century Crucifix by Juan de Juni, and a 16th-century portable organ.

Leaving the cathedral, cross the Avenida Generalísimo Franco. On the opposite side of the road is the Episcopal Palace. Pass this and head into the narrower streets of the old city. This was the tradesmen's area and many of the streets still bear names that show their speciality. It was also the Jewish Quarter, although nothing

164

The cathedral cloister, León

of this exists today. The 17th-century arcaded **Plaza Mayor** is still the heart of the city's café life, with numerous bars and restaurants. The 16th-century, arcaded **Plaza del Mercado**, a little further south, was the city's main market and the place where royal proclamations were read out. From here, turn north again towards the **Plaza de San Marcelo**, which has several fine buildings including the Plateresque Palacio de Los Guzmanes, built in the 16th century by Gil de Hontanón, the 16th-century Town Hall, built by Juan de Badajoz and Juan del Rivero Rada, and the

165

Casa de Botines, 19th-century, neo-Gothic creation of the extraordinary Catalán architect, Antoní Gaudí.

For the Camino de Santiago west to Villafrance del Bierzo, see page 167; for the route east to Burgos, see page 153.

León to Oviedo

This route, which connects León with Asturias and the coast, has very little sight-seeing, but for most of its distance, runs through superb mountain scenery, some of which is set aside as a National Park. It also offers an opportunity to visit the wonderful Valporquera Caves.

Leave León on the N621, but turn left almost immediately onto the road to Garrafe de Torio, which runs along the length of the Torio River. At **Navatereja**, a few kilometres from León, there is a Roman villa, with a small collection of mosaics. The road begins to climb almost immediately into the mountains, and about 36km on, you reach the Vegacervera Gorges, a spectacular river gorge formed by the Torio, with sheer cliffs, up to 100m high in places. The road runs alongside the gorge for several kilometres and there are plenty of opportunities to get out and have a look.

Keep going north until you reach Felmín, and turn off, following the signs for the **Valporquero Caves**, a few kilometres away. Little known outside the region, probably because there isn't a cave painting in sight, these are vast, superbly dramatic caverns that run some 4km into the mountain. Natural dyes such as iron and sulphur oxides have spilled a host of multi-coloured abstracts across the walls of great cathedral-like halls and narrow, twisting tunnels, all covered in magnificent, tortuous formations of stalactites and stalagmites. The final 1500m of the tour is along a vast passage with sheer, 40m high walls that looks like the perfect setting for a Star Wars battle. Carved from soft limestone by underground streams, the caves are permanently damp underfoot, and are at a constant 7°C, so wear sensible shoes with a good grip and take a jacket or sweater.

From here, back-track to the main road and keep going north to Cármenes, where you turn left onto a link road through to the main N630. When you reach this, turn right towards Oviedo. The road now climbs steeply towards the mountain passes. On your right, you will pass the Romanesque Collegiate Church of Santa María in **Arbás**, built in the 13th century, but heavily reconstructed in the 18th. Although this is the last village in León, the church actually comes under the jurisdiction of Oviedo. Behind it is the massive peak of the Braña Caballo, which reaches 2189m.

The border with Asturias is the **Puerto de Pajares**, a 1379m pass used since Roman times, with superb views over the peaks of the Cordillera Cantábrica. Above the snow-line for much of the year, this is the site of the Valdegrande-Pajares ski resort, which offers a variety of downhill and cross country runs at varying degrees of difficulty.

For the continuation of the route from the Puerto de Pajares to Oviedo, see page 65. To get to the triangular route around the Picos de Europa, which takes in part of León province, take the N621 from León via Cistierna to Riaño.

The Camino de Santiago – León to Villafranca del Bierzo

This route continues the relentless onward progress of the pilgrim way as it reaches the edge of the *meseta* and climbs once more into remote mountains on the border between Castilla-y-León and Galicia.

Leave León on the N120, heading south-west, signposted to Astorga. The first stop, 5km from the city centre, is the modern **Church of La Virgen del Camino**, the latest in a long line of sanctuaries in the same spot. An ultra-modern building, built in 1960 by the Portuguese Brother Coello, there is a huge cross outside, while the elongated bronze sculpture on the west front, showing the Virgin surrounded by the Apostles during Pentecost, is the work of Catalán sculptor, José María Subirachs. Inside there is a fine Baroque pietá.

A memorial slab on the 13th-century Puente del Paso Honroso (Bridge of the Passage of Arms) at **Orbigo**, 25km further on, marks the site of one of the more bizarre stories of chivalric Spain, said by some to have provided the inspiration for Cervantes' great classic, *Don Quixote*. In 1434, a Holy Year, a Spanish knight, Don Suero de Quinones, donned an iron collar and vowed, along with nine companions, to take and hold the bridge for 30 days, in honour of his lady, Leonor de Tovar. Anyone who wanted to pass had either to swear that she was the most beautiful woman they had seen or joust. Over the following month, they fought 727 courses, broke every lance they owned, killed one challenger and injured many others. The tragic corollary to this tale came 24 years later when Don Suero met again one of the knights he had defeated. The man had held a grudge ever since, and this time, he killed Don Suero.

In Roman times, Pliny described Asturica Augusta as 'a magnificent city'. Modern **Astorga** is no more than a small country town, capital of the bleak moorland region of La Maragatería, inhabited by a sturdy, taciturn people called the Maragatos. Everyone is agreed that their pedigree is long, but that is all they can agree on, some claiming they are Celts, others that they are direct descendants of the Visigoths, while others still say they are Moors or Mozarabs. Whatever the truth, until the early 19th century, Astorga was the northern end of the road from Madrid to Galicia, and the Maragatos soon became famous as muleteers, cornering the regional transport market.

Sections of the 6m thick Roman walls, complete with their circular bastions, still surround the old town. Work on the Cathedral which stands just inside them began in 1471, probably to a design by Simon of Cologne, was continued by Gil de Hontañon between 1530 and 1559, and did not end until the 17th century. As a result, even the exterior has a wide variety of styles, from the late Gothic east end, surrounded by quantities of elaborate flying buttresses, to the Renaissance west front, its two towers even built of different stones. The west front portal is a superb

Baroque work, completed in 1693, showing a number of scenes from the life of Christ. Inside, the high nave, with sweeping rib vaults is lit by clerestory windows containing 16th-century glass. The highlight however is the superb retable on the high altar, created in 1562 by three different artists: the relief sculptor, Gaspar Becerra; the sculptor, Gaspar de Palencia; and the painter, Gaspar de Hoyos. The choir-stalls, carved in 1551 from walnut, are also worth a look. The cloister, built originally in the 15th century, but heavily restored in the 18th, now houses a small Diocesan Museum with a number of Romanesque statues of the Virgin, a 10th century Mozarabic casket and several other church treasures.

Beside the Cathedral, a neo-Gothic fantasy to complement the Gothic one, is the Episcopal Palace. Built in 1889, one of the more wayward confections of Catalán architect, Antoní Gaudí, its decor is as flamboyant inside as outside. It houses the Museum of the Camino de Santiago, an essential stop for all those following the route. Alongside the expected collection of religious art, it has pilgrim memorabilia such as scallop-shells and staffs, and an excellent display of photographs, maps and documents related to the way.

From here, follow the narrow streets to the south-east to the Plaza Mayor, where the market is still held each Tuesday. The square itself and the surrounding streets house another group of interesting buildings, including several small churches and chapels. The 17th-century Baroque Town Hall has a fine clock. Two jacque-mart figures, wearing the Maragato national dress of baggy black breeches, embroidered shirt and round felt hat, strike the hour. Next to the town hall is the Roman slave prison, while in the Plaza Romana, there is an archaeological park.

On leaving Astorga, the route divides, leaving you with a choice of roads. The pilgrim route proper follows the shortest, relatively straight line through the high, wild Montes de León to Ponferrada. Narrow roads that are in places appallingly bad and even deteriorate to little more than muddy tracks lead through a series of tiny, ramshackle mountain villages, with only the wayside crosses and pilgrim fountains to remind them of their past. The road starts off easily enough, trailing across the last of the meseta through the thoroughly uninspiring villages of the Maragatería. At El Ganso, however you leave the plains as the road winds up to Rabanal del Camino, the ninth stop in the Codex Calixtus, now a dusty and decaying village, with only a small Romanesque church and the last remnants of its Templar monastery. From here, the road continues to climb, past the abandoned village of Foncebadón, to the 1504m **Manjarin-Foncebadón Pass**. At the summit stands the Cruz de Ferro, a massive iron pilgrim cross. It has been the custom for centuries, still followed by modern pilgrims, to add a stone to the vast cairn at its foot. Once past El Acebo, where you can see an overgrown stretch of the original medieval road, you can pick up a reasonable road again. The final section of this route drops rapidly to Riego de Ambros and Moulinaseca, and finally to Ponferrada.

The other, easier route, follows the line of the main NVI, a good, new road that crosses the Montes de León at the 1230m Puerta del Manzanal. From here, it loops south into the Tremor Valley, and follows this past Bembibre, which has a castle that once belonged to the Dukes of Frías. Just before you reach Ponferrada, a turning on the right leads to the tiny 10th-century Mozarabic **Church of Santo**

Tomás de las Ollas which has an oval apse, interesting vault and a number of horseshoe arches.

The first town to be built on the River Sil was the Roman Interamnium Flavium. The current town of **Ponferrada** was founded in the 11th century as a pilgrim base beside a long vanished iron bridge (the Puente de Ferro from which the town gets its name). There are still several interesting monuments here, and the town centre is old, charming and relatively untouched. The town as a whole has grown rapidly this century however, since the discovery of iron nearby, and it is now a centre for mining and heavy industry, with all the belching smoke and slag heaps that that entails.

The main body of the old town is on the right (east) bank of the river, dominated by the vast, imposing bulk of the Templar Castle. Built in the 12th century on the site of the original Roman camp, it was greatly enlarged in 1340, and has been heavily restored in recent years. Nonetheless, it is a splendid building, shaped like an irregular pentagon, with massive walls, and all the battlements and machicolated towers you could hope for.

A little way behind it is the Baroque Basilica de Nuestra Señora de la Encina, built in 1577, with a 1614 tower. Inside are a fine retable and a Gothic statue of the Virgin, which was formally adopted as the Patron saint of the town in 1958. A short way beyond this is the Plaza Mayor, where you can find the Baroque Town Hall, built in 1692. There are a number of other fine buildings, including the Hospital de la Reina, built in 1498 by Isabela the Catholic in celebration of the end of the Reconquista, the Puerta del Reloj, the last surviving medieval town gate, the Antiguo Consistorio, one of the earliest town halls in Spain, built on the orders of Felip II, and the Convento de las Concepcionistas Franciscanas, founded in 1542. Stroll through the streets of the old town to see the many attractive, but less important buildings.

Excursion to the Ancares de León

If you have the time, take a side trip from Ponferrada into the National Park of the **Ancares de León**, tucked into the north-west corner of the state on the borders of the Galicia and Asturias. To reach this remote mountain area, take the small road heading north to Vega de Espinareda and Candín.

Unlike national parks elsewhere in the world, the area is still inhabited and farmed, with some 3000 people living here, in 27 separate villages and hamlets, largely cut off from the world and even each other. It is an area of old traditions and crafts, steeped in tales of witchcraft and pagan folklore. The population is dwindling rapidly however, as the young head for the bright lights, and there is no intensive cultivation. The valleys are thick with forests of alder, willow, poplar, ash, elm, lime and hazel. There are several species of oak, including holm, Pyrenean, English, Durmast and rose, but perhaps most plentiful of all are the chestnuts that were the staple diet of the region until very recently. Further up the slopes are groves of birch and beech, while holly grows as big as trees and the ground beneath is rich with brambles, raspberries, and bilberries (used to make the local eau-de-vie) as well as bracken, heather and ivy. The high, open slopes above the treeline are used as summer grazing for sheep.

This national park was set up for two reasons. The first was to preserve the many endangered species of wildlife whose last few representatives cling on to life here (see page 66). The other was to preserve the Asturian-style rural architecture that has been handed down over thousands of years. To see the best of this, you need to go onto the even smaller roads beyond Candín. Pereda and Tejedo, in the Ancares River valley, are filled with fine examples of typical wood-framed double-storey houses with slate roofs. The ground floor is still used to house the animals, the heat from their bodies rising to help warm the living quarters above. The palloza is an even older style of building, thought to date back to the Celts, and used originally for summer camps by shepherds. Large round huts, that almost completely disappear under a steeply pitched thatched roof, some have now been given stouter walls and proper chimneys and are still used as homes, others have been turned into stables. The best place to see them is over the Puerta de Ancares in the village of Balouta, where they also still use the chillones (screamer) cart, a design that goes back to the Bronze Age, so called because of the frightful noise it makes. To get back to the main route from here, you have to back-track the whole way to Ponferrada.

Leave Ponferrada on the N120, and start off with another excursion, this time to the south, via Carucedo to the bizarre manmade moonscape of **Las Médulas**, formed by Roman mining. Asturian slaves were used to tunnel into the mountains, after which the tunnels were flooded and forced to collapse. The resulting sand was washed to extract some 3000 tonnes of gold before the mines eventually closed.

Backtrack into Ponferrada and turn left onto the old road to Villafranca del Bierzo. This runs across the Bierzo Basin, a roughly circular valley that was once a lake. Remote, well-watered, almost completely cut off from civilisation and well-protected against the ferocious winter weather of the surrounding mountains, it was a popular spot for hermits in the 7th and 9th centuries, and the area is littered with tiny ruined chapels. In 1809, the basin and the surrounding mountains were the scene of heavy fighting and enormous deprivation, with thousands dying during Sir John Moore's retreat from Ponferrada, ahead of the advancing French. At **Cacabelos**, there is a small Romanesque church with a statue of the Virgin on the portal. Turn left off the road here for a side trip to **Carracedo**, where there is a monastery first founded in 990, and rebuilt in 1138. The village also contains the remnants of a 13th-century palace, a number of 16th-century houses and a tower built in 1602.

Head back to Cacabelos and continue west. A little further on, on a hill top above Pieros, stands the ruined Suebic fort of Bergidum, from the which the region takes its name. 10km later, you will reach **Villafranca del Bierzo**. This pretty village huddles in a valley at the confluence of the Burbia and Valcárcel Rivers, ringed by superb views over the high mountains. Above the town hangs the huge bulk of the 16th-century Castle of the Counts of Peñarramiro, while the streets are filled by attractive houses and mansions, many bearing crests above the door. Of these, the finest is the Palacio de los Marqueses. Villafranca was the tenth stop on the pilgrim route, according to the Codex Calixtus, and as a result, has a large quota of churches and monasteries. The 12th-century Romanesque Church of Santiago has a main door known as the Puerta del Perdón. Only 170km from Santiago, some pilgrims were so weak that they were unable to complete the journey across the mountains, but if they reached this far and touched the door, they were considered to have made enough of an effort and could claim the full set of indulgences. Other churches worth a look are the 12th-century Romanesque Church of San Francisco, the 16th-century Convent of la Anunciata, which has a fine collection of religious art, and the Collegiate Church, built in 1726 on the site of the original Cluniac monastery and hospice around which the town was founded.

From here, follow the NVI west towards Lugo, crossing the border into Galicia at the 1109m Puerto de Pedrafita do Cebreiro.

For the last section of the pilgrim route, through to Santiago de Compostela, see page 195.

Castilla-y-León: General Information

Regional tourist office:
Junta de Castilla y León, Consejeria de Transportes, Turismo y Comercio, c/ Garcia Morato 36, 47008 Valladolid (tel. (983) 342 655).

Burgos Province

BURGOS
Tourist Office, Plaza Alonso Martinez, 7, 09003 (tel. (947) 203 125).
Where to stay:
Hotel Landa Palace, Carretera Madrid, 09000 (tel. (947) 206 343). One of the grandest hotels in the region, this is a Gothic fantasy built only 30 years ago by a friend of Franco's. The only old bit is a medieval tower moved here from a nearby village. Completely over the top, but great fun, for those who can afford it. On the main Madrid road, outside the centre. Expensive.
Mesón del Cid, Plaza Santa Maria 8, 09000 (tel. (947) 208 715). A modern building in the traditional style, beside Burgos cathedral. A little self-conscious it is however

very pleasant, the best of the city centre hotels, and the views of the cathedral are wonderful.
Moderate-expensive.
Hotel Norte y Londres, Plaza Alonso Martinez 10, 09003 (tel. (947) 264 125; fax (947) 277 375). Late 19th-century house right in the heart of the old city, pleasantly but simply renovated. Bed and breakfast only. Cheap-moderate.
Where to eat:
Landa Palace and **Méson del Cid**, as above.
Casa Ojeda, c/ Vitoria 5 (tel. (947) 209 052). Tapas bar with pavement tables downstairs, and a restaurant upstairs. Cheap-moderate.

León Province

ASTORGA
Where to stay:
Hotel Gaudí, Plaza Eduardo de Castro 6, 24700 (tel. (987) 615 654). A pleasant, well-furbished modern hotel right on the main square. Many of the rooms have balconies and excellent views over the cathedral and the bizarre Episcopal Palace built by Gaudí in 1889. Cheap-moderate.
Where to eat:
Gaudí, as above.
Mesón La Magdalena, Castrillo de los Polvazares (tel. (987) 618 539). Good, plentiful home cooking in attractive surroundings. Cheap.

LEÓN
Tourist Office, Plaza de la Regla, 3, 24003 (tel. (987) 237 082).
Where to stay:
Hotel San Marcos, Plaza de San Marcos 7, 24001 (tel. (987) 237 300; fax (987) 233 458). Reckoned to be one of the finest hotels in Spain, this magnificent building with a Plateresque façade was built in 1515 as a pilgrim hospice. It is now one of the main tourist sights in the city, and also houses a small museum, so visit even if you can't afford to stay there. If you feel extravagant, ask for a room in the old part of the building, although the modern extension is also beautiful, with fine views over the garden and river. Expensive.
Hotel Riosol, Avda de Palencia 3, 24002 (tel. (987) 216 650; fax (987) 216 997). Large, comfortable hotel near the river. There is a coffee shop, but no restaurant. Moderate.
Where to eat:
San Marcos, as above.
Mesón Leones del Racimo de Oro, Caño Badillo 2 (tel. (987) 257 575). A 16th-century building against the city wall, this has three small dining rooms and a garden patio, all serving good regional peasant food. Cheap-moderate.
Casa Pozo, Plaza San Marcelo 15, 24003 (tel. (987) 223 039).
A very traditional restaurant, serving fish and regional cuisine in an attractive square not far from the cathedral.
Moderate.

VALENCIA DE DON JUAN
Where to stay and eat:
Hostal El Palacio, Calle Palacio 3, 24200 (tel. (987) 750 474). Right in the centre of town, this is a small, family-run hotel in an ancient building decorated by various artefacts of folk history. There is a cider bar in the stables and a pleasant, shady patio at the back. Cheap.

VILLAFRANCA DEL BIERZO
Where to stay and eat:
Parador, Avenue de Calvo Sotelo, 24500 (tel. (987) 540 175; fax (987) 540 010). Pleasant, but one of the less inspiring paradors in the region, a low, white, modern building overlooking the industrial end of the valley. It is however a good base for exploring this section of the pilgrim route and the nearby mountains of the Sierra del Caurel and Picos de Ancares.

Palencia Province

CERVERA DE PISUERGA
Where to stay and eat:
Parador de Fuentes Carrionas, 34840 (tel. (988) 870 075; fax (988) 870 105). Although modern, both the building and furnishings in this rural retreat are charming. It also has splendid views over a lake and the lush foothills of the Picos de Europa. A few dead animals on the walls draw attention to the fact that this is a popular hunting centre in season. Moderate-expensive.

Galicia

Galicia, the land of the Gauls, is the largest of the states in north-west Spain, covering a total area of 29,434 square kilometres. Roughly square in shape, it is bordered on two sides by the sea and to the south by the Portuguese border, and is split into four provinces, Lugo in the north-east, La Coruña in the north-west, Orense in the south-east and Pontevedra in the south-west. It is a state that thrives on statistics and delights in telling you that it has 3000km of coast, 100 islands, 35,000 towns and villages and 1,000 rivers. Of all the rivers, by far the most important is the Miño. At 340km long, this is the seventh longest river in Spain, but in terms of volume it comes second only to the Ebro. It flows right through the centre of Galicia, rising in the northern Sierra de la Carba and meeting the Atlantic at LaGuardia. For the last 70km of its length it forms the border between Spain and Portugal. Effectively, the whole central area of the state acts as a giant drainage basin to feed the flow.

There are a good many megalithic and bronze age sites scattered across the region, but the first known people to live here were the Celts, who are thought to have arrived in about the 6th century BC, settling in this damp extremity of Europe, as they did in Brittany, Wales and Ireland. The Roman conquest began in 137 BC under the leadership of Decimus Junius Brutus, although it was Augustus Caesar himself who finally forced the region into submission, rapidly populating the landscape with a series of settlements and fortifications. In about 30 BC, the Greek geographer, Estrabón, visited the region, giving a detailed description of its warriors, who wore small, round shields, drank beer, ate cured hams and danced to flute and bugle music.

In 409 AD, the Suebians invaded, bringing Roman rule to an end, and setting up a kingdom of Galicia that included the whole of the modern state and northern Portugal. In 585, the Visigoths took over, but within their larger kingdom, the boundaries remained intact. In 713 came the first Moorish attack. For the next three centuries, the region was officially under Moorish rule, although surprisingly little physical evidence of their presence remains, and in fact, much of the area became a battleground for constant skirmishing between Muslim and Christian forces.

Meantime, in 813, came the miraculous discovery of the tomb of Santiago and the stage was set for the single largest influence on Galician culture, the pilgrim route to Santiago de Compostela (see pages 28 and 199). Pilgrims straggled in in

174

the early years, fearful of travelling although the Moors were remarkably tolerant of other religions. In the 11th century, however, the Reconquista in the region began in earnest under Alfonso VI, aided by various French nobles. In 1095, a grateful and victorious king handed the Duchy of Portugal, which roughly followed the old Suebian boundaries and included all of Galicia, over to Henry of Burgundy. The route to the Holy City was safe, the floodgates were opened and a period of building and expansion on a massive scale began. In 1128, his son, Alfonso, declared Portugal independent of Spain and the region was split along its current boundary. Galicia was sucked into León, and with it, eventually became part of the country of Spain.

The common image of Galicia is of rather gloomy peasants growing potatoes in a swirling Celtic mist, while 20m waves lash the rocky shore. There is a degree of truth in this, but it is only one aspect of a very complex state.

The coast is wild, for it is here that the rías, the drowned river valleys like low-lying fjords, come into their own. Much of the coast is made up of rocky cliffs and inlets, that earned a healthy respect from sailors, who named the section furthest to the west, the Costa da Morte (the Coast of Death). Much of this reputation was built of fear and superstition however, for at its tip, Cabo Finisterra is the westernmost point in mainland Europe. To the Romans who named it, it was the edge of the known world, a situation that changed only in 1492 when Columbus accidentally stumbled across Hispaniola. There is also another side to the coin, however, for between the fatal rocks are some fine, golden beaches and snug harbours that have provided a livelihood for fishermen for thousands of years and are now enthusiastically welcoming tourists.

The weather can be appalling in winter, with bitter cold and deep snow in the high mountains of the east, and ferocious storms along the coast. For much of the time and over the larger proportion of the state, however, the climate tends to be both mild and damp, while the summer does provide some brilliant sunshine and clear blue skies.

It is also true that the main crops here tend to be 'northern' vegetables such as cabbage, turnips and potatoes, but there are several pockets of countryside inland that are producing some fine wines, while even the coast can provide some surprises, with oranges and kiwi fruit, mimosas and palms flourishing in certain areas. Inland, much of the area is still heavily forested with massive oaks and chestnuts, eucalyptus and pine, while the higher hills are a scrubland of bracken and fern, broom and gorse.

The reputation for gloom and doom amongst the people tends to have been imposed by the Castilians, with whom the Galicians have little in common. The Galicians tend to be a tough people, their resilience brought about by centuries of struggling for survival, and they also have a good dose of Celtic introspection, that shows itself in a great love of poetry and music. They are far more hospitable to visitors than the Castilians themselves, willing to open their doors and hearts to those who express an interest. Although the culture still has strong Celtic roots, the language, Gallego, is Latin-based, more akin to Portuguese than to Spanish. Until the 12th century, it was the language of court, but as the state was submerged into Castille, its use became less widespread. It remained alive in the hills and villages,

Galician architecture

This huge state, buffeted by so many influences over the centuries, is notable for the extraordinary range of its architecture. Every farm or small-holding has its *horreo*, a grain store built up on stilts away from the teeth of the rats and other pests. While those further east are made of wood and thatch, the Galician *horreo* is typically rectangular, hewn from the local granite and adorned with a cross at one end. Further up the social scale, particularly in the Rías Bajas, the minor landed gentry of the 17th and 18th centuries built themselves *pazos*, elegant rural manor houses, while those in town glassed in their many ornate balconies until whole streets glitter in the evening sun.

In the remotest hills inland, a few people still live in *pallozzas*, the round, rough walled huts with steep pitched thatch that are a direct descendant of Celtic homes 3000 years old. Also up in the hills are still the remains of some 5000 *castros*, Celtic hill forts and villages with small round stone huts and deep defensive ditches gouged from the earth. The Romans left their mark, with a number of their bridges and viaducts and even a lighthouse still in use, together with such formidable defenses as the city walls of Lugo.

Above all, however, the converging routes of the pilgrimage to Santiago have ensured a superlative collection of religious monuments and buildings. Many of the towns and villages still have elaborately carved wayside crosses and there are literally thousands of churches, from great cathedrals to tiny chapels. The pilgrim route was the birthplace of Romanesque architecture and, astonishingly, it was never really replaced in Galicia, which virtually skipped the whole Gothic era. Gothic buildings are very scarce here and the rounded forms of the Romanesque continued to be built until the neo-classical lines of the Renaissance arrived in the early 16th century. It was only in the 18th century however that the builders really got underway again, refurbishing many of the churches and monasteries and building others from scratch to provide the state with a superb array of fine Baroque architecture.

however, and stayed popular amongst lyric poets and writers. In the mid-19th century came a revival. In 1906, the Galician Royal Academy was founded to promote the language, followed shortly afterwards by the first Gallegan magazine. Today, enthusiasm for Gallego continues, although it is not as widely spoken as Basque. Nevertheless, it is now taught in all Galician schools, there is a healthy volume of publishing in the language and, together with Spanish, it is an official language of government.

Today, Galicia is an autonomous community, largely dependent on the sea. Its major industries are deep-sea fishing, for cod, tuna and sardines, coastal fishing for shellfish, fish canning, commercial trade through its main ports of La Coruña and Vigo, and shipbuilding. Culturally, it is distinctive, never quite thinking of itself as Spanish, but without the ferocious and sometimes violent struggle for independence and national identity of the Basque Country or Catalunya. The pragmatic Gallegans seem content to trudge on through life, secure in their own identity and never seeing the need to prove it to anyone else.

As this book takes the pilgrim route to Santiago de Compostela as its southern boundary, only Lugo and Coruña provinces are included.

Ribadeo to Lugo

This route winds south through the pretty hill country of Galicia to connect the north coast with the ancient city of Lugo and the Camino de Santiago. *(For the Asturian coastal route east from Ribadeo, see page 59. For the coastal route west from Ribadeo to La Coruña, see page 184).*

Perched above the sea, looking out across the bay and the Eo Ría to Asturias, the busy little town of **Ribadeo** was founded in 775 around a long-vanished monastery, but grew, like all the other towns along this coast, as a small fishing port. As it expanded, the whitewashed cottages spread steadily up the steep slope, until today, the town centre is not around the fishing harbour at all, but on top of the hill around a large, dusty plaza filled by unexpected palm trees. The town has several rather undistinguished churches and a few fine buildings, such as the 18th-century, neo-classical Town Hall, built originally as the family home of the Marques de Sargadelos, and the flamboyant 1905 Casa de Moreno, also in the main plaza. The main reasons to come here however are for a walk through the delightful, if humble streets of the fishing quarter, and for the wonderful view across the ría to Castropol.

The ría is also one of the best centres for watersports in the region, its waters

The harbourside at Ribadeo

177

alive with the brightly coloured sails of dinghies and windsurfers. They take the water seriously here and many of the greatest of the summer festivities are focussed on swimming and canoe races, windsurfing and sailing regattas. There are sailing and canoeing schools for those who wish to learn. Amongst the boats, look out for those carrying the distinctive lateen sails (square on two sides and rising to a sharp curving point at the top of the mast) that are a local tradition. These boats were used originally as passenger ferries between the towns along the ría, but have been reinstated recently as pleasure craft.

Leave town on the small road south, the LU133, towards Vilela. Just outside the town at **Santa Cruz**, there is a fine view from beside the Hermitage of la Virgen de la Santa Cruz. There is also a monument here to el Gaitero Gallego (the Galician piper), sculpted by Failde in 1955. In early August each year, this is at the centre of one of the most colourful festivals in the area, the Xira a Santa Cruz, which is a tribute to the pipers of Galicia. Continue on, straight through Vilela, and 9km from Ribadeo, turn left, then right to Arante, where the Sanctuary of Nuestra Señora da Ponte has some interesting 16th-century murals.

Keep going along the same road to Villamar, and turn left onto the N634 to **Vilanova de Lourenzá**, where there is a splendid Benedictine Monastery. Although the monastery was founded in the 10th century, the existing buildings are mainly 17th- and 18th-century Baroque and include work by some of the finest craftsmen of the period. The abbey façade was the work of Asturian architect, José María Martínez Céliz, between 1712 and 1715, while the ornate church façade was created by Fernando Casas y Novoa between 1734 and 1738. Most of the work on the light and graceful interior was done in the mid-17th century, although the upper level and dome were created by Fray Juan de Samos and Fernando Casas in 1732. In the sacristy, there is a magnificent reliquary altarpiece, carved by Juan Vaamonde and decorated by Francisco de Andrade in 1680. Inside it is a wonderful collection of copper figurines. The tomb of the monastery's founder, the Conde Santo (Holy Count) is in the Chapel of Santa María de Valdeflores to the north of the nave, and in the cloisters (completed in 1637) is a small museum devoted to the history of the monastery.

Carry on down the N634 for 9km to **Mondoñedo**. This charming little town, set in the broad, green valley of the River Masma, has a population of only around 7000 today, but it has an illustrious past and is packed with wonderful buildings to prove it. Fragmentary archaeological evidence suggests that this valley was inhabited during the Neolithic, Bronze Age and the Roman era, but little is definitely known before 1117, when the diocese of Mondoñedo was moved here from the coastal town of San Martín de Mondoñedo. The town received its charter from Alfonso VII in 1156. When Galicia was broken up in the 15th century, the town became the capital of the northern province of Mondoñedo, a position it held until 1834.

Work on the Cathedral began in 1220 and continued for over a century. At that stage, it was designed along Cistercian lines to be large but simple. Some alterations were made in the late 15th and early 16th centuries, and more followed in the in the 18th century, under the auspices of Bishop Muñez y Salcedo, who is buried in the south aisle. The result is an unusual but pleasing west front that has retained its Romanesque portal, Gothic arches and rose window, framing them with

Baroque towers and pediment. The relief carvings on either side of the door show San Lorenzo and San Jerónimo. Inside, the main fabric of the building is still transitional Romanesque. On the walls, there are some lovely 15th-century frescoes, depicting the massacre of the innocents and the life of St Peter, and a fine early 18th-century organ. The elaborate main altarpiece was created in 1769 by a team of artists including Castro, Bahamonde and Riobóo. Amongst its many elements are an Assumption, and the figures of San Rosendo and San Martín Dumiense. Four of the apsidal chapels were remodelled in the 16th century. In the Chapel of the Holy Relics, the altarpiece is said to contain a fragment of the True Cross. In the south apsidal chapel is a polychrome wood statue known as the English Virgin. It shows the Virgin surrounded by seraphim and is said to have been brought here from St Paul's Cathedral in London at the time of the Reformation.

The 17th-century cloister houses part of the Diocesan Museum, a rich collection of religious art that also spreads into the Bishop's Palace. It also has a collection of 16th- to 18th-century furniture. Just outside the palace is a lovely fountain, the Fonte Vella, erected in 1548.

The Seminary was founded in 1565 and grew rapidly to become the third largest in Spain. It still has a superb library of more than 20,000 books and manuscripts. The Sanctuary of Os Remedios is a fine Baroque building, designed by Fray Lorenzo de Santa Teresa between 1733 and 1738. It has several beautiful altarpieces. Other buildings to look out for include the Convent of Alcantara (also designed by Fray Lorenzo), the Monastery of La Concepción, the Palace and Chapel of San Isidro and the tower of the Monastery of Os Picos. Surrounding these are a wonderful collection of mansions and houses, many emblazoned with coats of arms, some with wrought iron balconies and some with glassed-in solañas.

Those who wish to do a shorter route should keep going straight along the N634 to Villalba.

The route now turns east, along the twisting LU124 that leads across the 550m Puerto Cruz de Cancela to Villamea. Just beyond the village, turn right onto the N640, signposted to Lugo. The next 21km of the drive are through the hills of the Sierra de Meira, a particularly beautiful stretch of scenery, with dense woodland and lovely mountain views. The highest point on the road is about halfway along at the 575m Puerto Marco de Alvares. At the village of **Meira** itself, stop to look at the Cistercian Monastery Church of Santa María. The setting, when the abbey was founded in the mid-12th century, would have been typically Cistercian, in a wide, wooded valley beside a small river, in this case the Muiño. Today, only the abbey church remains, along with the small town that grew up around it. The church was built in the late 12th and early 13th century and is typically Cistercian, vast and austere, although the east end is round, instead of rectangular as laid down by St Bernard in the monastic rules. The main façade has a wide, round arched portal, topped by a huge rose window, while the nave is chiefly notable for its size, nine bays long, with an immensely high central aisle.

Follow the N640 for 2.5km to Parajes, then turn right onto the LU120, signposted to Villalba. At Tumbo, 18km on, turn left onto the LU112 and, at Feria do Monte, turn right to **Sistallo**. The parish church, founded by Miguel Verdes-Montenegro in 1754 has three fine 18th-century Baroque altarpieces. Look out also for the beautiful pazo de Clemente Sarela, one of the finest of these typically Galician houses in existence. Built by Francisco Verdes-Montenegro in 1750, it is privately owned and, sadly, not open to the public.

Follow the same small road on to the T-junction and turn left to **Villalba**. This is a small, very friendly little town with one architectural glory, the octagonal Torre de los Andrade, all that is left of a larger fortress built at the end of the 15th century. It has recently been restored and is now used as a parador. Ask to be taken up to the roof, as the views across the town and surrounding countryside are lovely.

Turn left here, and follow the C641 south for 22km to **Rábade**, where you should turn left onto the NVI for the last section of the journey into Lugo.

Two small villages, Robra and Meilán, just off the main road, both have small, simple late 12th-century Romanesque churches. At **Saamasas**, just on the edge of Lugo, near the old bridge across the Miño, are the remains of some Roman baths. They have been severely mauled over the centuries, and now live in the basement of a modern building. The church here contains some Visigothic reliefs.

For a description of the city of Lugo, see page 181. For the best onward route to Santiago de Compostela, follow the N640 south for 18km to Guntín de Pallares and join the Camino de Santiago, see page 195.

Alto de Acebo to Lugo

This route, which winds down the western end of the Cordillera Cantábrica into the gentle hills of the Miño River basin, is the continuation of the route across western Asturias from Oviedo. It follows one of the minor, northern branches of the pilgrim route to Santiago. Route directions are easy, just keep going along the C630, signposted to Lugo. *(For the section of the route from Oviedo to Alto de Acebo, see page 62).*

The 1030m **Alto de Acebo** marks the border between Asturias and Galicia, but it is not quite the end of the mountains. The western end of the range consists of a series of smaller, but still dramatic ranges, running north-south. The first half of this route winds through some spectacular scenery on the northern edge of the Sierra de Ancares. Granite grey villages cling to the thickly wooded hillsides, or crouch amongst their fields in the valley bottoms. Above, the skies open out across huge stretches of grasslands, bright with wild flowers in the spring and early summer.

Fonsagrada, the administrative centre of the region, is itself high up, at 952m. It is an attractive town without any specific sights, that is a good centre for exploring the remote lanes of the surrounding mountains. Shortly after this, the road climbs that little bit higher to the 960m Alto de Cerredo, swoops into the valley, and up again to the 930m Alto de Fontaneira. This is the last of the high passes, and from now on the route drops rapidly over a short distance, before evening out into rolling hill country, about 500m above sea level. About 15km from the pass, a small road on the right leads to the little village of **Vilabade** and the Church of Santa María. Built in the 16th century, by Juan Bautista Celma, this is one of the earliest works of the Galician school of architecture. Inside, it has some fine murals, and an 18th-century Baroque retable.

Back on the road, 1km on, is the splendid 14th-century Castle of Castroverde, positioned to guard the approach to Lugo and its surrounding plain. The city is 23km further west.

Lugo

When the Romans arrived in Galicia, they took the Celtic name '*lug*' (meaning 'sacred forest') and named their new town on the banks of the River Miño, Lucus Augusti, after their emperor. As time went by, and the Romans left, it slid back to being Lugo. Meantime, however, the Romans built a fine, big town from which to rule the western extremity of their empire. The city of Lugo became capital of a huge region that included all of Galicia and northern Portugal. In the 2nd century, they built it a massive wall of stone, but although the wall remained intact, the empire crumbled and by the early 5th century, the Romans had gone.

The Suebians moved straight into this marvellous citadel, which became their capital for the next two centuries. In the 8th century, it was captured briefly by the Moors, and for the next two centuries after that, it was the focus of countless battles between the Christian Asturian kings and the Muslims. By the early 11th century, the Moors were definitively beaten, but the city now became involved in numerous local squabbles between the kings, who were trying to centralise their power, and the nobility, who were determined to stop them doing so.

Meantime, with the popularity of the pilgrim route growing every day, Lugo became a favourite stopover for those who had travelled along the coast and were now cutting inland to Santiago. Within the walls, churches and hostels began to spring up and commerce flourished.

In the 15th century, however, the kingdom of Galicia was swallowed by Castilla-y-León, and the territory was split into smaller provinces. Even the province of Lugo itself was split in two, with the northern section given to Mondoñedo, while the city now controlled only a relatively small region in the south. This, and the drop in pilgrim numbers in the late 16th century ensured that the city gradually declined into a backwater, which it has remained virtually ever since. With the statute of autonomy, it did become the capital of a rejoined Lugo Province, and it has recently been attracting in new industry. The population is now up to about 85,000 and the attractive, lively old city is surrounded by an ugly sprawl of new development.

On arriving in the city, the first, inescapable sight is the vast bulk of the **Roman walls**, a massive ring of formidable grey stone, 2130m long. First built in the 2nd century AD, they still have 85 semi-circular bastions, although some have been destroyed and others razed to the level of the main wall (10–15m) by the combined pressures of attack over the centuries by the Suebians, Visigoths, Moors, Vikings

Back streets in Lugo, seen from the ancient city walls

and French. There are now also ten gates into the city, where once there would have been four. Nevertheless, the walls are still astonishingly well preserved, and are the one of the best surviving examples of Roman military architecture anywhere in the world. There is a path right round the ramparts, with fine views down across the city. For those who prefer to drive, they are also surrounded by a ring road.

Enter by the south gate, the Puerta Santiago and you find yourself in the Plaza Pio, facing the west front of the **Cathedral**. The first church to stand on this spot

182

was Visigothic, destroyed by the Moors in the 8th century. Work began on the existing cathedral in 1129, under the watchful eye of master builder, Raimundo de Monforte. The main body of the church was completed by the late 13th century, and this basic framework of a Romanesque, Latin cross still survives to this day. In the 14th century, however, the apsidal chapels were rebuilt in the Gothic style, while the 18th century produced a flurry of building work that has transformed much of the cathedral, including the main façade. This is now pure Baroque, created between 1769 and 1784, along with the three main towers. The north door is 14th-century Gothic, although its chief feature, a fine relief of Christ in Majesty, and the carving of the Last Supper on the capital beneath it, are Romanesque. The ironwork decoration on the doors themselves dates to the early 13th century. The east end still retains its Romanesque rotunda.

Inside, the cradle-vaulted nave is lined by galleries and side chapels. Partway along, it is blocked by a magnificent choir, carved in walnut by Francisco de Moure between 1621. There is a fine Romanesque chapel in the north transept, and both transepts have huge wooden Renaissance altarpieces. The one in the south transept is the work of Cornelis de Holanda in 1531. A door beside this leads into the elegant Baroque cloister, designed by Fernando Casas y Novoa, who was also responsible for much of the work in Santiago cathedral, between 1709 and 1714. Back in the main cathedral, there is a lovely Rococo Lady chapel behind the high altar, while at the east end of the cathedral is a superb Baroque chapel, dedicated to the Wide Eyed Virgin, patroness of the city. This was designed by Fernando Casas y Novoa in 1735, and follows the circle of the existing Romanesque walls, while the interior takes the form of a curved Greek cross, topped by a high dome. The overblown altarpiece, by Miguel de Romay, was inspired by the 'triumph' in Seville cathedral.

Leaving the cathedral by the north door, turn right and you arrive in the **Plaza Santa María**, a beautiful square, bordered to the west by the east end of the cathedral, and to the north by the Bishop's Palace, a long, low elegant building, typical of Galician pazo architecture. The first building here was the tower house of the Condes de Lemos, but in 1738, this was incorporated into a newer building by Bishop Gil Taboada, whose coat of arms is emblazoned on the doorway.

The east end of the plaza leads onto the formal **Alameda Gardens**, a paseo lined by shady arcades, under which huddle a host of cafés. At the far end, in the Plaza de España stands the Town Hall, constructed in 1738 by Ferro Caaveiro. The clock tower in the centre was added in 1871. Take the Calle de la Reina to the left past the Town Hall. This leads through to the huge **Plaza de Santo Domingo**, where a huge winged monument marks the geographical centre of the city. Recent excavations here have brought to light some fine Roman mosaics. On the north side of the plaza is the Convent of Santo Domingo, founded in the 12th century, although the church is mainly 14th-century Gothic, with a 15th-century Renaissance portal. The sacristy and cloister were both altered in the 18th century. There are several interesting retables and paintings inside, including one by Juan Antonio García de Bouzas, considered to be the finest of the Galician artists of the 18th century.

At the east end of the plaza is the **Church of San Francisco**, part of a monastery founded in the 12th century. The church itself is 16th-century Gothic and shows mudéjar influence in the design. The cloister was originally Romanesque but was heavily altered in 1452. It is an elegant square, surrounded by slim double columns. This, together with the convent refectory and kitchen, now houses the Provincial Museum, with a wide-ranging and eclectic collection from displays about Roman Lugo to religious sculpture, fine art, arms, nautical and musical instruments, furniture and ceramics.

Turn right into the **Rua Nova**. This is one of the prettiest streets in the city, lined by charming cottages and workshops, and ending in the lovely Plaza del Campo, which borders the north side of the cathedral. There is a charming 18th-century fountain in the square.

Excursion west from Lugo

Leave the city on the N640, heading south towards Orense and about 4km from the city, turn off onto the small road on the right to **Bóveda**, 14km from the city centre. The tiny subterranean Church of Santa Eulalia presents one of the most fascinating puzzles in the whole of northern Spain. Discovered in 1926, and the subject of several archaeological excavations, it is almost certainly the lower floor of a larger building, long since vanished. There are two sections. The first, reached down a small flight of steps from the street, contains two truncated pillars and some primitive low-relief stone carvings of geometric and floral patterns and a frieze of dancing people. The inner section, reached through a horseshoe arch, has a rectangular atrium or bath in the centre, and is covered by some wonderful late Roman frescoes. The interlinking pattern of geometric shapes and birds is very similar to mosaic design of the period. There is much dispute over the date and purpose of the building, but it is thought possibly to have started life as a Roman bathhouse or spring some time in the 3rd century. It seems to have been converted to Christian use in the late 4th century and to have been used, possibly as a crypt, throughout the 6th and 7th centuries. Fragments of pottery have led to one suggestion that it was used as a tomb, possibly even that of Santa Eulalia, although no body has been discovered.

For the best onward route to Santiago de Compostela, follow the N640 south for 18km to Guntín de Pallares and join the Camino de Santiago, see page 195.

The Coast Road West – Ribadeo to La Coruña

This route follows the gentler portion of the Galician coast, an area known as the Rías Altas. Most of the time it hugs the westernmost stretch of the Cantabrian sea, but where there are sights of interest just inland it loops round, away from the main road. This is a particularly beautiful stretch of coast, with many rocky inlets, small bays and fishing villages, virtually untouched by large scale tourism. *(For the next section of the coastal route east, from Ribadeo to Oviedo, see page 59).*

The Ría de Eo marks the eastern border between Galicia and Asturias. Leave Ribadeo on the N634 heading west, signposted to Foz and Mondoñedo. *(For a description of Ribideo, see page 177).* The picturesque little fishing port of Rinlo, famous for its lobsters, is off to the right, 4km from the town. A short way after this you come to the first of Galicia's 772 beaches, the long and lovely Playa del Castro, broken up by some beautiful hollow rock formations, known as As Catedrais (the Cathedral) and El Castro (the Castle). The area behind the beach, and for the next few kilometres contains a long series of caravan and camping sites. When you come to the main road junction, turn right onto the C642 that leads up the western edge of the Ría de Masma to Foz. *(Turn left if you wish to visit Vilanova de Lourenzá and Mondoñedo, described on the route to Lugo, page 178).*

Foz is one of the main towns in this area, with a population of about 9000 and a small, but thriving fishing fleet. There are several Celtic castros in the area, and ancient slag heaps also suggest that both Romans and Phoenicians mined the area. The existing town grew up as a whaling port in the Middle Ages and there is also a long tradition of shipbuilding, which survives to this day. The town itself has little of interest to see, but it does have two fine beaches, the Playa de Rapadoiro and the Playa de Llas, divided by a dramatic cliff.

There are two alternatives for the next section of the route. If you wish to remain beside the sea, continue along the C642 to Viveiro. There are several fine beaches on the way. At Fazouro, there is a well-preserved Celtic village. Burela is one of the prettiest of the fishing villages along the route, and the nearby Celtic village, the Castro do Chan was the discovery site of some magnificent gold jewellery, now on display in Lugo Museum. At Sargadelos, just inland from Cervo, you can see the Sargadelos potteries, founded in the early 19th century to produce imitation Toby jugs. It is still functioning as a pottery, although it has widened its repertoire, and the factory shop can be a good place to go souvenir hunting.

To follow the inland route, turn left onto the small road leading inland to **San Martín de Mondoñedo**. This was the seat of the diocese until 1112 and the magnificent early Romanesque Church of San Martín still exists, remarkably untouched by later architectural trends. Built in the mid- to late 11th century, the decoration throughout the church is superb, with a wonderful collection of primitive capitals, a simple sculpted stone altarpiece, and a series of murals dating from the 13th century. The typically Romanesque curves of the east end are supported by huge buttresses, and the whole church still has a timber roof.

Continue straight along to the crossroads with the LU152 and turn left to **Alfoz**, where you can see the Castro de Oro, a 15th-century fortress built by Mariscal Pardo de Cela. Recently renovated, it now houses the Town Hall. From beside the castle, there is a fine view across the Ouro River valley. Turn right here onto the LU160, which leads through the lovely valley to **Ferreira** (Valadouro), where the parish Church of Santo Tomé is the centre of a colourful festival on the first Sunday in August. From here, follow the LU161 for about 20km, via Vilacampa, Boimente to Chavin, where a small road on the right leads to the Church of San Pedro de Viveiro, founded in the 6th century, but basically Romanesque, with some attractive capitals.

Return to Chavin and follow the road along to the crossroads with the C640, where you turn right along the Landro River valley to Viveiro.

Situated at the foot of the ría, carefully sheltered from the open sea, **Viveiro** is the largest and most important of the towns along the north coast of Galicia, with a population of about 15,000. There is a lively modern centre and an attractive 12-arched bridge across the ría, but the real reason to stop here is for the lovely old town on the west bank. Some remnants of the medieval city walls and four of the ten original gates still survive. Of them all, the finest is the Puerta de Carlos V, a monumental, Plateresque arch beside the water, constructed in 1548. Others of interest are the Puerta do Valado, built in the 13th century as the entrance along the old Roman road and the Puerta da Villa (also known as the Puerta del Santo Cristo), which was the main entrance to the city, constructed in 1217, during the reign of Alfonso IX of León.

Once inside the walls, the old town is a charming huddle of narrow streets, tall, balconied buildings and little plazas. The Church of Santa María del Campo was built in the late 12th century and still preserves its Romanesque form although, sadly, it has been heavily altered over the years and its capitals have been lost. Other buildings worth a look include the 14th-century Gothic Church of San Francisco, part of a convent founded in 1219, and the Convent of Valdeflores.

Just to the east of the town, the Hermitage of San Roque stands on a small hill of the same name. There is a wonderful view across the town and the ría from here.

Leave Viveiro on the C642, heading up the western edge of the ría. There are several beaches along here, the finest of them, the Playa de Xilloi and the Playa de Arealonga looking out to the open sea and the little offshore Island of Coelleira. According to legend, when the Templars fled from France, a small band took refuge on this island, but the lord of Viveiro crept across one night and attacked. Only one of the knights survived, and he fled, disguised as a peasant, to the nearby village of O Vicedo, just off the main road to the right, overlooking the Ría del Barqueiro. He remained a peasant for the rest of his life, and his house is still known as the Casa del Paisano.

From O Vicedo, the main road crosses the ría on a bridge, but it is worth driving down the small road around the foot of the ría, as this is an enchanting garden area lined with camelias and azaleas in season. This ría, the estuary of the Sor River, marks the provincial boundary with A Coruña.

On the west bank of the ría stands the little whitewashed fishing village of Porto do Barqueiro. Take the small road to the north of this for some fine views across the estuary and to reach the best of the beaches, near the even smaller village of Bares. At the end of the peninsula, a lighthouse marks the Punta de la Estaca de Bares, the most northerly point along the whole Cantabrian coast.

Returning to Barqueira, carry on along the C642 which travels south-west past several fine beaches to **Ortigueira**, halfway down the huge and complex Ría de Santa María de Ortigueira, where the wriggling path of the Mera River estuary is joined by the rías of several smaller rivers. The town is a major centre with a population of about 17,000, but although it is neat and attractive, there is little of interest here. It is the scenery of the ría that is the real draw. Follow the road around to the foot of the ría at Mera, and turn right onto the C646 that winds up the dramatic west bank to Cariño, a little fishing port at the mouth of the ría beside

Cabo Ortegal. This effectively marks the end of the Cantabrian coast, as from now on, the shoreline slopes south-west, looking out into the Atlantic ocean.

The road crosses the cape and turns along the shore, offering wonderful views across wild cliffs and out to sea. Make sure you stop off at the little Sanctuary of San Andrés de Teixido and buy one of the small votive offerings of bread dough on sale from the caretaker, for it is said that those who fail in their duty to the saint will be reincarnated as a lizard or some other equally unpleasant creature! This is a particularly good place in which to pray for a healthy pregnancy, while one of the local herbs is said to make an extremely effective love potion.

Just before you reach the charming little port of Cedeira, there is a field on the side of the road known as El Curro. This is the scene each year of a colourful livestock festival, the *rapa das bestas*, held continuously since the middle ages. This was traditionally the time when all the animals that had been left to roam wild through the year were gathered together for sale. There are still wild horses in the area.

At **Cedeira**, you rejoin the C646 to travel around the foot of the Ría de Condomiñas. The last leg along the coast to El Ferrol is lined by virtually continuous beaches, many of the incredibly beautiful. Near Valdevino is a particularly lovely stretch of dunes surrounding a broad lagoon, the Punta Fruxeiro, that is a favourite stopping point for a wide variety of migratory birds.

At the end of this stretch of coast, because you arrive in the city of El Ferrol, a busy centre with a population of some 85,000, on the northern edge of the grandfather of all rías. No less than four main rías flow into this wide bay that is one of the busiest shipping areas in Spain, with the naval dockyards of Ferrol to the north and the huge commercial port of La Coruña to the south.

El Ferrol, named after the farol (lighthouse) that marked the entrance to the bay, has been a port since the middle ages, but it really came to life in the 18th century when a naval base was built here by Felipe V in 1726. Carlos III moved the naval arsenal here in 1769 and it has been one of Spain's main naval garrisons ever since. The dockyards themselves are hidden behind high walls and are closed to the public, but the streets are filled by happy sailors on shore leave. Surprisingly, for such a large town, there are no specific buildings of real interest, but it is worth taking the time for a walk, because there are a great many minor buildings of charm and elegance. The old town at the bottom of the hill is still laid out along the medieval street plan, and there are several attractive houses. After dark, however, this is very much port territory filled not by quaint bistros but raucous bars and red lights. The main centre of the town is the planned 18th-century district behind the parador. Stop and look at the detail of design on the windows, balconies and doorways, which is often delightful. These days, the city's greatest and somewhat dubious claim to fame is as the birthplace of General Franco.

Leave El Ferrol on the main road to La Coruña, the NVI, but be sure to take the route that heads along the estuary and do not cross the long modern bridge. At the foot of the estuary, in **Xubia**, the Church of San Martín is all that remains of a monastery first founded in the 9th century. It was taken over by Cluniac monks in 1113 and they were responsible for building the church in the second half of the 12th century. It is typically Romanesque in style, with a wooden roof, three naves,

Windows and solañas *in El Ferrol*

three apsidal chapels and some fine decorative detail including some wonderful capitals. Look out especially for the battle between two horsemen.

Continue through Neda and rejoin the NVI, now heading due south. 17km on, **Pontedeume** stands on the south bank of the Eume River estuary, the second of the four rivers flowing into the bay. As you cross the estuary, look out for the remains of the old bridge which gave the town its name. This originally had 58 arches. The village is one of the prettiest along the route, set between the river and the pine-clad slopes of Monte Breamo. It was home for many years to the Condes de Andrade, who were renowned as great builders, and the family passion rubbed off on the humbler houses nearby. At the centre of the village is a massive 14th-century keep, emblazoned with the family crest, that is all that now remains of the Palacio de los Andrades. There are two churches of interest. The Sanctuary of Nuestra Señora de las Virtudes was built between 1620 and 1680. The somewhat austere building is nothing particularly special, but it has a magnificent Baroque altarpiece, all barley-sugar and gilt, created by Alonso Gonzáles in 1679. The parish church was rebuilt by Archbishop Rajoy in the Baroque style, to designs by Alberto Ricoy. It has a fine façade with three towers, while inside are a lovely 13th-century statue of the seated Madonna, several 16th-century paintings and, in the Chapel of San Juan Bautista, a beautiful altarpiece. The best time to visit the old town, if possible, is during the Saturday afternoon market.

Before you continue south, take the time to drive inland along the small road beside the Eume River to **Caaveiro**. The setting of this ruined Benedictine monastery would be hard to beat, on a rocky promontory surrounded by thick woodland, overlooking the confluence of the Eume and Sesín Rivers. The monastery was founded in 934 by San Rosendo, but the buildings date from the second half of the 12th century. Although romantically overgrown, the apse and the fortified church door are still standing. The tympanum is carved with the Agnus Dei (lamb of God), while over the door, there is a baroque tower, designed in 1750 by Clemente Sarela, emblazoned with a coat of arms.

Return to Pontedeume and head south on the NVI. Along this road down to Betanzos, you will see the Church of San Miguel de Breamo, set off on its own. This is a classic Romanesque church, built in 1187 and thought to have belonged to an Augustine order which was disbanded in about 1500. The church is sober in design with graceful lines and a variety of lovely capitals. Further on, near Miño, is the Church of San Juan de Vilanova, one of the oldest churches in the region, built in the mid-11th century.

An alternative route heads inland on small roads from Campolongo, where you turn left to Taboada. About 2km along this road, a slip road on the left leads to the hilltop ruins of the 14th-century Castro de Andrade. There is a good view across the ría from beside the keep. From here, continue on to Taboada and turn right onto the LC152, a pretty road that leads south for about 10km to **Monfero**. Turn left here up the small road to the Monastery of Monfero. This began life as a grand, if isolated Cistercian house, but joined the Congregation of Castille in 1506. In the mid-16th century, the two cloisters were rebuilt, then, in 1620, the new church, designed by Simón de Monasterio was built. It has a striking façade with a grey-and-white chessboard pattern of slate and granite, with neo-classical pediments between high columns. Today, the monastery buildings are in ruin and only the church is in use. Return to Monfero, and turn south onto the road, which is now numbered the C640, and follow it round for 20 km to Betanzos.

Like almost every other town around, **Betanzos**, which stands at the foot of the third ría of the bay, began life as a fishing port. Over the centuries however, the estuary has silted up, and although there is still water, in terms of a harbour, the town has been left high and dry. It is a lovely place, with a population of about 12,000, and a great many very beautiful buildings, including some humble stone cottages and some town houses with glassed-in balconies. Many of the finest buildings line one square, the Plaza del Campo. At the centre of the square are a fountain that is a copy of of the Fountain of Diana at Versaille and a monument showing two 'Indiano' citizens of the town gazing towards America. The Convent of Santo Domingo was founded in the 16th century, but virtually rebuilt in the 18th. The church was sponsored by Archbishop Monroy (the rich Mexican who also paid for much of Santiago Cathedral), was designed by Domingo de Andrade, and built by Fernando Casas y Novoa. Opposite this, the Municipal Library was originally built in the 18th century as a school, while the 18th-century neo-classical palace now houses the National Archives of Galicia.

Very near this main square are three other lovely churches. Santa María del Azogue dates from the 14th and 15th centuries and is late Romanesque/Gothic in style, with a rounded portal, rose window, and small bell-wall to one side. There are sculptures of the Virgin and the Angel Gabriel in niches to either side of the portal, and a wayside cross stands in front of the church. Almost next door is the Church of San Francisco, built as part of a Franciscan monastery by Fernán Pérez de Andrade in 1387. The Count was a hunting fanatic and used the wild boar as his symbol. They keep reappearing all over the church, while the count's monumental tomb not only has a boar, but is covered in hunting scenes. There are many other fine tombs lining the walls of the church. The Church of Santiago was founded by the tailors' guild in the 15th century and has a fine equestrian carving of Santiago Matamoro above the main door.

Leave Betanzos on the NVI, heading towards La Coruña. About 10km along, you come to a crossroads. If you turn right, the road leads up to Sada, a pretty resort town with fine beaches, from where a picturesque road meanders along the coast and into La Coruña, offering fine views across to the city along the way. If you turn left, you cross the motorway and reach **Cambre**, where you will find the wonderful Romanesque Church of Santa María. This was built in the last quarter of the 12th century, but was part of an abbey that had been founded at least 300 years before. It has a simple façade with a rounded portal depicting the lamb of God, a rose window and small bell-wall. The rounded east end, surrounded by five apsidal chapels, is particularly lovely. Inside, the apsidal chapels have rib vaulting and there are numerous fine carvings and capitals. Look out in particular for the so-called Hydria of Jerusalem, dated 1519 and depicting the wedding at Cana.

Return to the NVI and turn left, and if you haven't yet had enough of Romanesque churches, there are others to see at Bergondo, Temple, O Burgo, Oza and Elviña before you reach the outskirts of the city.

La Coruña

The state capital of Galicia, as well as the provincial capital, **LA CORUÑA** is a large city, with a population of about 233,000, situated on the south bank of a great bay formed by four rías. There has been a settlement of some form here continuously since at least the 2nd century BC, although it seems to have gone under a remarkably varied list of names. It is thought that the town was founded by Phoenicians as a port for transporting tin. Captured by the Romans in 60 BC, it was renamed Ardobicum Corunium, but in the 2nd century AD, Ptolemy refers to it as Flavium Brigantium. In the 3rd century, it appears as Brigantia, while from the 6th to 8th centuries, several variations on the name Faro are suggested. The name Crunia only appears for the first time in the Codex Calixtus, written in 1140.

The city's history has been as varied as its names. Following the fall of Rome, it was taken over by the Suebians, then captured by the Moors in the 8th century. They were driven out, but the great Moorish General Almanzor captured it again in the 10th century and held it until his defeat in 1002. In 1371, King Fernando I of Portugal landed here on his way to try and claim the throne of Spain for himself. In 1386, John of Gaunt arrived here with 7000 men to claim the throne for his wife, Constance, who was the daughter of Pedro I (the Cruel). The city responded by building itself some hefty walls.

Numerous other royals passed through the city on various trips abroad, but Coruña really shot to fame in the 16th century. Most of Europe was at war at the time, but Catholic Spain and Elizabeth's Protestant England were particularly antagonistic. Not only had Elizabeth beheaded Mary Queen of Scots, but rivalry over the newly developing sea routes was intense, and England was threatening to support the Low Countries in their war against Spain. Felipe II amassed a huge flotilla of 130 men of war, containing 10,000 sailors and 19,000 soldiers at La Coruña. On 22 July, 1588, his invincible Armada, the greatest concentration of Spanish ships ever to gather in one place, set sail. Meanwhile, in Plymouth, Sir Francis Drake was finishing off a game of bowls . . . The English and Spanish fleets met in a stupendous sea battle that raged its way up the Channel to Flanders, but the Spanish suffered not only from the strength of the English navy, but from appalling weather and sheer bad luck. By the time the survivors broke free and limped back to Spain, they had lost 63 ships and over 15,000 men. Spain's position as a maritime power was lost forever and for the next 300 years, British naval power reigned supreme.

The saga was not yet over however, for in 1589, Drake, a villain known locally as 'the English pirate', swooped down on La Coruña, with 15,000 men and 30 ships. The alarm was raised by a local girl, María Pita, who managed to steal the English flag, raise the alarm and so save the town. She is the greatest of the local heroes now, with numerous streets, bars and sundry monuments in her name.

In the 18th century, things quietened down, and a regular passenger boat ran from England to La Coruña. In the early 19th century, however, it all started up again. In 1809, the English, retreating from the ferocity of Marshal Soult's attack, ended up in La Coruña harbour, in what became a tragic precursor of Dunkirk. As they struggled to load men and equipment onto the boats and sail for home, the French arrived. Sir John Moore stayed behind to hold them off and the two armies met at Elvina, just outside the city. The French and English both lost about 900 men, but the English were eventually defeated and Sir John himself was killed. He had, however, managed to delay the French while some 15,000 men got safely away by sea.

The city suffered from continuous social unrest during the rest of the 19th century, and lost many of its privileges along the way, but was captured by Nationalists within hours of the start of the Civil War, so escaped the worst reprisals during that period.

Today, it is a lively place with a thriving economy, based on the port, on its status as one of Spain's eleven naval garrison towns and on a wide variety of manufacturing industry.

Geographically, the town sits on a rocky peninsula, joined to the mainland by a narrow isthmus. It has two bays. The outer edges of the northern bay are rocky, but the inner curve, along the isthmus itself, is given over to three beaches, the Playa de Riazoa, the Playa de Orzan, and in the end, the little Playa de Matadero. It is a beautiful area, but the bay is open to the ocean and can be buffetted by high winds. The southern bay, almost totally enclosed since the addition of a long sea wall, is sheltered and calm, and is a positive hive of activity. The southern area beside the mainland houses the main commercial port, and the oil terminals, with a constant procession of supertankers and other massive ships ploughing their way in and out. Directly opposite this is the Darsena de la Marina, the brightly coloured fishing port, while at the other end of the old town area is the marina, with its hustle of super-rich yachts and gin palaces.

Although the city has long since spread along the mainland shore, and this is now the largest area of the city, the sites of real interest are those on the isthmus and peninsula. Begin your sightseeing on the **Avenida de la Marina**, and the **Paseo de la Darsena**, the long roads that curve around the southern bay. Not only are they lined by small restaurants and cafés, from where you get a wonderful view across the busy bay, but the houses that line the avenues are themselves spectacular. The whole length of the seafront is aglitter with beautifully designed *solañas* or glassed-in balconies with ornamental wooden, white-painted surrounds. They were all built in the late 18th and early 19th century and have become the city's trade mark, giving it the proud epithet of 'Crystal City'.

Follow the line of the bay around towards the marina and you will find yourself on the edge of the old city. Number 11, Calle Tabernas, beside the harbour, is a fine 18th-century mansion that was once the home of the distinguished 19th-century writer Doña Emilia Pardo Bazán. It is now the headquarters of the Royal Academy of Galicia, and houses a vast library of some 25,000 books and 10,000 manuscripts, along with various paintings and sculptures by eminent Galicians. On the first floor is a small museum dedicated to Doña Emilia.

At the far tip of the peninsula, guarding the entrance to the harbour is the **Castillo de San Antón**. Originally the site of a saintly hermitage, the first castle was built here in 1589, but the existing building dates from a refortification of the bay in 1779. These days it houses an Archaeological Museum, with an interesting collection of local Celtic material. Walking back towards the city, the **Paseo del Parrote** follows the line of the old city walls. Several of the gates along this section are still intact, including the 16th-century Puerta de San Miguel and the 17th-century Puerta del Clavo and Puerta de la Cruz.

Just to the right of the walls, in the centre of the old town, you come to the 18th-century Church of la Venerable Orden Tercera and the **Jardín de San Carlos**,

Town houses with elegant solañas *on the harbour front, La Coruña*

a charming garden laid out in 1843 inside the old fortress of San Carlos. At its centre is the granite tomb of the British general, Sir John Moore, who died in 1809 at the battle of Elvina. There are various commemorative texts carved on the surrounding walls, including tributes by the Duke of Wellington, the poet Charles Wolfe, and Gallegan poet, Rosalía de Castro. There is a wonderful view across the old city and harbour from the top of the citadel.

Walk through the park and at the far end on your right, you will come to the **Church and Convent of Santo Domingo**, a 17th-century Baroque church, with

193

an 18th-century façade, attributed to Alberto Ricoy. Inside are two fine chapels, both created by Melchor de Velasco. The Chapel de los Remedios was built in 1663 and the Chapel de la Virgen del Rosario in 1676. The latter has a beautiful altarpiece containing a statue of the Virgin of the Rosary, the patroness of the city. Just beyond here is an enchanting little square, the **Plazuela de Santa Bárbara**, used to hold chamber concerts in the summer. Part of the plaza is taken up by the Convent of Santa Bárbara. The existing building is 17th- and 18th-century, but the convent itself was founded in the 15th century on the spot of an older hermitage also dedicated to the saint. It now houses an enclosed order of Clarisan nuns.

The Calle Santa María leads up to the **Collegiate Church of Santa María del Campo**. Founded in about 1215, work on the building continued sporadically until the 15th century, and it now has various Romanesque and Gothic elements. The west front has three doorways with carved portals, the central one depicting the Adoration of the Magi. Inside, there are a number of fine polychrome statues, including one of the Annunciation and one of the Virgen del Poral, said to be the oldest in the city, along with several beautiful tombs.

To the left of the church, a small road leads down to the garden Plaza de Azcárraga, from where you can see the apsidal chapels of the **Church of Santiago**, the oldest church in the city, founded in the mid-12th century. It is basically Romanesque in design, although it has suffered from regular restoration and alteration over the centuries, and has, amongst other things, some 15th-century ogive arches and a 16th-century tower used as part of the city's defences. There are two fine portals, one depicting the Agnus Dei, the other Santiago Matamoro.

Keep going through the streets of the old town and out into the large **Plaza María Pita**, which marks the edge of the medieval city. The City Hall stands on the north side. On a side road just to the left of this is the 18th-century Baroque Church of San Jorge, designed principally by Domingo de Andrade. The church was dedicated at first to St Francis, whose image is still on display, was later switched to St Augustine, and was finally dedicated to St George only in 1838. Virtually opposite it is another fine Baroque church, San Nicolás, built by Clemente Sarela in the mid-18th century, but greatly altered in 1865.

On the far side of the Calle San Andrés, the **Museo de Belles Artes** is housed in the 18th-century building of the old Maritime Consulate. It has a fine collection of paintings, both by Galician artists and by a wide range of masters, Italian, French, Flemish, and Spanish, as well as local collections of ceramics and coins. Beside the museum is the 18th-century Church and Convent of the Capuchinas.

At the far northern end of the peninsula, staring out over the open sea is the **Torre de Hercules**. This lighthouse was built by the Romans in the 2nd century AD, on the orders of Emperor Trajan. Work was carried out under the direction of architect Cayo Servio Lupo. He would have good reason to be proud, for it has been working continuously ever since. A new surrounding wall was built in 1761 to protect the Roman construction: 105m above the sea, it has three floors, 242 steps, and its light can be seen for nearly 60km out to sea.

The last of the sights is out on a limb, on the mainland, in the Parque de Santa Margarita. The **Casa de las Ciencias** has several separate collections covering scientific theory, technology and the natural world. There is also a planetarium.

The Camino de Santiago – Villafranca del Bierzo to Santiago de Compostela

This route follows the last segment of the Camino Francés from the border with León at the Puerto de Pedrafita, just west of Villafranca del Bierzo on the NV1, across Galicia, until it finally reaches the Holy City, 800km from the Spanish border with France. *(For a description of the Puerto de Pedrafita and the next section east to León, see page 167).*

On the western slopes of the Puerto de Pedrafita lies the tiny hamlet of **Pedrafita do Cebreiro**. In the 12th century, Picaud described this as the 'most rugged of the mountains along the route', and even today it is easy to see why. Amongst the more modern buildings of the village huddle a group of Celtic-style *pallozas*, one of which is now a pilgrim hostel, while another houses a small Ethnographic Museum. The simple Church was built in the 9th century and is the oldest surviving on this branch of the pilgrim route, although it has been altered in successive centuries. In 1072, a monastery was set up here by Benedictine monks from the Abbey of San Giraldo de Aurillac in France to provide a hostel for pilgrims.

In about 1300, the little church was the scene of a famous miracle. One wet and windy day, only one peasant turned out to hear mass. While giving him communion, the disgruntled priest thought to himself that only a fool would have made the effort just for a little bread and wine. To his confusion, when he looked down, they had really turned to blood and flesh. News of the miracle and began to get confused with the story of the Holy Grail. The church became a major pilgrimage centre in its own right. In 1486, those good Catholics, Ferdinand and Isabela, arrived and presented the church with silver caskets in which to keep the relics. The chalice and paten are also on display, and there is a charming Romanesque statue of the Virgin holding the infant Jesus in her lap.

From here, the main road heads north-west to Lugo. Turn off to the left onto the LU634, which drops steeply before climbing again through the dramatic mountain landscape of the Sierra de O Courel to the 1337m Puerto del Poyo. This is the last high pass on the route, and pilgrims, ancient and modern, begin to drop thankfully to the less arduous hill country of central Galicia. There were several villages along this stretch that were important pilgrim stops – Liñares, Hospital da Condesa, and Fonfra amongst them. Today they are all but abandoned and few traces remain of the medieval bustle. At Triacastela, down in the river valley, began the twelfth and last stage of Picaud's route. The church here has been severely mauled but still has its Romanesque apse, and there is a pilgrim monument beside the road. It was traditional for pilgrims to pick up a stone here. They would carry this as far as Castañeda, over 100km further on, where it would be ground for mortar to help build the cathedral. Many modern pilgrims continue the tradition, but they now drop their stone on a large cairn, or *montjoie* that is the last stop before you enter Santiago.

About 10km on from here, still in the river valley, is the Benedictine **Monastery of San Julián de Samos**, thought to have been founded by San Martín Dumiense in the 6th century. This was not officially on the medieval route, but many made the short detour for the sake of a warm bed. There are small remnants from the earlier phases of the monastery's existence, such as the little 10th-century Chapel del Ciprés and one Romanesque doorway, but the main attraction is the 18th-century church, built by Fray Juan Velázquez between 1734 and 1748. The magnificent Baroque façade is by Fernando Casas y Novoa, who was also responsible for the facade of Santiago Cathedral. Inside, the church has a fine dome and several fine baroque altarpieces, some of which have incorporated earlier work into their panels. The cloister was begun in the 16th century and finished by Velázquez in the 18th. He was also responsible for the lovely Fountain of the Nereidas at its centre. The other buildings of the complex are modern, rebuilt after a major fire in 1951.

Keep following the same road west, now named the LU633, to **Sarria**. With a population of about 12,000, Sarria is one of the largest towns on this stretch of the route. This started life as the Roman town of Flavia Lambris, although the existing town grew up around the foot of the powerful medieval fortress of the Marquis of Sarria. It also became a popular stopping point on the pilgrim route with several churches, abbeys and hostels. Few remains are left of all this activity, and today the town is overwhelmingly modern, a production centre for cement and furniture. A single ruined tower of the fortress still stands on the hill above the town, while opposite this is the transitional 13th-century Church of El Salvador, which has an attractive portal. The Convent of los Padres Mercenarios dates from the 12th century, but was rebuilt in the 15th century in the Renaissance style. The church contains several fine tombs. The medieval pilgrim hospice later became the Monastery of La Magdalena and was almost entirely rebuilt in the 17th century.

Leave Sarria on the C535, heading west towards Portomarín. Just off the main route, the village of Barbadelo has a fine Romanesque church, while those in Paradela, Biville, Belante and Ferreiros are all small, pretty, but undistinguished. Twenty-four km from Sarria, you reach the Miño River and **Portomarín**. In 1963, a dam was built across the river, creating a huge new lake that snaked its way back along the river valley, threatening to drown one of the prettiest villages of the Galician pilgrim route. The answer was to move the village, so many of its finest buildings were dismantled stone by stone and carefully reconstructed away from the rising waters of the new Embalse de Belesar.

Along with several fine mansions and a token pillar and arch of the medieval bridge, which were built into the modern one, came two churches. The fortified Church of San Nicolás, which once belonged to the Knights of St John, was built in the late 12th and early 13th century. A solid rectangular block, topped by workmanlike battlements, the austerity of the exterior is alleviated by wonderful carved detail on the portals, thought to have been the work of the Maestro Mateo (see page 205) and his pupils. The west door shows the pantocrator surrounded by the old men of the apocalypse, all playing musical instruments. The north door depicts the Annunciation, and the south door, St Nicholas. Inside, it is remarkably simple, relying on the sheer grace of its proportions for its beauty. The other church is the charming 12th-century Church of San Pedro, with an ornate bell-wall above the main door and fine sculptural detail on its portal.

The area around here is one of the main wine-producing regions of Galicia and also makes *aguardiente*, a ferocious but popular spirit that is drunk neat during festivals, or flamed with sugar as the digestif *queimada*.

Continue west along the C535. A few kilometres on, the little village of Castromaior takes its name from the Celtic hill fort nearby. When you reach the main road, the N640, turn right (signposted to Lugo), and 9km on, you come to Guntín de Pallares.

If you wish to go to Lugo, keep going straight on, for 18km. For a description of the city, see page 181.

This route continues west along the L547 to Vilar de Doñas. The town is named after two 12th-century ladies who paid for the construction of the monastery and donated it to the Knights of Santiago, who owned it for nearly seven centuries. The existing church was built by the knights in about 1220. It is still primarily a Romanesque building, with a finely decorated portal and high vaults inside. The apse is covered in lovely frescoes, painted in 1386, showing Christ in glory surrounded by the evangelists, together with portraits of the church's lady benefactors. Along the walls are a number of fine tombs of various knights who died in battle.

Return to the junction with the C547 and turn right towards Santiago. Continue west to **Palas de Rei**, about 4km on. This was the twelfth and last of the 'official' stops of the Codex Calixtus, and it was also here that the northern route, via the coast and Lugo, finally joined the southern route for the last few miles to Santiago. There are two theories about the origin of the name. One states that the Visigothic king, Witiza, had a palace here, the other that it was a favoured stop of Alfonso XI. Whichever it was, the palace no longer survives and only the humble Romanesque façade of the Church of San Tirso is left to mark its importance.

A few kilometres west, still on the C547, in the little village of **Camiño**, is the pretty, rustic Romanesque Church of San Julián. Another few kilometres and you reach the delightful village of **Leboreiro**. After centuries when it seemed that hardly a stone had been added to these tumble-down houses, many have recently been restored, but so far, it is still a real working village, its streets more usually filled by peasants' carts than tourists' cars. It has an attractive Romanesque church with a Gothic portal, while there is a fine wayside cross in the centre of the village and a stretch of the old road remains visible on the edge of it. Leboreiro marks the border between the provinces of Lugo and Coruña.

Keep going to the west, past the village of Furelos, which has a pretty Gothic bridge, to **Melide**, officially the geographic centre of Galicia. Traditionally, when a new archbishop was sent from Rome, the mayor and corporation of Santiago would travel out from the city to meet him here.

There were a number of churches, chapels and hostels here, some of which still survive today. The finest of them is the Church of Santa María, a classic Romanesque church with a richly decorated façade. Inside, it has a series of lively late 12th-century frescoes in the apse, and the only 12th-century altar in Galicia. There is a lovely wayside cross outside. The other early church of note is San Pedro, whose transitional, 13th-century façade, was rescued ahead of the bulldozers when the new road went in, and moved to its current location, along with the pilgrim cross that is said to be the oldest in the state. In the centre of town, the former Convent of Sancti Spiritus, now the parish church, is a fine Baroque building, with an 18th-century portal and altarpiece, and several 16th-century frescoes that date back to the earlier church. The Church of the Pious Work of St Anthony was built by Archbishop Mateo Segade in 1671, to a design by Domingo de Andrade.

Amongst the other fine buildings in the town are the pilgrim hostel and the Town Hall, which is housed in a baroque chapel.

This route now takes a slight detour from the direct line of the pilgrim route (which, for purists, continues along the C547, via Castañeda, where the pilgrims used to drop their pebbles at the limekilns which no longer exist). This route turns north from Melide, heading along the small road to **Toques** where the Church of San Antolín still has traces of its pre-Romanesque routes under the eaves of the presbytery. The majority of the church is Romanesque, but inside, there are a fine 13th-century Calvary and some 16th-century frescoes.

Continue north to the T-junction, then turn left along the LC233 to **Sobrado**. This vast Monastery was founded in 1142 by the Cistercian order, whose members still live there today. There are some of the earlier buildings left, such as the 12th-century Chapel de la Magdalena and Chapterhouse, a 13th-century kitchen, a sacristy designed by Juan de Herrera in 1471, and hospice with a façade dating from 1555.

In about 1673, however, a major programme of rebuilding began that was to continue for the next 100 years, and today, the monastery is best known partly for its sheer size, partly for its wonderful Baroque architecture. The first part to be completed was the Chapel del Rosario, designed by Domingo de Andrade in 1673. Next came the façade of the church, designed by Pedro de Monteagudo and completed in 1676. The Great Cloister was finished in 1744 and the Garden Cloister in 1753.

Leave Sobrado heading west on the LC232 to Corredoiras, where you turn left onto the LC234 to **Arzúa**, back on the main pilgrim route. There is relatively little of interest on this last leg of the journey, so keep going until you reach **Labacolla**, right on the edge of the city. This is now thoroughly built up, with the airport runway actually following the line of the old road. In the Middle Ages, it was a peaceful sanctuary with a small stream in which the pilgrims used to wash and spruce before tackling the last 5km into the city. The stream is still there, between the Baroque Church of Labacolla and the little Sanctuary of San Roque. There is a lovely pilgrim cross in front of the church.

Just off the road, behind the little village of San Marcos, is the **Monte del Gozo**. On its summit is a huge cairn or *montjoie* where modern pilgrims all drop the stones they have carried from Triacastela. This hill offered the first view of the Holy City and, although it was slightly off the route, a trip to the top got you 100 days' more indulgence. Traditionally, every band of travellers would race to the top, and the one to arrive first would be declared their king. This custom contributed to the number of people in the world still called King, Leroi and other national variations today.

From here, the pilgrims would enter the city through the Concheiros district, where they would buy scallops from street traders, eat the contents and stick the shell in their hats.

Santiago de Compostela

For over a thousand years, millions of pilgrims have struggled their way across Europe, enduring untold hardships, just to reach this Holy City. Success, for the faithful, meant that they could halve their allotted time in purgatory. This, together with the many other indulgences and remissions they could pick up en route virtually assured them of an easy passage into heaven. It was felt to be a prize well worth the effort.

The earliest known settlement here was a Celtic village, which grew upon the Roman invasion into the city and port of Iria Flavia. This collapsed, along with the rest of the Western empire, in the early 5th century, but a small Suebian town remained in existence for the next couple of centuries.

The current city was founded after the miraculous rediscovery of the tomb of St James in 813 (see page 200). A small chapel was built on the site, and as the number of pilgrims began to grow, so too did the size of the church and the town. In 896, the first major church was built on the orders of King Alfonso III (el Magno – the Great). This was destroyed, along with most of the town, in 997 AD, when it was attacked by the Moorish general, Almanzor. Only the tomb itself remained intact. According to legend, Almanzor found a single monk still praying beside the tomb and was so impressed by his piety that he ordered his soldiers to keep it safe. He did however ride off with the two great bells from the cathedral tower, which he took back to Córdoba and placed, inverted, in the mosque as oil lamps.

The town and church were rebuilt in 1003 by Bishop Pedro Mezonzo and in the mid-11th century, another bishop, D. Cresconio built the city walls as a defence against further attack. Construction on the existing cathedral began in 1075 and in 1090, the see was officially moved here from Iria Flavia. In 1104, Bishop Gelmirez went to Rome and persuaded the Pope to turn the city into an archbishopric, and in 1189, a papal bull signed by Alexander III elevated its status to Holy City, one of only three in the world (the others are Rome and Jerusalem). In 1236, the bells were eventually rescued from Córdoba by King Fernando III (el Santo) and were returned to Santiago, carried on the shoulders of Moorish prisoners. Throughout the Middle Ages, Santiago was a magnet that drew millions from across Europe, completely altering the artistic heritage of the continent in the process. With this vast influx of visitors, the city itself grew and flourished.

In 1589, with Sir Francis Drake, known locally as the 'English pirate', rampaging along the coast, the relics of St James were hidden for safety. Their removal from view coincided with the height of the Reformation and the flood of pilgrims dried to a trickle. It was 1813, with Napoleon's French army finally defeated and off Spanish soil, before they were put back on display in the cathedral.

Today, the city has a permanent population of about 90,000 and over 1.5 million visitors a year. In Holy Years (when the Feast of St James falls on a Sunday and extra indulgences are handed out), up to two million flood in for the festival alone. The last two Holy Years of the 20th century are in 1993 and 1999.

The city has long outgrown its medieval walls, but while the streets outside are, in the main, wide and impersonal with far too many unlovely buildings, within

St James

Son of Zebedee and brother of John, St James was a fisherman from Galilee and one of Christ's disciples. Known as 'the Thunderer', on account of his loud voice, he is said to have left Palestine after the Ascension and travelled west, eventually reaching Hispania, where he was washed ashore at the mouth of the River Ulla, near Padrón in Galicia. The stone to which he theoretically moored his boat can be seen today under the altar of the parish church. He is credited with having introduced Christianity to Spain, although he seems to have made little real impact on the local populace. In 44 AD, he returned to Palestine, where he was beheaded by Herod, the first of the apostolic martyrs. One version of the story now says that his followers fled with his body, taking it back to Spain for burial near his original landing site. The other claims that they put his body in a marble sepulchre and pushed it out to sea in an unmanned boat which they found on the beach. This was then steered back to Galicia by the angels who deposited it near the Roman capital, Iria Flavia.

The eighth and ninth centuries saw St James's mutation into a warrior: the Christian victory against the Moors at Covadonga in 722 was attributed to his intervention, and later it was claimed an that he was seen on the battlefield, a shining knight on a white horse bearing a white standard with a red cross, during the Christian victories at Clavijas in 844 and Simancas in 939. It is difficult to know how this humble fishermen became a bloody warrior, but to a people desperately in need of a God-given hero, he became the symbol of Christian resistance, with the title of *Matamore* or 'Slayer of the Moors'.

The tomb was rediscovered in 813 when a star led, some say, a group of shepherds, some a hermit named Pelagro, to the spot. This is the origin, according to tradition, of the word Compostela, a corruption of the Latin *campus stellae*, or Field of the Star. More recent proof that it was the site of a Roman graveyard, however, makes it reasonable to suppose that it was in reality always *compostela*, the Latin word for cemetery. Whatever the truth behind the site, it was accepted by the local bishop, Theodomir, who built a church over the site, the place where the cathedral still stands today.

The fame of the site grew by leaps and bounds with numerous miracles being attributed to the tomb. As the pilgrimage grew (see page 28), St James mutated yet again, this time becoming the archetypal pilgrim, a gentle man with cape and broad-rimmed hat and staff.

To this day St James remains one of the most influential of the Catholic pantheon and the patron saint of Spain. His city, Santiago de Compostela, is one of only three holy cities in the world, the others being Jerusalem and Rome. His feast day, 25 July, is a Spanish national holiday.

the walls survives a near perfect old city that must surely rank amongst the most beautiful in the world. Every street is filled with charm, and every building touched with some fascinating detail. Every corner reveals some new and wonderful view, from a humble fountain to the magnficence of the cathedral itself. Best of all, in the midst of all this architectural splendour, the city is still alive, home to a real community, carefully preserved but never fossilised, while the plentiful tourist facilities have not been allowed to take over.

Start your tour in the huge **Plaza de Obradoiro** (also known as the Plaza de España) that stretches out in front of the west door of the cathedral. The square itself is

The sculpture of St James as a pilgrim, above the Puerta Santa of Santiago Cathedral

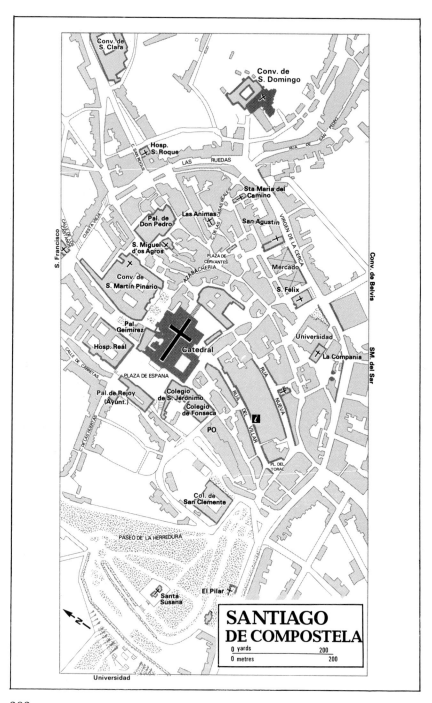

SANTIAGO
DE COMPOSTELA

0 yards   200
0 metres   200

wonderfully harmonious in spite of the fact that each of its magnificent buildings is of a different period, and represents a different aspect of life – charity, education, justice and religion.

To your left as you face the cathedral is the **Hotel de los Reyes Catholicos**. This was originally built as a pilgrim hostal on the orders of the Catholic monarchs, Ferdinand and Isabela, in 1492, and designed by Enrique de Egas. The superb Plateresque façade was the work of two French sculptors, Marín de Blas and Guillén Colas between 1501 and 1511. There are portraits of Ferdinand and Isabela in medallions above the main door. The Baroque balcony (the best place from which to watch any festivities) was added in 1678. Inside the building is laid out around four cloisters, two 16th-century Renaissance, two 17th-century Baroque, with a chapel at their centre. Even after the downturn in the pilgrim trade, the building remained in use as a hospital, but in 1954 it was converted into a hotel and is now one of the finest hotels in all Spain, run as part of the parador chain. Its marvellous collection of furnishings make it as good as most museums. The tradition of hospitality to pilgrims is still maintained, as those presenting a *compostela*, the official recognition that they have completed their pilgrimage, are entitled to a free meal.

To your right, at the opposite end of the square is the much smaller **Colegio Menor de San Jeronimo**. Built around the earlier doorway of an old hostel, this 15th-century building was erected as the home of the newly fledged University of Santiago, and still houses the Director's office today. Attached to the back of this, just off the plaza, is the **Colegio Mayor de Fonseca** (also known as the Colegio Mayor de Santiago Alfeo) which was for many years the main teaching block of the university, and is now a library. The building itself is a magnificent Renaissance work, founded by Don Alfonso III de Fonseca, who was Archbishop of Santiago from 1504 and Archbishop of Toledo from 1524 until his death in 1534. It was designed by Juan de Alava and built between 1532 and 1546. Inside it has a wonderfully ornate cloister and a fine hall with Mudéjar strapwork on the ceiling.

Back on the square, opposite the cathedral, the Town Hall and the Government of Galicia are both housed in the huge neo-classical **Palacio de Rajoy**, built in the 18th century by Archbishop Don Bartolomé Rajoy y Losada and designed by Ferro Caaveiro and Carlos Lemaur. The statue above the central pediment is a celebration of Santiago Matamore and the Christian victory at the Battle of Clavijo. Down the steep narrow street to the north of this, you will see the façade of the little Church of San Fructuoso.

Finally, turn back towards the Cathedral itself. To its right is the outer wall of the cloister, to the left, the **Palacio de Gelmírez**, the earliest of the buildings in the square, constructed in the 12th and 13th centuries, although the existing walls were built in the 16th and 18th centuries to stop its leaning walls from collapsing. The top two floors now house the Archbishop's palace. The lower Romanesque and Gothic apartments are open to the public. Particularly fine are the 20m long hall on the ground floor and the vast, 30m long Synod Hall with ogive vaulting, slender columns and fine capitals. Amongst the carvings are a full orchestra of musicians and servants carrying the makings of a magnificent feast.

The **cathedral** façade itself is much later in period than the main body of the

Gigantes in procession during the festival of St James in Santiago de Compostela

cathedral, which was constructed between 1075, consecrated 1124 and completed in about 1211. The right tower, the Tower of the Bells, was built in the 17th century by José Peña de Toro. The left tower, the Torre de la Carraca, was designed by master architect, Fernando Casas y Novoa in 1750, to match it. Casas also built the central portico at the same time, and the whole has become an elaborate triumph of ornate Baroque design. Between the two arms of the great stairway leading up to the west door, a small door leads into the Romanesque Crypt, built in 1175 as a way of evening up the slope on which the cathedral is built. It has many ornate capitals and also contains some of the early choir stalls and various other fine sculptures.

Just inside the Baroque façade however, the original 12th-century façade remains intact and, sheltered from the elements, it has retained not only all its detail, but even some of its paint. The **Portico de la Gloria** is probably the greatest single surviving work of Romanesque art in the world. It stretches the full width of the cathedral, with each of its three doorways corresponding to one of the naves. An inscription on one lintel shows it to be the work of one Maestro Mateo, completed in 1188, during the reign of Fernando II. In total there are 200 sculptures that between them tell almost the entire story of the Bible. Above the main arch, Christ sits in glory. Surrounding him, in all three arches are the evangelists, apostles, prophets and saints, angels carrying the instruments of the passion, the 24 old men of the apocalypse, each one playing a different musical instrument. There are visions of heaven and hell, the vices, mythical demons and various animals, wild and domestic. Even Adam and Eve and all the peoples of the world, Jews, Gentiles and Heathens are present. Part of what makes it all so special is the imagination and detail of the work, but above all, it is the vivid personality of every figure, their emotions written deep into the stone. Here, the maestro gave us a statue of a laughing St James at a time when most sculpture was still rigid and symbolic.

A Jesse tree, showing the genealogy of Christ, winds up the central column, also known as the Pilgrim Pillar. It is tradition for pilgrims to bend and kiss the base of the column in thanks for a safe journey. Over the centuries, so many have done so, that finger holes have been worn deep into the stone. After this, the pilgrim goes round to the far side of the pillar where there is a relief portrait of Maestro Mateo himself, kneeling and offering his work to God. Pilgrims tap their foreheads gently against the figure in hopes of gaining some of his wisdom. The custom has earned him the nickname of el Santo Dos Croques (the saint of cracked heads).

Inside most of the stonework of the cathedral is untouched Romanesque, with gracious, clean lines and curves alleviated only by a thousand capitals with every form of decoration from Visigothic knots to mythical beasts. Many of the windows of the clerestory have been filled in over the centuries however and at first glance the fabric of the building itself fades into the gloom, leaving only the flicker of gold and silver to fill the senses. Its pilgrims have brought the cathedral enormous wealth and it is literally filled with silver and gilt, huge canvases and fine sculptures.

There are only two chapels lining the left wall of the simple nave, the 17th-century Chapel of Christ of Burgos, in the shape of a Greek cross, and the Communion Chapel, founded in the 15th century, but rebuilt in the 18th century in the neo-classical style.

To the right of the main entrance is the Chapel of the Relics and the Royal Pantheon, designed by Juan de Alava in the 16th century. A great many relics are kept here, including a gold cross donated by Alfonso III in the 9th century, said to contain two fragments of the True Cross, and a silver reliquary ornamented with gem stones that contains the head of St James the Younger, the apostle who later became Bishop of Jerusalem. Amongst the tombs inside the chapel are several members of the royal family of the 12th to 14th centuries. Near to the entrance of the chapel stands an equestrian statue of Santiago Matomore that was carved in wood by Gambino in the 18th century. It is this that is carried in the religious procession on the saint's feastday.

A little further up the nave, also on the right, is the Treasury. Amongst the many dazzling pieces, probably the finest is the 16th-century Renaissance Monstrance of Antonio Arfe, made of gilded silver and showing scenes from the lives of Jesus and St James. There are several other gold pieces including another monstrance, a chalice and cruets, all donated by a Mexican devotee, Archbishop Monroy, in the 17th century, and a number of magnificent silver pieces including two great shells and the silver hammer used to open the Holy Door (see page 208).

Overpowering the whole cathedral is the enormous high altar clearly visible from the other end of the church since the 16th-century choir was removed earlier this century. Donated by Archbishop Monroy in the 17th century, the altar itself was made from Mexican silver by two local silversmiths, Montaos and Figueroa. A small silver statue of the Virgin by Pecul stands above the tabernacle. Behind the main altar is a vast 17th-century altarpiece, an elaborate Baroque creation of gilded wood and marble, jasper and paint. It is crowned by a statue of St James on horseback by Mateo de Pedro, but the main focus of it all is a central niche which contains a seated stone statue of St James, carved in 1211 by Maestro Mateo or one of his pupils. The statue itself is 12th-century, but its seat and mantle, of silver inset with precious stones, were donated by Archbishop Monroy. Pilgrims queue to walk round behind the altar, kiss the mantle and make their prayers to the saint. On either side of the altar are fine silver grills both made in the 18th century and above hang two enormous chandeliers, also of silver. The chapel also contains two fine bronze pulpits, the work of Juan Bautista de Celma in the 16th century.

Directly underneath the high altar is a crypt. The outer ambulatory of this is part of the 9th-century church of Alfonso III, the inner wall is Roman. On the main altar, a huge silver reliquary, made by Rey y Martinez in the 19th century, houses the remains of St James and his two disciples, St Anastasius and St Theodore.

The octagonal dome just before the high altar, created in 1445, is used to hang the botafumeiro, an enormous brass incensor that replaced a silver one stolen by Napoleon's troops. Used only on feast-days, it takes eight men to swing this huge contraption which swoops low over the heads of the crowd billowing sweet smoke that hangs in the air for hours afterwards. The rest of the time, it is displayed in the library.

Ten small chapels surround the ambulatory behind the high altar. All of them have great works of art, but the finest must be the second on the right, the Chapel of Mondragón, which has a superb renaissance grill made by Juan Francés, and a 15th-century terracotta relief by Miguel Ramón. At the head of the church, in the centre, is the Chapel of the Saviour, a beautiful Romanesque chapel in which the very first stone of the cathedral was laid in 1075.

Traditionally, pilgrims were given communion here, and also came here to receive their compostela. This was a sort of certificate of merit that proved they had completed the journey and that they were entitled to spiritual benefit. It also did them a great deal of material good, such as opening the door to free board and lodging on the way home. These days, pilgrims should ask for their *compostela* at the Cathedral secretariat.

In the north transept, on your right, up a small flight of steps, is the Chapel of La Corticela, which has a lovely Romanesque doorway depicting the adoration of the Magi.

In the south transept, a Plateresque doorway leads through to the cloister. This was built in the 16th century to designs by Juan de Alava and Gil de Hontanon to replace the Romanesque one. One of the largest cloisters in Spain, the actual decor is remarkably plain, although the arcades have fine ribbed vaulting, and there is a delicate filigree balustrade above. The Cathedral Museum is housed in the west wing. This starts with the Archives. The most important book here is the 12th-century *Codex Calixtus*, an illustrated manuscript recounting the adventures of Charlemagne and containing Picaud's account of the pilgrim route. Next door is the Library, decorated by a series of 18th-century frescoes by Arias Varela depicting the life of St James. This is where the *botafumeiro* is displayed when it is not in use, and there are also various parchment books and hymnals.

The Capitular Room marks the start of the cathedral's superb tapestry collection, which continues right through the first floor. These tapestries are mainly of the 17th and 18th centuries and include Flemish and Gobelin works as well as some from Spain. In the first room upstairs, most are copied from works by Rubens, while in the second, the designs are by Teniers and the fourth, Goya. The range of subjects is vast, from Hannibal and his elephants to hunting scenes, smugglers and even a guitar player. The archaelogical collection on the second floor is made up mainly of finds from in and around the cathedral itself including many details from the Romanesque cathedral that were removed by later generations.

Leave the cathedral by the main door and turn right, past the Palacio de Gelmírez. The Calle de San Francisco leads up to the **Convent of San Francisco**. This was founded by St Francis of Assisi himself in 1214, while on pilgrimage here. The land was donated by the Benedictines for the rent of one basket of fish a year. There are a few fragments of the early monastery here, and the present building dates to the 18th century. An ornate stone cross representing the life of St Francis, carved in the 18th century by Miguel Ferro Caaveiro, stands in front of the main entrance.

Turn right along the Cuesta Vieja, and right again along the Puerta de la Pena and you come to the **Plaza de San Martín** and the Church of San Martín, the church belonging to the Monastery of San Martín Pinario. This is an early 17th-century building with a Renaissance-style façade designed by Gines Martínez. It has a huge Baroque altarpiece created by Fernando Casas y Novoa in 1733 that is considered to be the sculptor's finest work.

Walk up the Plaza San Miguel opposite the entrance to the church. On your right is the 18th-century Baroque **Church of San Miguel dos Agros** and at the top of the road, the 15th-century Gothic **Palacio de Don Pedro** contains the Museum of Pilgrimage. Turn right and walk through to the Plaza de Cervantes. Tucked in to the east of the square is the Church of San Benito, with Romanesque, Gothic and neo-classical elements, while on the south side is the 17th-century former Town Hall. Turn west along the Calle Azabachería, which leads down into the

Plaza de la Azabachería (also known as the Plaza Inmaculada) on the north side of the cathedral.

This marked the official end of the pilgrim route, and pilgrims stopped here to rest and wash in the fountain before entering the cathedral. Many arrived in tatters and the cathedral canons would hand out new clothes. The old ones were left beneath the iron cross, the *Crus d'os farrapos*, to be taken away for burning. The square takes its name from the *azabacheros*, or jet carvers, who were one of the two biggest manufacturing guilds in the city. They would set up stalls here, carving little souvenir figures of St James to sell to pilgrims.

For a long while this north door, the Puerta del Paraso (the Paradise Door) was the cathedral's main entrance. Today, the entire north façade is an ornate neo-classical work by Rodriguez Ventura, completed in 1770.

On the north side of the square is the **Monastery of San Martín Pinario**. This Benedictine institution was founded in 912 AD. Over the next few centuries it grew in power and importance, to control some 30 other monasteries and came to rival even the Cathedral. The existing building was constructed in the 16th century to be more in keeping with the monastery's illustrious status, while the doorway is 17th-century Baroque, by Fray Manuel de los Martires. Inside, there are two cloisters, one Baroque, one with a beautiful fountain by Fernando Casas y Novoa. Beside this is a huge, beautiful unsupported stairway topped by an ornate Baroque dome.

Take the small road around the back of the cathedral into the **Plaza de la Quintana de Muertos**. Its name means the 'square of the cemetery where food was sold'. It stands on one of the largest sections of the Roman cemetery, and was, by the Middle Ages, a sort of fast-food paradise, full of street stalls and wandering vendors. There are two distinct sections to this plaza, connected by wide steps. In the upper section stands the Casa de la Parra (the House of the Bunch of Grapes), a fine 17th-century Baroque mansion decorated with ornate carvings of fruit, interspersed with garlands, and real vines growing from the wrought iron balconies. In the lower section, at the east end of the cathedral, is the Puerta Santa (Holy Door), designed by Fernández Lechuga in 1611. An elegant neo-classical framework has been provided for a number of beautiful 12th-century Romanesque statues carved by Maestro Mateo that originally stood in the choir. The wonderful statue of St James as pilgrim above the door is 17th-century. The door is normally kept locked, and is opened only during Holy Years. From here, you can also get the best view of the Berenguela Tower (Clock Tower), the tallest of the cathedral at 80m high. The first level is 14th-century, and the top is 17th-century Baroque, by Domingo de Andrade.

Walk round the clock tower into the **Plaza de las Platerías**, the last of the squares surrounding the cathedral. This is named after the silversmiths who were, together with the jet workers, one of the two main guilds of medieval Santiago. The arches under the cathedral were once used as silversmiths' shops. This square is also on two levels, and is literally surrounded by a feast of wonderful buildings, including sections of the Romanesque apse and the east wall of the cloister. To your right, on the upper level is the Puerta de las Plateras (the Silversmiths' Door), a magnificent Romanesque portal with two arches, both covered in fine, low relief carvings. In the lower level, both the central Fountain of the Horses and the Chapter House are the work of 18th-century Baroque architect, Fernández Sarela.

There are so many other wonderful mansions and churches scattered across the streets of both the old city and the modern town that it is impossible to list them all here. The best thing to do is to put on comfortable shoes, arm yourself with a street plan, and just set off. It is hard to get lost for more than a few minutes and every new street and alley is a delight.

There are three particularly fine spots in the modern town. The **Collegiate Church**

Regional costume at the festival of St James, Santiago de Compostela (SNTO)

of Santa María del Sar, to the south-east, was built between 1133 and 1170 and contains some of the finest Romanesque art in the city. Particularly beautiful is the exterior of the apse, with its classic Romanesque curves and decorated arches. The flying buttresses along the nave were added in the 18th century. Inside, the columns lean curiously, probably due to subsidence. One side of the cloister has retained its superb Romanesque style with a wonderful array of decoration on the arches and capitals. The **Convento de Santo Domingo de Bonaval,** just outside the old town, almost due east of the cathedral, is thought to have been founded by the saint himself, during his second pilgrimage in 1220. It has a fine Baroque façade and an extraordinary, three-tier spiral staircase, both designed by by Domingo de Andrade in about 1667, while there is also a beautiful Renaissance façade of 1561. The convent buildings now house the Museum of the Galician People, while the chapel is home to the Pantheon of Illustrious Galicians. Among those buried here are the poet, Rosalía de Castro, Alfredo Branas, the founder of Galician nationalism, and the sculptor, Asorey.

From the Paseo de la Herradura, the small park to the south, encircling the Church of St Susan, there is a fine panoramic view across the old city.

Without a doubt, the best time to be here is over the Apostle's feast-day of 25 July, although the town is heaving with people then, and you will need to book accommodation well in advance. The festivities have stretched out these days to a jamboree nearly three weeks long, but on the night of 24 July, there is a massive and spectacular firework display over the Plaza del Obradoiro, with even the façade of the cathedral brought into play. The feast-day itself starts with a formal military review followed by a formal mass, usually attended by a member of the royal family. After this, the *gigantes*, folk dancers and musicians take to the streets. With formal concerts, classical and rock, as well as every other form of entertainment you can think of, it is a giddy whirl of sound and colour that continues round the clock. If you get tired, just find yourself a good seat in a pavement café and let the celebrations come to you. In the year that I attended, however, there was a clear example of the trend of things to come in the new Spain. In this Holiest of cities, with thousands of pilgrims queuing to pay their homage to the saint, they had forgotten to put the religious procession itself onto the festival programme. It took a call to the bishop before anyone could tell me when and where it would be.

Galicia:
General Information

Regional tourist office:
Junta de Galicia, Consejera de Turismo, Juventud y Deportes, Plaza de Pontevedra 22, 2°, 15003 La Coruña (tel. (981) 220 043).

La Coruña Province

LA CORUÑA
Tourist Office, Darsena de la Marina, s/n, 15001 (tel. (981) 221 822).
Where to stay:
Hotel Finisterre, Paseo del Parrote 22, 15001 (tel. (981) 205 400; fax (981) 208 462). The best hotel in town. It is situated in the centre of town, beside the marina with excellent views over the bay. It has a swimming pool and tennis court. Expensive.
Ciudad de la Coruña, Poligono Adormideras, 15002 (tel. (981) 211 100; fax (985) 224 610). Large hotel set in a wonderful location on the end of the peninsula beside the Torre de Hercules, with a swimming pool and sea views. Moderate.
Hotel España, Juana de Vega 7, 15004 (tel. (981) 224 506). Large modern hotel right in the centre of town, within easy walking distance of both the port and the beach. Cafeteria only. Cheap-moderate.
Where to eat:
Coral, La Estrella 2, 15003 (tel. (981) 221 082). Unexciting surroundings, but good traditional regional cuisine. Moderate-expensive.
El Rapido, c/ La Estrella 7 (tel. (981) 226 785). The best seafood restaurant in the city, with a formal restaurant upstairs and an informal bar on the ground floor. Expensive.
Yéboles, c/ Troncoso 14 (Zona Plaza Maria Pita) (tel. (981) 206 220). Popular place for drinks, tapas and affordable food. Cheap.

EL FERROL
Where to stay and eat:
Parador de Ferrol, Plaza Eduardo Pondal, 15400 (tel. (981) 365 720; fax (981) 356 720). A large, imposing white building on the edge of the modern city,

211

overlooking the docks. Decorated on a nautical theme, with everything from anchors to globes and back again. Moderate.

Hotel Almirante, Maria 2, 15400 (tel. and fax (981) 325 311). Large modern hotel with its own good restaurant, the Gavia. Moderate.

NEDA

Where to stay:

Pazo de la Merced, 15510 (tel. (981) 382 200; fax (981) 380 104). A delightful 17th-century manor with only five rooms, all well-restored and furnished. There is a swimming pool in the garden and a good view over the Ferrol estuary. Only a few kilometres from El Ferrol, this would be a good alternative for those who prefer not to stay in town. Bed and breakfast only. Top end of mid-range.

SANTIAGO DE COMPOSTELA

Tourist Office, Rua del Villar, 43, 15705 (tel. (981) 584 081).

Where to stay:

Hotel Reyes Catolicos, Plaza de España, 1, 15705 (tel. (981) 582 200; fax (981) 563 094). Named after Ferdinand and Isabela, who built it in 1499 as a pilgrim hospice, this is a vast and stunningly beautiful building planned round four cloisters, right beside the cathedral. The furnishings are as sumptuous as the building. It is now one of Spain's finest hotels, and if you are ever going to splash out, this is the place to do so, especially if you are planning to visit during the fiesta, as the hotel has a long balcony, open only to guests, from where you get a bird's eye view of all the celebrations and parades. Expensive.

Hotel Compostela, Hórreo 1, 15702 (tel. (981) 585 700; fax (981) 563 269). Large, comfortable modern hotel just outside the walls of the old city, within easy walking distance of the cathedral. Moderate.

La Estela, Rajoy, 1 (tel. (981) 582 796). A small family-run bed and breakfast in the heart of the old city, just off the main plaza beside the cathedral. Cheap.

Hostal Suso, Ría de Villar 65, 15700 (tel. (981) 581 159). Small, simple family-run hotel right in the heart of the old city, with its own, popular tapas bar. Cheap.

Where to eat:

Restaurante Don Gaiferos, Rúa Nova 23 (tel. (981) 583 894). Small, elegant restaurant in the centre of the old city. Expensive.

Anexo Vilas, Av Villagarcía 21, 15706 (tel. (981) 598 637). Founded in 1915, this restaurant has grown into one of the finest in the city, serving traditional regional food. Expensive.

El Asesino, Plaza de la Universidad 16 (tel. (991) 581 568). A friendly welcome and home cooking. Cheap.

Metate, Callejón de San Pelayo (tel. (981) 581 916). Run by students and doubling as an art gallery, this popular place serves chocolate-flavoured cocktails to celebrate its home in an old chocolate factory. Cheap.

Bodega Abrigadoiro, c/ Carrera del Conde 5 (tel. (981) 563 163). A lively, cheerful tapas bar where the bottles are kept cool by a working water wheel. Cheap.

SOBRADO DO LOS MONJES

Where to stay and eat:

Hotel San Marcus, 15312 (tel. (981) 787 527). Small modern hotel, built in the traditional style with glazed balconies, overlooking the marketplace and monastery. The rooms are attractively furnished, the food traditional. Cheap.

Lugo Province

CERVO
Where to stay and eat:
Posada O Almacén, Ctra de Sargadelos (tel. (982) 557 836). A simply, but charmingly, converted 18th-century warehouse in a small hamlet near Cervo. Cheap.

LUGO
Tourist Office, Plaza de España, 27–29, 27001 (tel. (982) 231 361).
Where to stay:
Gran Hotel Lugo, Av Ramón Ferreiro 21, 27002 (tel. (982) 224 152; fax (982) 241 660). Large, luxury hotel with all the trimmings, including a swimming pool. Moderate-expensive.
Hotel Méndez Núñez, Reina 1, 27001 (tel. (982) 230 711; fax (982) 229 738). Large modern hotel in the city centre. Bed and breakfast only. Moderate.
Where to eat:
Mesón de Alberto, Cruz 4, 27001 (tel. (982) 228 310). A little bit of everything here, with a bar, *bodega*, and restaurant. The food ranges from *raciones* to full meals, and is based on traditional Galician recipes. Moderate.

MONDOÑEDO
Where to stay:
Hotel Montero II, Avenida Candido Martinez 8, Plaza de España, 27740 (tel. (982) 521 041). Small, prettily furnished hotel in a typical Galician town house beside the cathedral. Bed and breakfast only. Moderate.

RIBADEO
Where to stay:
Parador de Ribadeo, Amador Fernández, s/n, 27700 (tel. (982) 110 825; fax (982) 110 346). One of relatively few modern paradors around, and the best hotel in the town. Best of all are its views, overlooking the mouth of the ría, the fishing harbour, and, on the far shore, the town of Castropol. Moderate.
Where to eat:
Parador de Robadeo, as above.
O'Xardin, Reinante 20, 27700 (tel. (982) 110 222). Pretty restaurant. The food is good, with no pretensions to *haute cuisine*. Moderate.

VILLALBA
Where to stay and eat:
Parador Condes de Villalba, Valeriano Valesuso, 27800 (tel. (982) 510 011; fax (982) 510 090). This tiny parador, in the 13th-century octagonal tower of Los Andrade, is the main reason for visiting Villalba. It has thick stone walls, Rapunzel-like windows, murals in the foyer – and only 6 rooms. Ask to visit the roof, from where the views are stupendous. My favourite hotel in the whole region. Expensive.

VIVEIRO
Where to stay and eat:
Hotel Ego, Playa de Area, 27850 (tel. (982) 560 987; fax (982) 561 762). Light, airy and elegant modern hotel out of the town, beside the sea, with a specialist fish restaurant and terrace. Moderate.

Navarra

Navarra is one of the great ancient kingdoms of Spain, once extending over the Pyrenees into southern France. Today, it covers an area of 10,420 square kilometres, a divided land with continually changing scenery. The northern border is the border with France, a dramatic mountainscape of rocky peaks and lush forest, much of which is set aside in a series of stunningly beautiful national parks and hunting preserves. Hunting is still a favourite activity here. Game is on every menu, and in season, some 70,000 pigeons are shot each year. Surprisingly, there is still plenty of wildlife, including wild boar and red and roe deer, to be seen by those who are prepared to be patient.

To the north-east of Pamplona lies the great Irati Forest. Covering a total of about 300 square kilometres, of which two-thirds are in Navarra, this is thought to be one of the largest beech woods left in Europe. Directly to the north, around the Roncesvalles area is the Quinto Real, while further west still, as the land tapers down to the Atlantic coast, you reach the Señorio de Bertiz, a rich forest land of oaks, beeches and chestnuts. This is probably the most accessible of the forest reserves and also now includes a botanical garden with some 120 different species of tree. Closer still to the coast, you reach the gentle dairy pastures of the foothills, more typical of the Basque Country.

To the south of the mountains, the rain-shadow turns the plains into an almost Mediterranean-style sea of wheat, vines and even olives. Further south still, the area known as the Ribera leads from irrigated vegetable fields to windswept and twisted desert lands.

The earliest known inhabitants of the region were the enigmatic Basques, who still make up a sizeable proportion of the population, but historically, this has been the crossroads through which wave after wave of invaders have entered Spain. First came the Romans, who settled the central plains. Then came the Visigoths, and shortly afterwards the Moors. Charlemagne's great battles against the Moors were fought here. Throughout it all, however, the Basques, secure in their impenetrable mountain strongholds, retained an extraordinary degree of independence.

The county of Navarra was officially formed in the 9th century, and in 905 AD, it was turned into a kingdom by Sancho I. In the 12th century, during the reign of Sancho VI (the Wise), the first *fueros* were agreed. These rules of common law enshrined an agreement between the monarchy and people, in which the king swore to respect local traditional law and gain the approval of his subjects for any laws which he might enact. They also held a remarkably useful loophole that said the inhabitants of Navarra might 'regard but not act upon' any laws with which they didn't agree. Needless to say, this led to later complications, the only surprise being that the clash didn't arrive until the aftermath of the Carlist Wars in the 19th century. In 1238, these rights were enshrined in the kingdom's first written constitution.

For the next three hundred years, Navarra was involved in numerous small wars with the neighbouring states until it was finally incorporated into the Castillian kingdom by the marriage of Ferdinand of Navarra and Isabela of Castille (see page 139). In 1515, the merger was officially recognised by the parliament of Burgos, but Navarra retained its status as a separate kingdom, with its own parliament, and the traditional *fueros* continued to be recognised.

The status quo only changed in 1841, when the kingdom was converted into a province of Spain, although Navarra still had more autonomy than most other provinces. In 1936, the majority of people here supported Franco's Nationalists, and as a result, during the ensuing 40-year dictatorship, the province retained a far greater degree of independence and wealth than most others in this northern strip. After the 1978 democratic constitution was put in place, this became one of the first states to be given its autonomy.

Today, the state has a total population of only around half a million, of whom about a third live in the state capital, Pamplona. Although the articles of autonomy forbid the different Basque states to combine, the north-west of Navarra, at least, has a strongly Basque culture.

Basque sports in Tafalla (SNTO)

216

Since the 1960s, the region has been heavily industrialised, until today, only 15 per cent of the population work in agriculture. Nevertheless, it is still best known as an agricultural region, for its market gardens, and particularly for its truly delicious white asparagus. The area near the Rioja border is a major producer of fine wine, with some 23,500 hectares of vineyards. Production over the centuries has been so fruitful that some of the local churches have used wine instead of water to mix their mortar as a way of using up the stock. Reds, whites and rosés are produced, but of them all, the rosés are particularly famous. Navarra does have its own *appellation d'origine*, but its lack of international recognition can be attributed to the fact that since 1946, the best of its vintages have been marketed as Riojas.

For the tourist, there are three main reasons for visiting Navarra – the annual festival of San Fermín in Pamplona, the great forest reserves of the Pyrenees, but perhaps above all, for the first section of the Camino de Santiago, which crossed the border at Roncesvalles and headed south through Pamplona to the Rioja border at Logroño (see page 28). All along the way are magnificent architectural jewels, religious and secular. This route is the southern boundary of 'Green Spain', so only the north-western corner of Navarra (the Basque region) is included in this book.

Pamplona

At first sight, Pamplona is a large, ugly, noisy city with little to recommend it. It has grown rapidly since Franco's industrialisation, with its population doubling, to just over 180,000 since 1960. Battle your way through the outskirts and into the heart of the old city and it is a very different matter. Perched on a clifftop above a loop in the Ría Arga, it is an old fortress city, its dark, narrow streets – still extremely noisy – built high to cram as many people as possible within the lines of the walls. Some of these have now been demolished, to make room for the growing modern city, but there are still enough in existence to show how very solid they once were.

Originally the site of an obscure Basque village, Pamplona takes its name from the Roman general Pompey, who founded a camp here in 78–79 BC. Ever since, the strategically sited town, which controls the two major passes in the Western Pyrenees, has been the major city of the Navarra region.

Over the years, it has been a particularly tempting target to all invaders. It was taken by the Goths in 466, and by the Franks in 542. In 738, it was the turn of the Moors, who remained for ten years, until they were thrown out by the the the Christians in 748. Charlemagne sacked it in 778, tearing down the city walls, an action which led to the massacre of his rearguard at Roncesvalles later the same year (see page 221). It became the capital of Navarra in the 9th century, a status it still holds today.

In 1276, the cathedral was sacked by the French and in 1512, the city was captured by Castille, who installed a Viceroy as governor. Heavily fortified by Felipe II in 1571, when the existing citadel was built, the city had a respite for the next 250 years, until the Napoleonic Wars, when it was taken by the French in 1808, and by Wellington, after a four-month siege, in 1813.

The roughly square-shaped old town is bordered on two sides by the river, and the old city walls. A shady paseo or walkway leads right round the top of the walls, offering good views of the river valley and the formidable 16th-century bastions. Do the walk in the cool of the day, or join the many old people who choose seats round here to sit out the scorching midday heat. On the third side, the main through road, the Avenida Taconera separates the old city from the huge Parque Taconera. The best bit of this beautiful park is set within the star-shaped 16th-century **Citadel**, designed by Jose Palearzo and based on the one in Antwerp. Steps up onto the walls offer a good view over this cool, shady area with its central pond and water sculpture.

The fourth side of the fortress was destroyed in two sections, in 1890 and 1912, to make way for the growing modern city centre with its wide boulevards and luxurious shops. Now the very distinct change from old to new city is marked by the wide Paseo de Sarasate, which leads from the citadel to the **Plaza de Castillo**, a large, lively square ringed with cafés that is the effective centre of the old city. This is where everyone comes for the evening paseo, to stroll and sit and sip a drink, to see and be seen.

A few minutes walk from here, on the city walls, above the river is the **Plaza Toros**, the bullring at the heart of Pamplona's modern fame. Pamplona's great moment each year is from the 6–14 July, during the Festival of San Fermín. Ernest Hemingway wrote a novel, *Fiesta*, (also published under the title *The Sun Also Rises*), about the festival, and ever since people have been flocking from around the world, to run with the bulls and see the bullfights that are at the core of the celebrations (see page 219). In gratitude to the man who singlehandly put Pamplona on the tourist map, a statue of Hemingway stands beside the main entrance to the bullring, while the leafy paseo which runs alongside it is called after him. Plan well ahead if you wish to visit Pamplona during the week of San Fermín, as hotel rooms are booked up literally years in advance. If you are at all squeamish about bullfights, avoid it like the plague.

From the bullring, take the Rúa Dormiteleria down to the left, following the line of the ramparts along the river, and you will come first to the Episcopal Palace, and then to the **Diocesan Museum**, housed in the Canons' kitchens and refectory, built in 1330. A number of religious objects from all over Navarra are on display here, including an interesting collection of polychrome wooden statues. Look out also for the central lantern and chimneys in the kitchen, and for the Unicorn chase on the reader's rostrum in the refectory.

Next door to this is the **Cathedral**. From the outside, by far the best view of this is from the back, so make sure you wander through the tiny alleys that lead round the side and onto the bastions to get a good look at its Gothic glory. The west front, designed by Ventura Rodríguez to replace the Romanesque one and completed in 1783, is sadly dull.

There has been a cathedral on this site since the 11th century, but the existing one was built between 1397 and 1525. In a country known for dark churches, this must be one of the darkest, but it is worth visiting if you can peer through the gloom. The nave is fairly plain, but there are interesting retables and paintings in some of the side chapels, while the alabaster tomb of Charles III (the Noble) and his wife, Queen Leonor, is particularly beautiful. Charles, who founded the

The Corrida

In spite of a growing groundswell of opinion against it, bullfighting is still one of the most popular entertainments in Spain. Most of the larger cities have a bullring and, thanks to Hemingway, the fiesta of San Fermín in Pamplona, a two-week extravaganza each July that revolves around daily *corridas*, is the most famous of all Spain's thousands of fiestas.

Each morning during the festival, the bulls to be fought that afternoon are let loose to run through the streets between the town hall and the bullring. Those with secret yearnings to be a matador dress in the *aficionado*'s colours of white with red belt and scarf and run before them. Few days pass without someone being gored or tossed. Once in the ring, the bulls are corralled, then brought in one by one and put through their paces so that the crowd can judge their fighting spirit. The bulls are specially bred for their aggressiveness in Andalusia and Castile. They come into the ring at the age of four, weighing about 450kg.

The bullfight itself normally takes place in late afternoon. Ticket prices vary according to the quality of the matadors, how near the ringside your seat is and whether it is on the sunny or shady side of the ring. Advance booking is almost always essential. There are normally six bulls and three matadors in a full fight programme.

After the triumphal procession of all the teams which opens the event, each fight is divided into three acts or *tercios*. In the first, the foot followers or *peones* will enter the ring to distract the bull and build up his aggression, after which the *matador* will work the bull using the full cape, testing his reactions and showing off the classic passes. Next the *picadors* enter on horseback. The horses are heavily padded to protect them from the horns, but frequently also have their vocal chords cut so that their screams of fear cannot be heard by the crowd. The *picadors* carry pikes which they thrust into the bull's hump as he charges the horses, after which the *matador*'s assistant will plant two colourfully decorated sticks or *bandilleras* in the bull's back. Finally, the matador will again enter the ring, playing the bull with a *muleta* in his left hand and a sword in his right. Once the bull is still, he closes in for the kill, reaching over the horns to stab it between the shoulder blades to the heart.

The crowd has plenty of opportunities to show its pleasure or displeasure and takes full advantage. A brilliant fight will end with the matador being awarded one or both ears and occasionally the tail. A blue kerchief honours the bull, which is then dragged around the ring on a lap of honour. A green kerchief is the mark of disgrace for a poor fight and will result in the bull being allowed to leave the ring alive. They are always killed, however. A bull that has fought once is said to have learnt too much and be too dangerous to fight again. The meat is sold and fetches premium prices, with many butchers displaying special signs.

cathedral, commissioned the tomb himself when his wife died in 1416. The highlight of the visit however has to be the cloister. Built between 1277 and 1472, it is claimed to be the most beautiful in Europe. It is lovely, with delicate, classic Gothic tracery and a light, almost English feel. A number of intricately carved doorways lead off it, the best of them leading to the Sala de la Preciosa, once the meeting place of the Cortes of Navarra. There are also several sculpted tombs.

The narrow, bustling **Calle Mercaderes Curia**, a good shopping street, leads down the hill from the cathedral to the Plaza Consistorial, where you will find the attractive Baroque town hall. A small rocket, fired from the balcony, is the signal that starts the festival going, and this is also part of the route for the running of the bulls. Nearby is the **Church of Santo Saturnino,** said to be on the spot where the saint baptised 40,000 pagans. It is a bit of a mixture with a 13th-century Gothic porch, Romanesque brick towers and a little bit of almost everything else. The Calle de Santo Domingo leads down between the town hall and church to the Museum of Navarra, with a collection of Roman mosaics, Romanesque capitals and Gothic and Renaissance paintings. At the time of writing, it is closed, but it is due to reopen fairly shortly.

The Pyrenees – Pamplona to Irún

This route covers the short stretch of the Camino de Santiago between Pamplona and the French border before turning west towards Irún and the coast. On the map distances are not great, but most of the driving is on mountain roads, and the lie of the valleys means that it is necessary to back-track several times.

Leave Pamplona on the C135, signposted towards Roncesvalles and France, and follow it for 45km to Burguete, where you turn left for Roncesvalles. Keep climbing through the village and about 2km further on, you will reach the top of the **Ibañeta Pass.** This was the site of the battle in 778 between the rearguard of the Carolingian army and the Basques that was later immortalised in the *Chanson de Roland* (see page 221). On the grass beside the road, supposedly at the very spot where Roland chose to lie down and die, there is a megalithic memorial to the super hero, erected in 1967. The views are stupendous. Nearby are the ruins of the church Charlemagne built in memory of his dead.

Unless you are planning to continue across to Valcarlos and the French border, turn back now and head back down into **Roncesvalles.** For the many thousands of pilgrims who trudged their way up the steep tracks of the Pyrenees, arrival here was a moment to celebrate. Not only was it their first stop inside Spain, but it marked the start of a downhill stretch, followed by a plain. A fit person is said to be able to do the walk from here to Santiago de Compostela in 20 days. Not for another two weeks, until they reached the Montes de León would anything be as punishing as the section they had just conquered. There is a tiny hamlet here, but it is completely dwarfed by the massive buildings of the zinc-roofed **Augustinian Abbey,** founded by Sancho VII (the Strong) of Navarre in the early 13th century. The Collegiate Church, originally modelled on churches in the Ile-de-France, was first consecrated in 1219, but has been much altered and restored over the centuries. There is a fine 13th-century statue of the Virgin and Child on the high altar, made of wood and silver plated. The gothic chapter house, off the cloister, contains the tombs of Sancho VII and his wife, Clemencia. A treasury museum, housed in the former stables, contains a variety of offerings made to the community over the centuries, including a gold-embroidered cope donated by Elizabeth of Portugal, a 14th-century enam-elled reliquary known as Charlemagne's chessboard, a Romanesque gospel, and

The Song of Roland

"The County Roland with pain and anguish winds His Olifant, and blows with all his might.

Blood from his mouth comes spurting scarlet-bright

He's burst the veins of his temples outright."

(1937 translation by Dorothy Sayers, for Penguin Classics.)

One of the great moments of medieval literature is that attempt to recall Charlemagne's army back to the assistance of his hopelessly outnumbered rearguard. The tragic, heroic Roland blows his great horn, Olifant, so hard that he bursts the veins in his temples. By the time the emperor arrives back at the pass of Roncesvaux (Roncesvalles), all are dead, but the battle is won. The rest of the poem concerns itself with the emperor's revenge for his nephew's death, against the infidel Moors.

The *Chanson de Roland*, as it is now known to us, was written in the 11th century. Roland is seven feet tall, and a hero of super-human strength and perfect chivalry, armed with his great horn and the jewel-incrusted, relic-holding Christian sword, Durandel. The Moorish army that rides against him is 60,000 strong, yet his small band defeats them and Roland himself kills several hundred. He dies not from wounds, but from his own efforts at blowing the horn, and before he goes, the Moors have fled. Roland chooses the place to die, facing towards Spain like a conqueror, and angels come down to carry his soul to heaven. It was a story perfectly in tune with the times, as Christians all over Europe gathered for the Crusades, and moreover, it took place at the very pass used by the pilgrim route to Compostela, then at the height of its popularity.

The reality, needless to say, was somewhat different. The first written report of the incident was by the chronicler Eginhardt in his *Vita Caroli* in 830. In 778, the beleaguered city of Pamplona asked for Charlemagne's assistance against Moorish attack. The emperor arrived as requested and defeated the Moors, but before he left he pulled down the city walls, so that it could never stand against him. He then headed back across the Pyrenees, leaving Roland, Duke of the Marches of Brittany and, as far as we know, no relation to the emperor, to head the rearguard of his army. This was attacked at Roncesvalles not by the Moors but by a small army of Basques, infuriated by his treatment of their city. Roland, along with most of his army was killed, in a battle which should have become nothing more than a minor footnote in history.

a 16th-century Flemish triptych. There are also a 12th-century funerary chapel, the Chapel of the Holy Spirit, much altered in the 15th century, and the pilgrim hostel within the complex.

From here, you have to back-track along the main Pamplona road until you reach **Zubiri**, where you turn right onto a narrow mountain road that winds its way across a 894m pass to Olague, where you turn right onto the main N121. As ever, on this road, you begin to climb again immediately, crossing the Puerto de Velate, where there is a ruined castle, at 863m. This whole area was hotly disputed in 1813 during the Peninsula Wars, when Napoleonic General Soult attempted to cross the Pyrenees and break the Allied siege of Pamplona. In all, some 40,000 men, French and English, were killed during that summer's campaigns in these mountains.

When you reach Mugaire, turn right for the next side trip through the oak, beech and chestnut forests of the Val de Baztán to **Elizondo**. This is the largest village in

The collegiate church at Roncesvalles (SNTO)

the area, and was, for a time, an independent state. Look out for the 16th-century Governor's Palace. Several of the small villages in the area have some surprisingly grand mansions, decorated with coats of arms. Many of them were built by the 'Indianos', locals who headed off to Latin America to make their fortunes, retiring to their home town with a stash to spend on a lifestyle fit to make the other villagers weep. The **Señorio de Bertiz**, with its magnificent botanical gardens and arboretum are near here. If you have time to spare, keep going up into the mountains to the remote village of **Zugarramurdi**, huddled in dense forest. It is famed throughout Navarra as a place of legend and witchcraft as local covens were said to hold their meetings in the nearby caves.

You now have to back-track the whole way down the valley again, and turn right at Mugaire, back onto the N121, which winds its way along the right bank of the Bidassoa River. A signpost to the left will point the way across the river to the lovely village of **Lesaca**, which was Wellington's headquarters while crossing the Pyrenees. It is a beautiful place, with several tower-houses, and other attractive regional architecture. The church contains a number of medieval statues that were gold-plated in the 16th century. Lesaca has a unique Christmas tradition: the *Olentzero*, or charcoal-burner, arrives from the mountains to bring the glad tidings.

His image is also carried in procession around many of the other small towns and villages in this mountain region.

Go back again to the main road, and turn left for **Vera de Bidassoa**. This, along with Lesaca and three other towns, Aranaz, Yanci and Echalar, make up the ancient confederation of 'Cinco Villas' or Five Towns. Another beautiful place, its houses have overhanging eaves designed for winter snows, and are decorated by coats of arms and delicate wooden balconies. Look out for the ruined castle of Alzate, the church, the old bridge, and the town hall, which was built in 1776. Shortly before arriving in Irún, you will pass the confluence of the Bidasoa and Baztán Rivers. From here, the road leads straight through to Irún.

The route along the coast road from Irún to San Sebastián is covered on page 98.

Royal Navarra – Pamplona to Logroño via Olite

This route heads due south from Pamplona before looping west, to join the Camino de Santiago at Puente la Reina. The distances are small, but there is so much to see that you should allow at least two days to reach Logroño. For the section from Puente La Reina to Logroño, see page 225.

Leave Pamplona on the N121 heading south, signposted to Soria. This runs parallel with the A15 motorway, on which you can do the first section of the journey, if you prefer.

The first stop is at **Tafalla**, 35km away. A small market town surrounded by wheat fields, in the late 13th and early 14th centuries, during the reign of Charles III (the Noble), this was the site of the massive Fortress of Santa Lucia. Only a few fragments of the royal palace remain, but it is still worth a visit, with a number of mansions with fine façades clustered in the streets around the Plaza de Los Fueros, the typically Navarrese central square. Look inside the Church of Santa María, which has a 16th-century Renaissance retable by Basque sculptor Juan de Ancheta, and a Baroque organ loft. The Convent of La Concepción has an altarpiece by Rolam de Moys, which came originally from the 12th-century Cistercian abbey of La Oliva, about 30km away.

From Tafalla, head east on the C132 for 10km to the charming medieval walled village of **San Martín de Unx**, which has a Gothic church, built on earlier foundations. Keep going on the same road for a further 9km to **Ujué**, a small medieval hill town. Seemingly unchanged for centuries, the narrow streets and ancient rough stone houses of Ujué crowd up the sides of the hill, dwarfed by the massive fortified Church of Santa María. Incorporated into a castle, of which only the encircling walls and covered gallery still remain, it was first built in the 11th century. Most of the church is now Gothic however, built in the 14th century by Charles II (the Bad). Only the Romanesque chancel remains. There is a silver-plated wooden statue of Santa María la Blanca in the central chapel. This is the centre of a pilgrimage cult, dating back to the 14th century. Usually on the night of 30 April, a *romería* procession of penitent pilgrims led by the 'Twelve Apostles' dress in black robes and hoods, with string tied around their waists, and, carrying lanterns and crosses, walks the 17km from Tafalla to the shrine of Santa María la Blanca in Ujué. This is one of the local *mayos*, pagan spring festivals adopted, like many others, by the Church.

You now have to back-track as far as Tafalla, before turning south along the N121 to **Olite**, 7km away. Now a village of only about 2500 people, it is a wonderful place, literally steeped in history. This is the site of the Roman town of Ologicus and some sections of the Roman walls still remain. In the 15th century, the fortress, built between 1406 and 1419 by Charles III (the Noble), became the court of the Kings of Navarre. An extraordinary mix of styles, it was designed by French architects, but built by Moorish workmen. The result is a formidable, solid exterior of red sandstone, with 15 square towers, and battlemented walkways. Within the thickness of the walls is a defensive labyrinth of hidden corridors and stairs. Behind the defences however lies an enchanted world of hanging gardens and intricately decorated halls. It was said to have a room for every day of the year, and even had a lions' den and aviary. One section has now been restored and is used as a parador. Climb at least one of the towers to get a good view over the town and surrounding countryside.

The former royal chapel, now the Church of Santa María la Real has a beautiful 14th-century Gothic façade, with an intricately carved portal and multi-arched porch. Only some sections of the 14th-century cloister now remain. The town's other Church, San Pedro, is a more polyglot affair, with a Romanesque façade and cloister, and a Gothic spire. The Convents of San Francisco and Santa Clara both date from the Middle Ages, but were heavily restored and altered in the 18th century.

Yet again, you will need to return to Tafalla, this time, turning west, along the NA603 towards **Artajona**, 11km away. Looming over the horizon for miles around, this incredibly imposing medieval walled town with its high walls and square towers, is one of the best preserved fortresses in Navarra. Known as the Cerco de Artajona, it belonged to the Templars in the 12th century. Of the three churches within the walls, the most interesting is the 13th-century Church of St Saturnino at the top of the hill, itself fortified. It has a finely carved west front, and a gold altarpiece dating from 1497. From here, walk down through the golden stone houses of the old town to the modern church, centre of the newer settlement, and look back through the archway for a finely framed view of the town.

Continue along the same road to reach Puente La Reina and join up with the Camino de Santiago.

The Camino de Santiago – Pamplona to Logroño

This 92km route follows the main road, the N111, the whole way, and takes in the very best of the sights en route. It would be easy to do in a day, but for those who wish to linger, which is well worth doing, there is plenty to keep you occupied. The local tourist offices have brochures with suggested routes from both Pamplona and Estella which take in many of the smaller or more isolated churches and palaces that litter the area.

Leave Pamplona on the N111 signposted to Logroño. The road runs across vast open plains, with wide skies and only a distant rim of purple to mark the mountains of the Sierra de Andía to the north. Tiny, neat hill villages rise like beacons from the wheat, each top heavy with a massive church amidst the minute cottages. The first stop is at the tiny octagonal Church of Santa María, at **Eunate**. Built in the 12th century by the Templars, this is thought to have been a funerary chapel, modelled on the Church of the Holy Sepulchre, Jerusalem. There are several others along the route of the same design. The outside gallery, used as a pilgrim shelter, would have been connected to other buildings.

Five kilometres on, you will reach the small town of **Puente la Reina**. From the road, this looks like nothing very much, but the old walled village hiding behind the row of modern houses is extremely pretty, built around an imposing central square. The hump-backed bridge across the Ría Arga which gives the town its name was built in the 11th century on the orders of Queen Uracca, wife of Alfonso VI of Navarra. This is where the two last branches of the French pilgrim routes, from Paris and Arles, finally met. There are two churches worth visiting. The Church of Santiago beside the bridge has a fine, but badly eroded portal, while inside there is a charming statue, in gilded wood, of St James as a pilgrim. The Church of the Crucifijo, originally 12th-century, but substantially rebuilt in the 15th, is a Templar church, with a porch that connected it to the pilgrim hospital. It gets its name from a Y-shaped wooden crucifix thought to have been brought here from Germany in the 14th century.

As you proceed along the N111 towards **Ciraqui**, the landscape begins to change, as the hills build up and the forest begins to close in. Ciraqui is a small, huddled place that climbs almost cliff-like from the river. Steep alleys lined by steps lead past beautifully decorated houses with arched doorways, coats of arms, cornices and wrought iron balconies. The Church of San Román at the top of the village has a fine, richly carved 13th-century portal.

Allow plenty of time for your next stop, at **Estella**, roughly halfway between Pamplona and Logroño. This is a pure product of the pilgrim route – and probably one of the most beautiful towns in the whole of north-west Spain. In 1085, it is said, a shepherd, guided by a shower of falling stars, found a miraculous statue of the Virgin on a small hill above the Ría Ega. The hill has been known since as the Puy de Virgen, and a church has stood there almost from the beginning. The last, a Baroque chapel, was in a ruinous state when it was pulled down at the beginning of the century, and the current modern Puy Basilica was built in its place by Navarrese architect, Victor Eusa. It was inaugurated in 1951. It is a stiff climb up to the church, but it is worth it, not only for the building and the Gothic statue of the Virgen del Puy (now the patron saint of Estella), but also for the spectacular view from the terrace over the town and surrounding valley.

Partly because of the statue, partly because of its convenient geographical loca-tion, in 1090, King Sancho Ramírez I founded a town of *francos*, free men who had no feudal ties, either to local nobles or the church, who were to set up inns and shops as a base for pilgrims. The town grew rapidly more affluent and the various religious houses moved in, followed shortly after by a number of noble families who built palaces and hospitals.

In 1270, another miracle occurred when strange lights appeared and opened up a grave in the cloister of San Pedro. The grave was said to be that of the Greek bishop of Patras, where the Apostle Andrew had been martyred. The bishop had died en route to Santiago with the apostle's shoulder blade in his possession and this was now found in his coffin. Estella's position as a pilgrimage centre in its own right was assured.

The town was nicknamed Estella La Bella by the pilgrims. The name is as apt today. It is an architectural jewel, with a dozen churches and almost as many palaces, monasteries and convents. It is also a small, peaceful place, that is perfectly designed for those who wish to take a leisurely stroll through narrow streets and tiny, leafy squares, past mansions and cottages, antique shops and backstreet cafs, across the tiny, triangular Romanesque bridge or along the shady paseo on the north bank of the river to a small swimming beach.

The oldest part of the town is the area surrounding San Pedro de la Rua, on the south bank of the river. San Pedro itself, reached by an imposing modern staircase, is a 12th- to 13th-century church, with a magnificent Mozarabic portal. The baroque chapel to the left inside still houses St Andrew's shoulder blade. Only two galleries of the cloister remain, the other two having been destroyed by falling masonry in 1572, when the castle on the clifftop above was blown up. Those that remain, however, are enchanting, with a magnificent collection of carved capitals. The square below the church, the Plaza de San Martín contains two buildings of interest. On the west side, the Palace of the Kings of Navarre, built in the 12th century and one of the earliest surviving buildings in the whole of Spain, has a series of carved capitals which tell the story of Roland's heroic victory over the giant Ferragut. The old town hall, with a Baroque façade, is now the local court. The detail on the central fountain is also worth looking at. The Calle de la Rúa, just to the right, contains a number of fine houses, including the 16th-century, Plateresque Casa de Fray Diego de Estella, which is now in use as the Casa de Cultura, and the early 17th-century Governor's Palace. At the far end of the street is the Church of Santo Sepulcro, which has a fine Gothic portal. It supposedly contains a Museum of the Pilgrim Route, but getting in can take more effort than its worth. On the crest of the hill above San Pedro stand the ruins of the old castle. The area just below this is the old Jewish quarter. The Church of Santa María de Jus del Castillo, at the foot of the castle walls, was originally built as a synagogue.

The more modern section of the town, on the right bank, was divided until the 16th century into two separate and extremely competitive parishes, both with their own markets, rights, traditions and mayors, based around the Church of San Miguel, on Calle Ruiz de Alda, and the Church of San Juan Bautista, on the Plaza de los Fueros. San Miguel, surrounded still by narrow stepped alleys and tiny cottages has a particularly fine Romanesque north portal. San Juan is much more of a mixture, with a façade that includes Gothic and 18th-century elements, but was

Sculpture of Christ in majesty in the church of San Pedro de la Rua, Estella

finally only completed in 1902. Other sites worth visiting include the Hermitage of Rocamadour, the Convent of Recoletas, and the Capuchin Convent.

Before you continue on, you should also allow a little time to make two short detours. The **Monastery of Iranzu** is about 12-km north of Estella, just past Abárzuza. A Cistercian monastery, built at the end of the 12th century, in a remote and beautiful gorge, it typifies its period, as styles began to change from the elegant simplicity of the Romanesque to the more flamboyant decoration of the Gothic period. The **Monastery of Irache** is about 3km south of Estella, just off the main road. First founded by the Benedictines in the 10th century, it rose to fame as a

227

Cistercian monastery and a major stop on the pilgrim route. In the 16th century, it became a Benedictine University, and eventually only closed in 1833. The church is an odd, but pleasing combination of styles, with a Romanesque apse, and Renaissance dome and cloister, while the main façade and most of the monastery buildings date from the 17th century.

Back on the main road, you will shortly arrive at **Torres del Río** where there is a small octagonal church, which is a virtual twin to the one at Eunate (see page 225). 17km from Estella, **Los Arcos** is an attractive small village, with a central square reached through a 17th-century gateway and lined by brick built houses. The Church of La Asunción has a 15th-century cloister, Baroque retable and fine organ.

The final stop on the route, only a few kilometres from Logroño, is the medieval village of **Viana**. In 1423, Carlos III of Navarra turned Viana into the capital of the fiefdom of the heir to the throne, who took the title of Prince of Viana. There are still several fine mansions, adorned with coats of arms, within the town, along with the now ruinous Torre de San Pedro. Of most interest is the Church of Santa María with an imposing Renaissance portal dating to its reconstruction from 1549 to 1567. Look down just before you enter the church and you will see a simple slab which marks the grave of Cesare Borgia, who was killed here in 1507 while besieging the town. Only 32 when he died, he was the son of Pope Alexander VI and the brother of Lucretia Borgia. He became a cardinal before leaving the church to marry, taking the title of Duke of Valence. With the backing of a French army, he then set out on a massive military campaign, aiming to unite all Europe under the rule of the Pope. Deeply unpopular at the time, he is said to have been the model for Machiavelli's *The Prince*, and has gone down in history as one of the all-time great villains. He was originally buried inside the church, but his body was moved by a 19th-century bishop, who carefully positioned it so that anyone entering the church should step on his tomb.

Navarra:
General Information

Regional tourist office:
Diputación Foral de Navarra, Departamento de Industria, Comercio y Turismo, Av de San Ignacio 1, 31002 Pamplona (tel. (948) 227 200).

ARIZKUN
Where to stay:
Fonda Etxeberria, 31713 (tel. (948) 453 013). A simple, but pleasant inn in a converted farmhouse in a small working village, within easy reach of Pamplona and San Sebastián. Ask for a room in the old house. Cheap.

ESTELLA
Tourist Office, c/ San Nicolas, 1, 31200 (tel. (948) 554 011).
Where to stay: Perhaps surprisingly for such a pretty town, Estella has no hotels worth picking out for special mention. There are a number of small hotels and fondas that are clean, comfortable and perfectly satisfactory.
Where to eat:
Restaurante Navarra, Gustavo de Maeztu 16 (Los Llanos), 31200 (tel. (948) 551 069). An attractive villa, decorated in the Navarrese-medieval style and standing in its own lovely gardens. The food is regional. Moderate-expensive.

PAMPLONA (IRUÑEA)
Tourist Office, Duque de Ahumada, 3, 31020 (tel. (948) 220 741 or 211 462).
Where to stay:
Los Tres Reyes, Jardines de la Taconera 1, 31001 (tel. (948) 226 600; fax (948) 222 930). Large modern hotel with all the trimmings, including a swimming pool, just on the edge of the old city, within easy walking distance of everything of interest. Expensive.
La Perla, Plaza de Castillo (tel. (948) 227 705). This is where Hemingway used to stay and, as a result, it can get very booked up. An old-fashioned hotel, with an air of faded elegance, it is cheerful and friendly. Moderate.
Hotel Eslava, Plaza Virgen de la 0–7, 31001 (tel. (948) 222 270; fax (948) 225 157). Small modern hotel on the edge of the old city. This is near the park and river, so is slightly quieter than most. Bed and breakfast only. Cheap-moderate.

Otano, c/ San Nicolas 5 (tel. (948) 225 095). Somewhat spartan, but convenient. Best known for its regional restaurant and tapas bar. Cheap.

Most of the fondas are huddled together in the streets of the old city, near the Plaza del Castillo and Paseo de Sarasate.

Where to eat:

Joisetxo, pl Principe de Viana 1, 31002 (tel. (948) 222 097). Highly elegant and upmarket restaurant with strings of stars. Expensive.

Hartza, Juan de Labrit 19, 31001 (tel. (948) 224 568). A comfortable family-run restaurant specialising in interesting variations on regional cuisine, this is another of the most famous restaurants in the city. Expensive.

Other restaurants that come highly recommended are the **Rodero** (Arrieta 3, tel. (948) 228 035) and the **Sarasate** (Garcia Castañon 12–1°; tel. (948) 225 102). Both are also expensive. In the mid-range are the **Otano** (see above), and the **Shanti** (Castillo de Maya 39; tel. (948) 231 004).

RONCESVALLES

Where to stay and eat:

La Posada, 31650 (tel. (948) 760 225). Built in the 18th century for pilgrims, this simple hotel is still owned by the church and is still a regular stopping point for pilgrims. Cheap.

The Picos de Europa

In global terms, the Picos de Europa are not particularly high, reaching a maximum altitude of 2642m at Peña Cerredo, yet they must be some of the most dramatic mountains in Europe, rising almost vertically from the coast to give a far greater impression of height than they actually achieve. They were given their name by sailors in the early days of the Spanish empire. As they sailed into the Bay of Biscay and towards their homes, after voyages often lasting over a year, these peaks were the first land visible on the horizon, an eagerly awaited landmark that told them they had finally reached Europe.

Up on the top, great rocky crags and ridges of shale scree pierce the sky, reflected in pale mountain lakes that still survive in the circular bowls left behind by ancient glaciers. Far beyond the tree line, with views that stretch north to the coast and out to sea and south to the Castillian meseta, you really can feel that you are on top of the world. Yet nowhere is it inaccessible. There is some heavy climbing and serious hiking, but the majority of areas can be reached by anyone who is reasonably fit, and even the old or disabled can get access to the various miradors. It is perhaps no wonder that these fabulous mountains are one of the top tourist attractions in northern Spain. In spite of this, however, it is possible to get away from the crowds and only in a few places does the press of people get depressing.

The road is good, although a lot of the land is mountainous, and in terms of simple mileage, the tour could be covered in two days. To rush it would be to cheat yourself of a magnificent experience however. Unless the weather is foul (always a sad possibility), allow yourself plenty of time.

Detailed walking maps and guidebooks are available in all the surrounding towns. For the more adventurous, numerous tour companies in Potes and Cangas de Onís will hire you a jeep, organise a walking tour, either with a group or individual guide, or take you pony trekking, climbing, caving, and even paragliding. In winter, there is some cross-country skiing, but the terrain is not suitable for downhill.

The Picos de Europa stand at the border of three states, Cantabria, Asturias and Castilla-y-León. This tour follows a roughly triangular route through all three, starting at Panes and travelling clockwise, with access routes into the highest, impassable mountains at regular intervals. It can be reached on good roads from several places in all three states, namely Unquera (page 131), Ribadasella (page 55), Burgos

231

or León via Riaño (page 167), and Cervera de Pisuerga (page 158), as well as along a host of smaller roads.

Panes, the market town just a few kilometres from the coast, on the Deva River, is trying without much success to set itself up as one of the main tourist centres for the region. It is in reality a small, rather dreary place that is a useful shopping stop, but not much else. Its only historic monument is the crumbling remnants of a 10th-century Mozarabic church.

Leave here, heading south along the Deva River on the N621 and almost immediately you enter the **Desfilada de la Hermida** (Defile of Hermida). This is the start of the Liébana Valley, an area of high mountains and fertile valleys first repopulated in 818 during the earliest stages of the Reconquista. For a short time in the 19th century, it became an independent state, and although it is now part of Cantabria, it doesn't quite know it.

Astonishingly, in this area, a bizarre micro-climate leads to small pockets of the most unlikely crops, with citrus, olives and vines rubbing shoulders with apples, chestnuts and dairy herds in the shadow of the snow-capped peaks.

Little can grow in the almost permanently shadowed Desfilada, however, so it is best known to locals for its superb trout and salmon fishing. You will see plenty of eager fishermen with rods strung out along the river bank. The 17km long gorge is dramatically beautiful, with small patches of rich chestnut forest clinging to the gaps between the vast, sheer slabs of rock that slide down into the tumbling river. Partway through, with the gorge briefly opening out, the tiny 10th-century Church of Santa María de Lebeña clings to the hillside, surrounded by trees. The tower and porch are 20th-century additions, but the rest of the church is classic Mozarabic design, built in about 925 AD for Count Alfonso de Liébana, who came originally from Andalucía. It has an external gallery, three aisles, with semi-circular vaulting, horseshoe arches and corinthian capitals, and is probably the finest surviving Mozarabic monument in Cantabria.

A little way after this, a road on the right leads to **Colio**, at the foot of the Eastern Massif, once the site of a military barracks used for training soldiers to fight the French. High up above the village, there is a slow-growing glacier that every so often cracks with a massively noisy fall of ice, rock and mud. The resulting rumbles are said to result from the playful antics of the 'little devils of Colio'. Just after this, a road off to the left leads up to Castro, where a local man has opened a small, privately owned ethnographic museum.

As the Desfilada ends and the valley opens, the next side strip leads from Ojedo to the left along the N627. At **Cabezón de Liébana**, a small road off to the right leads to the Monastery of Santa María de Piasca. Founded originally in 857, this was one of the most powerful houses in Cantabria. All that now remains of it is the church, begun in 1172, but not completely finished until 1439, and showing both Romanesque and Gothic elements. It has a simple, but attractive façade that still retains remnants of polychrome decoration, with wonderful 12th-century statues of Sts Peter and Paul, on either side of a 16th-century statue of the Virgin. In the portal arch itself, look for the carving of the 'kiss of Piasca'. Inside, the mainly Gothic church has some fine capitals.

Santa María de Lebeña in the Desfilada de la Hermida, Picos de Europa

Returning to Ojedo and the main road, turn left and you come finally to a beautiful, broad river basin, in which is nestled the town of **Potes**. This is the capital of the Liébana region, and a bustling market town with an excellent Monday market, which draws all the villagers from miles around. Perhaps more importantly, it is also the main tourist centre for the Picos, humming with activity and a permanently festive, holiday atmosphere. If you wish to stay here in late July and August, when the Spaniards and French are all on holiday, book ahead or you could find

233

yourself sleeping in the car. The 15th-century Torre del Infantado was originally built by the family of local hero, Orejón de la Lama, but has been restored now for use as the Town Hall. There are no other buildings of note here, but there are many pretty houses in the back streets of the old town, and along the river bank. Some are genuinely old, some are sympathetic reconstructions after massive damage during the Civil War.

The road off to the right, actually the continuation of the N621 signposted towards Fuente Dé, is the real focus of activity, leading up into the high peaks. Most of the best hotels and restaurants in the district are also strung out along its length. Before you head into the mountains however, a road off to the left, shortly after leaving Potes, leads to the Franciscan **Monastery of Santo Toribio de Liébana**. Known at first as St Martín de Turieno, legend surrounds its origins, some saying its founder was St Toribio of Astorga in the 5th century, others that it was the 6th-century St Toribio of Palencia. Whichever saint it was travelled on pilgrimage to the Holy Land, bringing back with him the single largest fragment of the True Cross in existence, part of the left arm of the cross, complete with a nail hole for authenticity.

The earliest factual record of the monastery, by now called St Toribio, was in 828 and the more likely story is that St Toribio was a bishop of Astorga, who removed the cross here for safekeeping ahead of a Moorish attack in the 9th century. The existing church dates from 1250, at the transition between the Romanesque and Gothic.

The fragment of the cross was split in two in the 16th century and mounted in a richly bejewelled, silver gilt reliquary. This now stands in an ornate 18th-century Baroque chapel, with an octagonal cupola, reached from the cloister. In 1958, the fragment of wood was extensively tested, and was found to be from a type of conifer native to Palestine, while C14 dating placed its age at around 2000 years old. In Jubilee Years (when the feast of St Toribio, 16 April, falls on a Sunday), plenary indulgences are granted and the monastery becomes a major pilgrimage centre. There are several small hermitages in the surrounding hills.

The road continues west past the villages of Mogrojevo, with a 13th-century tower, and Cosgaya, and comes to an end in the vast natural amphitheatre of **Fuente Dé**, carved out by a glacier during the last Ice Age. Said to be so beautiful that this was the site of Paradise, Fuente Dé and the River Deva take their name from the Fountain of Eve. Within the cirque itself there is a comfortable, but stupendously ugly parador, while to the left is the bottom end of the Cable Car. Both were built in 1966. Aim at arriving early in high summer because huge queues for the cable car can build up by about 11am. It takes about three minutes to ascend the 800m to the top of the cliff and the superb viewpoint of the Mirador del Cable (named not after the cable car, but an earlier mining cable built in 1903). A rather alarming but spectacular viewing platform with an open metal grill for a floor hangs out over the valley, offering magnificent views to the south. The area around the cable car and mirador is always busy, but walk only a few hundred metres and you will find yourself in glorious solitude. This area is a national hunting preserve, so there is a chance of seeing some wildlife if you get far enough away from the crowds. Long distance footpaths lead across to Caín, the Cares Gorges (see below) and Sotres (page 240), and there are several mountain refuge huts within easy access. For the truly energetic, a narrow path winds back down the cliff.

From Fuente Dé, backtrack the whole way down to Potes, and turn south, onto the N621. The first part of the journey is across the Quiviesa River valley, lush and green and relatively gentle. At La Vega, a side route to the left turns off up the Frio River valley, and, after some fairly hair-raising hairpin bends, eventually reaches the Mirador de Liébana, with fine views across the Liébana Valley and the remote, utterly unspoilt mountain village of Cucayo.

The main route continues south from La Vega, as the mountains close in and the road begins to climb to the **Puerto de San Glorio**, which, at 1609m, is the highest road pass west of the Pyrenees. It also marks the border between Cantabria and Castilla-y-León. There is a long-distance footpath from here that leads up to Fuente Dé, and links in with the routes across the high massif. A much shorter path leads up to the 1675m Mirador de Llesba, marked by a grand statue of a bear, from where there are superb views across the highest peaks.

The road drops rapidly on the far side of the pass until you reach Llánaves de la Reina, from where a short tunnel leads into the entrance to the Yuso River Gorge, another spectacular rocky defile which continues through to Portilla La Reina. The easier route from here continues south-west to Riaño, currently the building site of a massive dam, which is due, in the course of time, to flood the town, and then north-west along the C637 to the Puerto del Pondón.

The more interesting route takes a smaller road to the right, which climbs again for 17km to the 1562m **Puerto de Pandetrave**, which has a magnificent view over all three massifs of the Picos – the eastern Andara Europa, the central Picos de los Urrieles, and the western Picos Cornión. This is the edge of the Valdeón region, a high, green, farming valley tucked into the heart of the mountains, and frequently cut off in winter by snow on the surrounding passes. The road winds around the edge of the mountains to San Marina de Valdeón, the highest village in the Picos, and once the site of a medieval monastery. The road on from here is good, but very narrow, so beware of oncoming traffic. The next village along is **Posada de Valdeón**, which derived its name from a guest house once run here by the monks of St Toribio de Liébana. Today, it is once again a hospitality centre, with several small hotels and restaurants.

A narrow road leads north on an excursion along the Cares River to Cordiñañes, the Mirador del Tombo, built in 1964 as a memorial to architect and mountaineer, Julián Delgado Ulbeda, and marked by a statue of an ibex, and to La Majada de Corona, traditionally the site of Pelayo's coronation by the Christian refugees in 714. Finally, at **Caín**, you reach the end of the road and the start of the most popular footpath in the Picos, an 11km hike along the Cares Gorges to Poncebos, a route that can get horribly overcrowded at weekends and on national holidays. This dramatic gash through the mountains, at times nearly 1000m deep, splits the Urrieles and Cornión Massifs and also marks the boundary between the hunting preserve and the Covadonga National Park. The first section runs through a steep defile, beside a canal built in 1917 to supply hydro-electric power, with both canal and footpath winding through tunnels in the cliffs. About 4km after leaving Caín,

The cable car at Fuente Dé

you reach the border between Castilla-y-León and Asturias, an area of scree slopes used by the Muslim armies to flee after their defeat at the battle of Covadonga (see page 238). Shortly after this, a steep section drops some 300m to the water's edge (which is why it is better to do the route in this direction), and from then on, the path follows an easy line along the river valley. It is possible to hire a four-wheel drive car and driver in either Caín or Poncebos to return you over the mountain tracks to where you left your own car.

Back in Posada de Valdeón, keep going to the right and the road widens again to climb to the 1450m Puerto de Panderruedas, at the western end of the Valdeón Valley. A track to the right leads to the Mirador de Piedrafitas, built in 1966 in honour of General Franco. There is a viewing table which points out the main sights, including the massive cirque which surrounds the end of the Valdeón Valley and the 2648m Peña Cerredo, the highest mountain in the Picos. From here, the road drops slighty to join the C637 from Riaño. Turn right, and about 2km on, you reach the 1280m Puerto del Pontón, the last of the high mountain passes on the route, with excellent views over the Sajambre Valley.

From here, the road winds steeply down through elm forests to **Oseja de Sajambre**, the centre of another small mountain region, the village itself once centred around a long vanished monastery. Just beyond the village, a mirador offers the very best view across the Sajambre Valley, pierced at the centre by the needle of Niaja rock. This is also the start of the 10km **Desfilada de los Beyos**, (Defile of Los Beyos) probably the most dramatic set of gorges accessible by car on the route. The road winds its way along the Sella River, between sheets of sheer rock, hardly broken by a tree. About halfway along, you cross the border from Castilla-y-León into Asturias. At Sames, a road off to the left leads to another stupendous gorge, this time on the Ponga River, where a narrow road squeezes its way past massive boulders that almost block the valley. It is possible to loop round via Viego, rather than returning on the same road. Once back in Sames, the road follows a relatively gentle path through to **Cangas de Onís**, at the north-west corner of the Picos triangle.

At a much lower altitude, effectively at the edge of the coastal plain, this small market town stands at the confluence of the Sella and Güeña Rivers, surrounded by agricultural land and deciduous woods. The town has an illustrious past, not only as a Celtic village and Roman town, but in effect, as the first ever capital of Christian Spain. Pelayo, the hero of Covadonga (see page 238), set up court here in the early 8th century, ruling for 18 years. Next came Favila, whose main accomplishment was to have been eaten by a bear in 739, thus turning the animal into the Asturian symbol. After him came Alfonso I, who finally got round to spreading the boundaries of the kingdom, and the last of the line was Fruela I, who was murdered at his palace in Cangas de Onís. After that, the title and court moved elsewhere. In 1907, Alfonso XIII granted the town the title of city, in honour of its status. A regional centre of government and the main tourist centre for the Cornión Massif, Cangas de Onís is a lively attractive place, with few specific monuments of importance. Best of these is the 13th-century stone bridge, with a cross of St James hanging beneath, that has been so frequently photographed that it is almost another Asturian symbol. There are a number of fine domestic buildings around the streets, including the 16th-century Palacio de Cortes. In nearby Contranquil, the Hermitage of Santa Cruz was theoretically founded in 437 by Bishop Astemo, was rebuilt in 735 by Favila to celebrate the victory at Covadonga, again in 1632, and again this century after being blown up during the civil war. The blast which destroyed the 17th-century church also uncovered the only known dolmen in the region.

A couple of kilometres west of the town, on the C631 to Ribadasella, is the Benedictine **Monastery of San Pedro de Villanueva**. Founded originally by Afonso I in 746, it has a 12th-century Romanesque church, but most of the rest of the monastery dates from a further rebuilding in 1687. There are some interesting capitals inside, but the best of the church is the portal, which illustrates Favila's grisly end at the paws of the bear.

Leave Cangas de Onís on the C6312, which runs east, along the northern edge of the Picos. Three km out of town, a small road on the left leads to the **El Buxu Caves**, which have a small but fine collection of cave paintings dating back around 15,000 years to the Magdalenian era (see page 130). Only 25 people a day are admitted, on a first come, first served basis, so get there very early if you are keen to see them.

Shortly after this, a road on the right leads back into the mountains to the major pilgrimage site of **Covadonga**, possibly the biggest tourist trap in the whole region, and all in the name of religion. Set in a superb site, the streets are lined with poor quality souvenir stalls selling plastic, light-up Virgins and armed guards are used to keep the lines of the faithful moving. It is fascinating, but it left me, at least, with a bad taste in my mouth.

Covadonga first came to fame for a totally different reason however. By the early 8th century, the Moors had swept right across the Iberian Peninsula, as far as the north coast, leaving the court and its Christian followers to take refuge in the mountains. In 714, a Visigothic nobleman named Pelayo was elected as their leader, and in 718, he began a small-scale resistance movement. By 722, he was sufficiently irritating for the Emir Alçama to send an army against him. The two forces met in the remote, steep-sided valley of Covadonga, and with the aid of a major – and Heaven-sent – rockfall, which rained down upon the heads of the attackers, Pelayo won the first Christian victory against the Moors. Soon afterwards, the Moors abandoned the north coast, and the kingdom of Asturias, with its capital at Cangas de Onís, came into being. Symbolically at least, the start of the Reconquista, Covadonga has always had a major significance in the life of Spain.

There is a statue of Pelayo on the main terrace of the sanctuary, and in the 12th century, his sarcophagus, together with those of his wife, Gaudiosa, their daughter, Erminsinda, and son-in-law, Alfonso I, was moved here. Today, they rest in an insignificant alcove on the way to the Cueva Santa, a small chapel in a cave that is now the focus of activity. As with many historically important sites in Spain, Covadonga has been hi-jacked by the church.

In 740, Alfonso I built a small shrine to Our Lady of the Battlefield (Nuestra Señora de las Batallas) in the cave beside the battle site and founded a Benedictine monastery to tend it. In the 12th century, this was taken over by the Augustinians and in the mid-17th century, they built the first Collegiate Church of San Fernando.

In 1777, a serious fire destroyed the chapel and its statue of the Virgin, and another had to be sculpted. Ever since, it has been this 18th-century statue and not the battle that has been the major focus of the village. Supposedly miraculous, the 'Santina', as it is known, is now the Patron Saint of Asturias. The collegiate church was completely rebuilt between 1886 and 1901 and is now a large, neo-Romanesque/Gothic and rather overblown basilica. The chapel in the Cueva Santa was rebuilt at much the same time, and again after another fire in 1936. The Santina now stands in a small, rather soulless modern chapel, with a constant stream of pilgrims being allowed little more time than is necessary to genuflect and leave their offering before being moved on to make way for the next. Just below it is a waterfall and pool, known as the Fuente del Matrimonio. If you drink the water, you are meant to marry within a year. Most people content themselves with throwing in money and wishing.

Perhaps the most interesting of the sights here is the treasury museum next to the basilica. Here are displayed just some of the enormous number of offerings made to the Virgin over the centuries, from enough robes, many encrusted with gold and jewels, for her to change every day of the year, to a crown containing over 1000 diamonds. The sheer wealth of it all is staggering, but at the other end of the scale, and far more poignant, is a cheap, scruffy ball point pen.

Covadonga stands on the northern edge of the **Covadonga National Park**, created in 1918 as the very first national park in Spain. At 16,925 hectares, it is still the largest in the country, covering virtually the entire Cornión massif of the Picos de Europa. There is some wildlife here, but the area is busy, and you will have to get a long way from the crowds before you can hope to see anything much. A 13km road leads from Covadonga up into the mountains. The journey is well worth it, but be very careful as the road is narrow, has hairpin bends the whole way and is a very popular route not only with tourists, but with daytrippers from nearby Oviedo and Gijón. About halfway up, you come to the Mirador de la Reina, with superb views out across the high peaks and valleys of the national park. At the top, you come to the two pale mountain lakes of Enol and Ercina, both formed in rock cirques carved out by glaciers. Although both are generally busy with people, they are stunningly beautiful, and there are plenty of easy strolls, as well as longer walks around the lakes and long distance footpaths leading over to the Cares Gorges (see page 235).

From here, you will have to back-track the whole way down to the C6312 below Covadonga, and turn right. This road runs along fairly flat, and relatively uninteresting terrain, in comparison to the magnificence of earlier section of the route, but there are still a couple of worthwhile stops. Near Benia, the heavily restored 12th-century Church of Santa Eulalia de Abamia is all that remains of a much larger monastery, said to have been the original burial site of Pelayo. It has two fine portals.

Las Arenas de Cabrales is famous, above all, as the centre of production of Cabrales, one of the most famous cheeses in Spain. Over 60,000 kilos a year are made of this blue cheese, a mix of cows', goats' and sheeps' milk, matured for 90 days in the nearby caves. Blue cheese is uncommon in Spain and the production method is said to have been introduced by French travellers on the pilgrim route to Santiago. A Cheese Festival is held here on the last Saturday in August for the real devotee.

Turn right here, along the O204 to Poncebos, 6 km from the main road. This small village is an increasingly busy tourist centre and the starting point for several excursions into the heart of the central massif of the Picos de Europa. Of these, the most popular is the walk through the Cares Gorges to Caín (see page 235). A driveable road leads to the left, climbing through the tiny village of Tielve to **Sotres**, a charmingly attractive, and as yet unspoiled mountain fastness. There is also a footpath between the two. The route takes about five hours each way, involves both climbs and steep descents, but if you want to do one way only, Sotres is about 1000 metres higher than Poncebos, so it is far easier to hire a driver to take you to Sotres and walk back. The route is worth doing, if you have the energy, as it covers some spectacular scenery, with fine views over the 2519m Peña de Naranjo de Bulnes, one of the highest peaks in the range, and one that has come to symbolise the region. From here, the path leads through to the tiny hamlet of Bulnes, still without a proper road and supplied by mule or horse, drops steeply into the Cares Gorge and follows the broad track through to Poncebos.

Returning to Arenas de Cabrales, turn right again onto the C6312, and follow the road through the far more gentle, but still attractive lower Cares Gorges. At El Pontón, just before you reach Trescares, there is a medieval bridge, the Puente de Lavidre. Follow the road along the valley into the open countryside and back to Panes.

Picos de Europa: General Information

POTES

Where to stay and eat:

Hotel del Oso, 39539 Cosgaya (tel. (942) 730 418). An attractive modern hotel built in stone to a traditional style in the heart of the Picos, on the road between Potes and the cable car at Fuente Dé. It has a tennis court and smimming pool. Cheap-moderate.

Parador del Río Deva, 39588 Fuente Dé (tel. and fax (942) 730 001). A concrete monstrosity on the outside, this is the least attractive of the paradors, although it is pleasant inside. The setting is spectacular, in a massive natural amphitheatre right beside the cable car, high in the Picos, about 20km from Potes. Moderate prices.

Posada de la Casona, 39539 Cosgaya (tel. (942) 730 977). Family-run inn dating back to the 17th century. Comfortable, friendly and attractive. Dinner on request. About 10km from Potes, on the road to Fuente Dé. Cheap.

For accommodation in Cangas de Onís and Coradonga, see page 69.

La Rioja

La Rioja is one of the smallest of the Autonomous states in Spain, covering an area of 5000 square kilometres, and with a population of only 250,000 of whom half live in and around the state capital, Logroño. It takes its name from the Ría Oja, itself a tributary of the Ebro River, which flows across the north-east corner of the state.

The state is split into three distinctive geographical zones. The Rioja Alta is the northern section, bordered to the north by the Basque Country, Navarrese and Castillian borders, and to the south (roughly) by the Camino de Santiago. This is the charmed region, which seems to have everything – the most fertile ground and finest climate, most of the vines and the best quality wines, and a good proportion of the state's industry and wealth. If that were not enough, it even has the most beautiful historic monuments and the bulk of the tourist industry. It is lush, rolling country, intensively cultivated and patchworked by the neat green rows of the vines on the best chalky slopes, while the land between is used for wheat and vegetables.

The south-eastern region of the Rioja Baja, bordering southern Navarra, Aragón and Soria is still wine country, but it is more open and drier. The main centre here is Calahorra, a city with an impeccable pedigree, but much damaged over the centuries.

In the south-west, the land begins to climb again to the Sierra de la Demanda, a mountain land of sheep and cattle breeding, of green forests and remote villages, the main watershed for the entire region. There is some winter skiing, but the main reason people visit is to hike, shoot and fish, with some of the best trout streams in Spain to be found here.

Historically, La Rioja has had little distinctive identity.

It became a region in its own right only in the constitutional shake-up of the early 1980s. Before that this was a border land, partly belonging to Navarra, partly to Castille. Probably its main claim to fame was the Battle of Clavijo in 844, when Ramiro I won one of the first great Christian victories in the war against the Moors, supposedly with the miraculous aid of St James (see page 200). Only a ruined castle now remains at Clavijo, 17km south of Logroño.

For the tourist, there are two main reasons for visiting Rioja. One is the stretch of the Camino de Santiago, with its attendant churches and monuments, which runs across the northern section of the state. The other is for the wine, the finest in Spain, which is not only one of the state's main industries, but also the local obsession. Luckily for visitors, it is easily possible to combine both.

As the Camino de Santiago forms the southern boundary of this book, only the Rioja Alta and a small section of the Sierra are covered here.

Logroño

Capital of La Rioja, Logroño lies on the eastern border of the state, on the plains to the south of the Ebro River.

Originally the site of the Roman town of Julia Briga, it later became a major stop on the Camino de Santiago. Only a small section of the medieval centre has survived its massive growth this century however and today, it is a noisy, hot and dusty place with a population of around 120,000, and a few attractive corners within a basically unattractive city. Having said that, it is worth a stop, but although it has most of the hotels in the region, head out to Santo Domingo de la Calzada or Haro if you want to stay in the area.

To the north of the city centre, there are three interesting bridges. The stone Puente de Piedra, built in 1770, and the iron Puente de Hierro, built in 1884, both span the river and offer fine views, while between the two, on the south bank, stands the last remaining arch of the 1138 Romanesque bridge. All three lead directly into the heart of the old city where there are, inevitably, a number of interesting churches.

The Cathedral of Santa María de la Redonda, in the Plaza del Mercado, was first built in the 15th century, a hall church with elegant star-vaulting. In 1769 however, it was given a new, rather strangely contrasting Baroque façade and twin towers. Inside, the main altarpiece is also Baroque, and there are some fine side chapels, the octagonal, rococo Capella de Nostra Senora de los Angeles, and the Capella de los Reyes and the Capella de Santo Ildefonsus, both of which have interesting altarpieces.

At the foot of the Puente de Piedra, on the c/ Marqués de San Nicolás, is the Church of Santa María del Palacio. According to some, and with little basis in fact, this was founded by Emperor Constantine (the Great). It did form part of the 11th-century royal palace donated by King Alfonso VII in 1130 to the Order of the Holy Sepulchre. The church was rebuilt in the late 12th century, enlarged in the 16th, and altered again in the 18th. The 45m high pyramidal spire, known for obvious reasons as La Aguja (the Needle), dates from the early 13th century. The cloister is late Gothic, with Baroque frescoes, while the retable on the main altar is Renaissance.

A little further in to town, on Barriocepo, is the 16th-century **Church of Santiago le Real**, which has a Renaissance retable and two statues of St James, showing him as soldier and pilgrim. Across the road is the Fuente de los Peregrinos, the pilgrim fountain. The **Church of San Bartolomé**, in the Plaza de San Bartolomé, dates from the early 13th century, but has an early 14th-century Gothic façade with some lovely carvings showing the life of St Bartholomew. The 17th-century brick tower shows signs of Mudéjar influence. At several points around the old town, sections still remain of the city walls and gates put up by King Carlos V.

The heart of the city today is the large and leafy **Plaza de Espolón**, on the southern edge of the old town. In the middle is a statue of the guerilla leader, General Espartero, on an extremely well-endowed horse. The General himself is buried in the cathedral.

His former home, the **Espartero Palace**, in the Plaza de San Agustín, was built in the 18th century in the Baroque style. Bought by the state in 1884, with the idea of turning it into an Episcopal Palace (a plan that never came to fruition), today it houses the regional museum, with a fine collection of religious art.

Like everywhere else in this region, Logroño is a wine town, and along with plenty of wine shops, and quite a few good wine bars, there are several *bodegas* here. The two easiest to visit (and two of the most interesting, in very different ways) are the **Bodegas Marqués de Murrietta**, Finca YGAY, Ctra de Zaragoza, km 403 (tel. 258 100) and the **Bodegas Campo Viejo**, Poligono de Cascajos, c/ Gustavo Becquer 3 (tel. 238 000). The Murrietta claims to be the oldest in the region, founded by a Galician count in 1848, and still owned by the same family. The Campo Viejo is a vast modern affair owned by Savin, Spain's biggest producer. Both offer tastings and sell wine on the premises. The city's main festival, officially dedicated to San Mateo, starts on 21 September and lasts a week, happily coinciding with the *vendimia* (grape harvest).

For the pilgrim route east from Logroño to Pamplona, see page 224; for the pilgrim route west to Burgos, see page 247.

Logroño to Haro

There are actually three main roads travelling the 57km between these two towns, the two largest, the A68 motorway, and the N232, running along the south bank of the Ebro River. The most interesting however is the road, confusingly also labelled as the N232, which wanders along the border between Rioja and the Basque Country on the north bank of the river.

Leave Logroño on the main N111 north, signposted towards Pamplona. A couple of kilometres out of town, turn left and go about 20km to **Laguardia**, a small town at the foot of the Sierra Cantabrica which is actually in the Basque Country, but belongs at least in spirit to La Rioja. It is a splendid place, perched on a hill, its town wall, square bastions and ancient gateways still dramatically intact, and set in a sea of vines against a mountain backdrop. Inside, ancient stone houses with wrought iron balconies line the streets that lead up to the ruined castle. The Church of Santa María de los Reyes has a wonderful 15th-century portal and a Baroque retable and interesting collection of polychrome sculptures inside. Like so many other places nearby, this is a wine producing centre, with two *bodegas*, the 19th-century Bodegas Palacio and the modern Bodegas Alavesas.

From here, continue west along the N232. The road begins to climb dramatically up the side of the Sierra Cantabrica until you reach the Puerto de Herrera (1100m). On the south side, just before you go over the pass, stop at the viewing point known as the Rioja Balcony, for a superb view along the dusty brown length of the Ebro Valley. As the road descends on the other side, you will come to a junction with the other, larger branch of the N232. Turn left for the last few kilometres back across the Ebro to Haro.

Haro is a small market town perched on a rocky ledge above the confluence of the Tirón and Ebro Rivers. Built around a large arcaded plaza, it is an attractive place to stroll and sit with a number of fine old houses built between the 16th and 18th centuries. Look out, in particular, for the 16th-century Casa de Paternina, and the Town Hall, built in 1769. The most interesting of its three churches is the Church of Santo Tómas. The nave is Gothic, but its best features are the delicate Plateresque south portal, carved in 1516 by Felipe de Vigarni, and the Baroque altarpiece.

The real reason for coming here, however, is for the wine. At the heart of the

Riojan Wine

The first vines were planted here in the 12th century by Benedictine monks, to cater for thirsty pilgrims on their way to Santiago. It wasn't until the late 19th century however that the wines began to be transformed from rough and ready table wines to the great vintages we know today. The catalyst came from France. In the 1860s virtually the entire Bordeaux harvest was destroyed by phylloxera and the region's vintners, on the verge of ruin, had to look around for a suitable alternative site. They found it in Rioja and over the next few years, many of Bordeaux's finest manufacturers opened up vineyards and *bodegas* in the region. By the time the dreaded phylloxera finally crept down over the Pyrenees, and they had begun to plant Bordeaux with new, disease-resistant stock, Rioja was firmly on the wine map.

The next big jump came in the post-Franco years of the late 1970s, when the wines began to attract international acclaim and sales. To the existing houses, still using the traditions of 19th century-Bordeaux, were suddenly added a whole new breed of multi-national producers with their shiny vats and scientific technology. Today, while Rioja continues to produce

its traditional rich reds, increasingly, they are being joined by a variety of lighter wines, including some fine whites and rosés.

There are now nearly 48,000 hectares of vineyards in Rioja, nearly half of them under Tempranillo grapes, used for red wines. The other main variety, with a third of production, is Garnacha, while small quantities of Mazuelo and Graciano are also grown. Most of the whites are made from the Viura grape, but some Garnacha Blanca and Malvasa are also grown.

The traditional oak barrels create a full-bodied, slightly tawny red that should be aged for many years before drinking, and a rich, golden white. Both are smooth, tasting slightly of the oak and vanilla. The newer wines are the much lighter red *claretes*, and light, dry whites, fermented at low temperatures and drunk young.

A visit to La Rioja should include at least one tour of a *bodega*. Most are open to visitors, but few are geared up to regular public tours, and you might have to arrange your visit in advance. Sadly, too, a large number are closed at the height of the tourist season in August.

wine-growing regions of the Rioja Alta, this is the centre of the Rioja wine industry, capital of the Denominación and home to the Oenological Institute which is at the forefront of the scientific study of wine and wine production.

Even the town's main festival is related to wine. Held on 29 June, St Peter's Day, it starts with everyone dressing in white and pouring into the streets and bars to drink *zurracapote*, a punch similar to sangria, made from red wine, fruit (mainly citrus) and cinnamon. The action then moves 3km to the small chapel of San Felices for mass. As the service ends, and people move out onto the small rocky

Rioja wine on sale in Haro, the wine-growing centre of the Rioja region

hill of the Peña de Bilibio, the Batalla del Vino begins. A ferocious, no-holds-barred battle, fought with wine, some 50,000 litres are used each year. The *bota*, a traditional goatskin wine bag, is the normal weapon, but in one memorable year, someone even hired a helicopter. The other good time to be here is in late September for the *vendimia* (harvest).

There are dozens of *bodegas* in and around Haro, along with several wine shops selling a good selection from them all. Amongst the most interesting to visit are the Bodegas Muga, Barrio de la Estación (tel. 310 498), an old, mellow place oozing in tradition, and the Compañía Vinícola del Norte de España, Av Costa del Vino 21 (tel. 310 650), a much larger place, with a wide range of wines, that runs regular organised tours. There is also the chance to see and buy several local crafts, as a number of traditional craftsmen and artists have studios and workshops in the town. Amongst them are wineskin makers, cabinet and barrel makers, potters, and one blacksmith and one glassblower.

The Camino de Santiago — Logroño to Burgos

Leave Logrono on the main N232 signposted to Haro, south of the Ebro River. About 10 km from the city, turn left onto the N120, signposted to Burgos. The first stop is at **Nájera**, about 20km further on.

Huddled at the foot of a massive rocky abutment, this pretty, but rather run-down town was the capital of Navarra until 1076, when La Rioja became part of Castilla. Today little remains of its glorious past, except for a ruined castle and the imposing bulk of the Monastery of Santa María la Real. This was originally built between 1032 and 1056 by King Garcia III of Navarra, next to a cave where an image of the Virgin had been found. The cave is still accessible from the church, but the polychrome statue in it is 13th-century. From the first, the church was used as the royal pantheon and it contains a number of 11th- and 12th-century tombs of princes of Navarra, León and Castilla. Of them all, the most beautiful is that of Doña Blanca, wife of Sancho III, who died in childbirth in 1155. Her son survived and later became King Alfonso VIII. The kneeling statues of the founders, Garcia and his wife Estefania, are 16th-century. Ferdinand III (the Saint) was crowned here in 1217.

In spite of this illustrious Romanesque pedigree, little remains of the early church however, as the whole thing was rebuilt in 1453, and today it is almost wholly late Gothic in style. The beautifully carved choir-stalls date from 1495, and the intricate lacy cloister dates from 1528.

The area between Nájera and the small village of Navarrete was the site of a famous battle. Enrique de Trastámara, with the aid of the French, had overthrown his half-brother, King Pedro (the Cruel). Probably because the French were involved on the other side, the Black Prince agreed to help Pedro. After several months of manoeuvring and skirmishes, the two armies met here in April 1367, and the English won in the proverbial river of blood. The Black Prince received his famous ruby (now in the State Crown) as part payment, but also picked up the fever which eventually killed him. Pedro went back on his deals and received no further aid.

He was eventually defeated and killed by Enrique in 1369, and the Trastámara dynasty came to power (see page 28).

The castle at Nájera was also the site of the earlier, legendary battle between superhero Roland and the giant Farragut, during which Roland threw a stone from the hill some two miles away, with precise enough aim and power to kill the giant. The hill is now known as Puyo Roldan in his honour.

From here, turn left onto the C113 which leads south; after 6km turn west onto the L0832 for the twin Benedictine monasteries of **San Millán de la Cogolla**. San Millán was a hermit who lived in these remote hills in the 6th century, tending sheep and cows. He died in 574 at the age of 100, and his hermitage rapidly became a pilgrimage site. Although there is said to have been a monastery here since the 6th century, the earliest of the existing buildings, the Monastery of Suso, dates back to the early 10th. Perched high on a wooded hill, with wonderful views over the terraces of Cárdenas Valley and the later monastery, it is an extraordinarily atmospheric place, with a Visigothic chapel carved out from the rock, while the east end of the church has Mozarabic horseshoe arches and the west end is classic Romanesque. The saint's empty sarcophagus is on display. Legend has it that his body melted into the stone, and that when attempts were made later to move the tomb, it grew so heavy that no one could lift it. Other tombs include those of the Infantes de Lara, and the poet Gonzalo de Berceo, who died in about 1264. A local boy who became a priest at the shrine, he is the first known person to write in Castillian.

Lower down the hill is the much later and more elaborate Monastery of Yuso, begun in 1554 and added to over the next 200 years. The Benedictines left in 1835, and there is now an Augustinian community here. The church is basically Renaissance, while the sacristy is neo-classical and the portals Baroque. The whole place is large, luxurious and a little overblown. There is a 16th-century retable by Juan Rizi on the main altar, depicting the life of San Millán. There is a magnificent and priceless library in which were found a few pages of a late 10th-century codex which includes the earliest written examples of both the Castillian and Basque languages. In the treasury, there is a set of wonderful ivory plaques, originally part of an 11th-century reliquary, showing scenes from the life of San Millán.

From here, turn right onto the small road that leads north-west towards Santo Domingo de la Calzada. 5km on lies the unfinished Cistercian Convent of Santa María de Cañas, founded in 1171. Work on the existing buildings began in 1236, but only the transepts and presbytery were completed, along with a chapterhouse that contains the tomb of Abbess Urraca López de Haro, who died in about 1260.

Santo Domingo de la Calzada was founded in the 11th century by another famous saint as a halt on the pilgrim route. Santo Domingo, whose name literally means 'St Dominic of the Causeway', was born in 1019 in Viloria La Rioja. He came to the area intending to join the community at San Millán, but never got there, becoming a hermit instead. Until this time, the pilgrim route took a different road, through Valpierre, Ochánduri and Leira, but Domingo set to work and built a massive 24-arched bridge across the Oja, followed by an inn and hospital. In doing so, he successfully rerouted the Camino onto its present course. In honour of his achievements, he is now patron saint of civil engineers!

The town today is a small, sleepy, charming place built of a rich honey-coloured stone. Large sections of the walls erected in 1367 by Pedro the Cruel still remain intact, while the main road in from Logroño enters through one of the original gates. Near this is a large plaza ringed by low arcaded buildings and attractive old houses crowd the narrow streets. The highlight of any visit however must be the great cathedral which dominates the town centre. The first major church on the site was consecrated in 1106 by the Bishop of Nájera, Don Pedro Aznar. Only a few traces of this have survived however, although the plan remains essentially Romanesque. The main body of the existing cathedral is early Gothic in style, dating from 1138 to 1235. In 1232, it became the regional diocesan headquarters, taking over from Nájera. In 1959, it gained even more status as the Bishopric of Calahorra, La Calzada and Logroño – effectively of the whole of La Rioja.

The exterior of the church was greatly altered in 1767 by Martin Beratúa, who created the neo-classical portal at the same time as he built the free-standing belfry tower beside the ancient Chapel of Nostra Señora de la Plaza. This was the cathedral's third tower, the first having been destroyed by lightning in 1450, and the second virtually in ruins and thoroughly dangerous when it was dismantled in 1760.

The roast that crowed

Once upon a time, a young pilgrim, Hugonell, son of the Archbishop of Cologne in Germany, stopped for the night at an inn in Santo Domingo de la Calzada, where he caught the eye of a serving girl. She offered herself to him, but he refused her advances. Furious and humiliated, she hid a silver cup in his bag, and next morning, accused him of stealing it. He was arrested and in spite of all his protests and prayers, was condemned to death and hung.

Several weeks later, his parents arrived to claim the body. To their delighted surprise, he was still alive and spoke to them, saying that he had been saved by the intervention of Santo Domingo. They rushed in to tell the mayor who was just sitting down to dinner. Irritated at the interruption, he declared that they were talking nonsense and that the boy was no more alive than the roast chicken on his plate. The chicken promptly got up, started crowing, and flapped its way across the room. The stunned official realised that the boy was innocent and that only a miracle had saved him from a severe miscarriage of justice. Ever since, a live white cock and hen have been kept in the cathedral, where pilgrims traditionally bring them crumbs. It is said that if they eat, the journey will succeed, but if they spurn your offering, you will die along the way. A piece of the gallows is kept in a niche below the window opposite.

Inside, the cathedral is one of the most lavish in northern Spain. Just inside the door, in the south transept is the tomb of Santo Domingo himself, a vast, elaborate, gilded and painted affair designed by Felipe de Vigarni, erected in 1517 and extended in 1529. Opposite, in a gilded cage, are kept a white cock and hen in memory of the saint's most famous miracle (see box). On the 12 May each year, they are killed and eaten and replaced by a new set. Amidst the cathedral's many other treasures are a Baroque, high relief walnut retable on the main altar, carved in 1541 by Damián Forment, and some charmingly ornate Plateresque choirstalls dating from 1531 to 1536, the work of Andrés de Nájera to designs by Guillén de Holanda. The cloister dates from 1380, and is Gothic with Mudéjar influences, and later 16th-century alterations. Numerous chapels line both the church and cloister, many containing other fine works of art. Look out in particular for the Plateresque screen in the Chapel of La Magdalena, some fine 15th- and 16th-century sculptures of the Counts of Civiñuela in the Chapel of San Juan Bautista and a 15th-century Flemish sculpture of St Veronica near the entrance to the Sacristy. A monument on the wall beside the Chapterhouse door marks the spot where the heart of Enrique de Trastámara was buried on his death here in 1379.

On the edge of town stands the 16th-century Monastery of San Francisco, designed by Juan de Herrera. It contains a beautiful stone retable and the alabaster tomb of the monastery's founder, Bernardo de Fresneda, the confessor to King Felipe II, who died in 1587. Santo Domingo's original hospital, later extended, stands on the small square beside the Cathedral, its rather dour exterior belying the beauty inside. This is now in use as a parador.

From here, you have a choice of routes. The first continues straight along the N120 for the 69km into Burgos, crossing the frontier into Castilla-y-León about 15km after leaving Santo Domingo. It is a beautiful drive, at first across open country, then climbing through the Montes de Oca to the Puerto de Pedraja (1130m). There are several pretty villages en route, including Belorado, Villafranca-Montes de Oca and San Juan de Ortega, but little of historic importance for you to stop and see.

The backroads alternative heads south along the L0810 for 14km from Santo Domingo along the Oja Valley to **Ezcaray**, an attractive village with some fine houses, including grander sandstone mansions emblazoned with coats of arms, and humbler cottages, and a small Diocesan Museum. The real interest near here is up in the mountains, a few kilometres from the village. Firstly, there is the Hermitage of La Virgen de Allende, a Baroque building containing five extraordinary paintings of St Michael, dressed as an 18th-century officer and armed with a harquebus. Secondly, there is the ski resort of **Valdezcaray**, with 300 hectares of run and eleven ski lifts.

Back in Ezcaray, you can head west on the smaller road which leads over the border into Castilla-y-León and into Burgos via Pradoluengo and Arlanzón.

For Burgos, see page 140; for the next section of the Camino de Santiago, from Burgos to León, see page 153.

Rioja:
General Information

Regional tourist office:
Comunidad Autónoma de La Rioja, Consejera de Industria, Comercio y Turismo, c/ Portales 1, 1°, Logroño (tel. (941) 227 654).

HARO
Where to stay:
Hotel Los Agustinos, c/ San Agustin 2, 26200 (tel. (941) 311 308; fax (941) 303 148). A 14th-century building that has served time as a monastery, hospital and jail, now transformed into a luxurious hotel. Expensive.
Iturrimurri, Ctra. N-232, km 41, 26200 (tel. (941) 311 213; fax (941) 311 121). Comfortable but uninspiring hotel about 1km from Haro. It stands in its own grounds and and good views and a swimming pool. Cheap-moderate.
Where to eat:
Terete, c/ Lucrecia Arana 17 (tel. (941) 310 023). Cheerful and popular, with home-style food and own label wines. Moderate.
Beethoven I y II, Santo Tomás 3, 26200 (tel. (941) 311 181). Friendly family-run restaurant with good regional food. Moderate.
There are several charming cafés in the main square which serve good *raciones* and local wines.

LOGROÑO
Tourist Office, Miguel Villanueva, 10, 26001 (tel. (941) 291 260).
Where to stay:
Hotel Los Bracos Sol, Bretón de los Herreros 29, 26001 (tel. (941) 226 608; fax (941) 226 754). Large modern business-style hotel. Cafeteria only. Expensive.
Marqués de Vallejo, c/ Marqués de Vallejo 6, 26001 (tel. (941) 248 333; fax (941) 240 288). Simple but attractive bed and breakfast in a side street town house. Cheap-moderate.
Where to eat:
La Merced, c/ Marqués de San Nicolás 109 (tel. (941) 221 166). There are no less than nine small dining rooms in this 18th-century town house. The food is good regional fare; the wine list is extraordinary. They boast of a cellar of 40,000 bottles, representing every *bodega* in Rioja. Expensive.

Mesón Lorenzo, Marqués de San Nicolás 136, 26001 (tel. (941) 259 140). Housed within a *bodega*, this serves lighter versions of traditional regional cuisine. Moderate.

SANTO DOMINGO DE LA CALZADA
Where to stay and eat:
Parador, Plaza del Santo, 3, 26250 (tel. (941) 340 300; fax (941) 340 325). Closed for renovation at the time of writing, but due to reopen some time in 1993. Originally a palace of the Kings of Navarre, this was later taken over as a pilgrim hospice by Santo Domingo himself. Right beside the cathedral, its plain exterior belies an enchanting interior of Gothic arches and great stairways. Moderate.
Mesón El Peregrino, Zumalacárregui 18, 26250 (tel. (941) 340 202). Best known as a restaurant, with rustic decoration and good, plain food, this also has a number of comfortable, if simple rooms. Cheap.

Section Three: Language

Glossary

bodega	wine-vault or cellar and winery
brañas	Celtic-style thatched settlements built in the high Asturian mountains by nomadic shepherds
castro	Celtic hill fort or village
fuero	charter, act of common law, in which those in authority would swear to respect local traditions and to consult the people in the enactment of new laws, particularly in the Basque country
gigantes/gegants	'giants' – people dressed in costumes and on stilts, participating in festival parades
meseta	plateau
mirador	observatory, panoramic viewpoint
mozarabs	early Christians who fled during the Moorish conquest, bringing with them some elements of Arabic architecture such as the horseshoe arch
mudéjar	art forms based on Arabic design, e.g. ornately stuccoed ceilings, usually the work of Moorish converts to Christianity, or Muslims left in Christian territory during the Reconquista
parador	state-run hotel often converted from a castle or palace (not necessarily very expensive)
raciones	large helpings of *tapas*, often sufficient as a light meal
ría	fjord-like estuary
romería	pilgrimage-cum-picnic with festive celebrations
solaña	glassed-in balcony
tapas	small savoury dishes served in a bar to accompany drinks

253

Survival Spanish

This is an extremely brief list, covering only the most essential phrases you might need to use. As few people in this region seem to speak much English, I would strongly recommend taking a good phrase book and a pocket dictionary if you can't speak Spanish.

GREETINGS AND BASICS

buenos días	good morning	*buenas tardes*	good afternoon/good evening
buenas noches	good night	*ola*	hello
adiós	good bye	*hasta luego*	see you soon
si	yes	*no*	no
por favor	please	*gracias*	thank you
de nada	Don't mention it/ that's OK	*perdóneme*	excuse me/I beg your pardon
lo siento	sorry	*váyase*	go away
i ciudado!	look out!	*i peligro!*	danger!
i socorro!	help!	*no entiendo/no comprendo*	I don't understand
no hablo mucho español	I don't speak much Spanish	*¿Habla usted inglés?*	do you speak English?
¿puede usted hablar más despacio?	could you speak more slowly?	*¿podría usted repetir eso?*	could you repeat that?
escríbelo, por favor	please write it down	*¿dónde?*	where?
¿cuándo?	when?	*¿dónde está (están) . . . ?*	where is (are) . . . ?
¿cuánto cuesta?	how much does it cost?	*¿A qué hora . . . ?*	what time . . . ?
¿puede darme..	can I have . . . ?	*¿Me puede decir cómo se va a . . . ?*	can you tell me the way to . . . ?
¿tiene . . . ?	do you have . . . ?		

BANKS AND SERVICES

el banco	bank	*la oficina de cambio*	bureau de change
el cheque de viajero	traveller's cheque	*la tarjeta de credito*	credit card
el cambio	exchange rate	*quiero cambiar . . . .*	I want to change . . .
¿cómo está el cambio?	what's the exchange rate?	*¿que comisión cargan?*	how much commission do you charge?
la oficina de correos	post office	*el sello*	stamp
la carta	letter	*la tarjeta postal*	postcard
la lista de correos	poste restante	*el paquete*	parcel
por correo aéreo	airmail	*el teléfono*	telephone
el indicativo	area code	*la guía de teléfonos*	telephone directory
con cobro revertido	reverse charges		

ACCOMMODATION

¿tiene una habitación?	do you have a room?	sencilla	single
doble/con dos camas	twin	una cama matrimonial	double bed
con baño	with a bath	con ducha	with a shower
con balcón	with a balcony	con vista	with a view
barato	cheap	caro	expensive
la reserva	reservation	la cuenta	bill
dormir y desayunar	bed and breakfast	media pensión	half board
pensión completa	full board	el piso	floor/storey
los servicios	toilet	la llave	key

EATING

el camarero/la camarera	waiter/waitress	el menú/la carta	menu
el menú del día	menu of the day	el plato combinado	set meal
especialidades de la casa	house speciality	especialidades locales/platos típicos	local speciality
las tapas	canapés	las aceitunas	olives
las nueces	nuts	las raciones	snacks
los entremeses	starters	el jamón	ham
el chorizo	sausage	las ensaladas	salads
la tortilla	omelette	los huevos	eggs
la sopa	soup	los pescados y mariscos	fish and shellfish
las gambas	shrimps	los langostinos	prawns
las almejas	clams	los calamares/los chiperones	squid
los cangrejos	crab	los mejillones	mussels
las ostras	oysters	el salmón	salmon
las sardinas	sardines	el bacalao	cod
la merluza	hake	el pulpo	octopus
el rape	monkfish	los salmonetes	red mullet
la trucha	trout	la carne	meat
el buey	beef	el cordero	lamb
el cerdo	pork	la ternera	veal
los aves	poultry	el pollo	chicken
la carne de caza	game	el conejo	rabbit
el venado	venison	la liebre	hare
el jabalí	wild boar	el biftec	beef steak
el filete	steak	la chuleta	chop

las legumbres/la verdura	vegetables	el arroz	rice
la patata	potato	las judías	beans
los pimientos	peppers	la macedonia de legumbres	mixed vegetables
el queso	cheese	los postres	pudding/dessert
el arroz con leche	rice pudding	el flan	creme caramel
el bizcocho	sponge cake	el helado	ice cream
el pastel de queso	cheesecake	la tarta de manzana	apple tart
la tarta helada	ice cream tart	las frutas	fruit
las almendras	almonds	las cerezas	cherries
las ciruelas	plums	las frambuesas	raspberries
las fresas	strawberries	la lima	lime
el limón	lemon	la manzana	apple
el melocotón	peach	la naranja	orange
la piña	pineapple	el plátano	banana
el pomelo	grapefruit	el melón	melon
las uvas	grapes	el pan	bread
la mantequilla	butter		
la sal	salt		
la pimienta	pepper	las bebidas	drinks
el agua mineral	mineral water	sin alcohol	without alcohol
el jugo de fruta	fruit juice	el jugo de naranja	orange juice
el té	tea	el café	coffee
solo	black	con leche	with milk
con limón	with lemon	con azúcar	with sugar
los aperitivos	aperitifs	el vino	wine
tinto	red	blanco	white
seco	dry	dulce	sweet
espumoso	sparkling	el vino de la casa	house wine
la cerveza	beer	los licores	spirits and liqueurs

TRANSPORT

el billete	ticket	la tarifa	fare
ida	single	ida y vuelta	return
primera/segunda classe	first/second class	la reserva	reservation
llegada	arrival	salida	departure/exit
el aduana	Customs	el pasaporte	passport
el equipaje	luggage	el avión	aeroplane
el transbordador	ferry	el tren	train
el autobús	bus	el autocar	coach
el coche	car	el taxi	taxi
aquiler de coches	car hire	el permiso de conducir	driving licence

el seguro	insurance	la carretera	road
el autopista	motorway	el mapa	map
el plano	street plan	el estacionamiento	car park
el garaje	garage	la gasolinera	filling station
la gasolina	petrol	super/normal/sin plomo	super/normal/ unleaded
diesel	diesel	el aceite	oil
llénelo, por favor	full tank, please		

NUMBERS

cero	0	treinta y uno	31
uno	1	cuarenta	40
dos	2	cincuenta	50
tres	3	sesenta	60
cuatro	4	setenta	70
cinco	5	ochenta	80
seis	6	noventa	90
siete	7	cien/ciento	100
ocho	8	ciento uno	101
nueve	9	doscientos	200
diez	10	trescientos	300
once	11	cuatrocientos	400
doce	12	quinientos	500
trece	13	seiscientos	600
catorce	14	setecientos	700
quince	15	ochocientos	800
dieciséis	16	novecientos	900
diecisiete	17	mil	1,000
dieciocho	18	mil cien	1,100
diecenueve	19	dos mil	2,000
veinte	20	diez mil	10,000
veintiuno	21	cien mil	100,000
treinta	30	un millón	1,000,000

DATES

el día	day	la semana	week
el fin de la semana	weekend	el mes	month
el año	year	el siglo	century
la mañana	morning/tomorrow	la tarde	afternoon/evening
la noche	night	la primavera	spring
el verano	summer	el otoño	autumn
el invierno	winter	domingo	Sunday
lunes	Monday	martes	Tuesday
miércoles	Wednesday	jueves	Thursday
viernes	Friday	sábado	Saturday

enero	January	febrero	February
marzo	March	abril	April
mayo	May	junio	June
julio	July	agosto	August
septiembre	September	octubre	October
noviembre	November	diciembre	December

Metric Conversion Tables

All measurements are given in metric units. For readers more familiar with the imperial system, the accompanying tables are designed to facilitate quick conversion to imperial units. Bold figures in the central columns can be read as either metric or imperial: e.g. 1kg = 2.20lb or 1lb = 0.45kg.

mm		in	cm		in	m		yds
25.4	1	.039	2.54	1	0.39	0.91	1	1.09
50.8	2	.079	5.08	2	0.79	1.83	2	2.19
76.2	3	.118	7.62	3	1.18	2.74	3	3.28
101.6	4	.157	10.16	4	1.57	3.66	4	4.37
127.0	5	.197	12.70	5	1.97	4.57	5	5.47
152.4	6	.236	15.24	6	2.36	5.49	6	6.56
177.8	7	.276	17.78	7	2.76	6.40	7	7.66
203.2	8	.315	20.32	8	3.15	7.32	8	8.75
228.6	9	.354	22.86	9	3.54	8.23	9	9.84

g		oz	kg		lb	km		miles
28.35	1	.04	0.45	1	2.20	1.61	1	0.62
56.70	2	.07	0.91	2	4.41	3.22	2	1.24
85.05	3	.11	1.36	3	6.61	4.83	3	1.86
113.40	4	.14	1.81	4	8.82	6.44	4	2.48
141.75	5	.18	2.27	5	11.02	8.05	5	3.11
170.10	6	.21	2.72	6	13.23	9.65	6	3.73
198.45	7	.25	3.18	7	15.43	11.26	7	4.35
226.80	8	.28	3.63	8	17.64	12.87	8	4.97
255.15	9	.32	4.08	9	19.84	14.48	9	5.59

ha		acres	Metric to imperial conversion formulae	
0.40	1	2.47		multiply by
0.81	2	4.94	cm to inches	0.3937
1.21	3	7.41	m to feet	3.281
1.62	4	9.88	m to yards	1.094
2.02	5	12.36	km to miles	0.6214
2.43	6	14.83	km^2 to square miles	0.3861
2.83	7	17.30	ha to acres	2.4721
3.24	8	19.77	g to ounces	0.03527
3.64	9	22.24	kg to pounds	2.205

Further reading

One of the problems for travellers to northern Spain is that relatively little has been written on the area. Most authors seem to have passed through with a brief comment on their way south to Madrid and Andalusia, while the majority of guidebooks cover the entire country. I have selected those that I feel would be of most use to people visiting the north-west exclusively.

Guidebooks
Blue Guide to Spain, *Ian Robertson* (A & C Black, London and WW Norton, New York). Excellent touring guide with a wealth of cultural information for the committed sightseer.

Michelin Green Guide to Spain, and **Michelin Red Guide to Spain and Portugal**. Regularly updated, the Green Guide has a wealth of historical and cultural information, while the Red Guide series is one of Europe's best guides to top quality hotels and restaurants.

Field Guide to the Birds of Britain and Europe, *Peterson*; **Field Guide to the Flowers of Britain and Europe**, *Schauer* and *Caspari*; **Handguide to the Wildflowers of Britain and Europe**, *Blamey* and *Fitter* (all published by HarperCollins). In the absence of any good English language guide to the flora and fauna of the Iberian peninsula in particular, these three guides together should give the keen amateur naturalist a reasonable hand.

Foods and Wines of Spain, *Penelope Casas* (Penguin/Knopf).
Pocket Guide to Spanish Wine, *Jan Read* (Mitchell Beazley/Simon and Schuster).
Castles in Spain, *Michael Busselle* (Pavilion).

History
A Traveller's History of Spain, *Juan Lalaguna* (Windrush Press). Easy to read potted history of Spain with gazetteer and charts for easy reference to people, places or dates.
Spanish Civil War, *Hugh Thomas* (Penguin/Harper & Row).
Imperial Spain 1469–1716, *JH Eliot* (Penguin).
Modern Spain 1875–1980, *Raymond Carr* (Oxford University Press).

Spain and the Spanish Today
Spain, Change of a Nation, *Robert Graham* (Michael Joseph). Analysis of Spain's transition to democracy in the post-Franco era.

The Spaniards – A Portrait of the New Spain, *John Hooper* (Viking/Penguin). The Spanish and their society today.
The Spanish Temper, *VS Pritchett* (Hogarth/Greenwood).
The Basques, *Roger Collins* (Blackwells).

Travels in Spain
Iberia, *James Michener* (Secker & Warburg/Corgi).
Spain, *Jan Morris* (Penguin/Oxford University Press).
As I Walked Out One Midsummer Morning and **A Rose for Winter**, *Laurie Lee* (Penguin/Norton).
In Spain, *Ted Walker* (Secker & Warburg/Corgi).
Northern Spain, *Cedric Salter* (Batsford/Hastings).
The Road to Compostela, *Rob Neillands* (Moorland).
The Pilgrimage to Santiago, *Edwin Mullins* (Secker & Warburg/Taplinger).

Maps
Michelin Nos. **441** (North-West Spain) and **442** (Northern Spain). 1:400 000.
Bartholomew World Travel Series – **Spain and Portugal**.

Useful Addresses

CAMPING
Federacion Española de Empresarios de Campings y C.V., General Oraa, 52–2°D, 28006 Madrid (tel. 262 9994; fax 563 7094).

CAR HIRE – UK BOOKING
ATESA, 65 Wigmore St, London W1M 9AG. (tel. 071-224 0504).

AVIS, Trident House, Station Rd, Hayes, Middx UB3 4DJ (tel: 081-848 8733).

HERTZ, Radnor House, 1272 London Rd, Norbury, London S16 4XW (tel. 081-679 1799).

MELIA, 273 Regent St, London W1R 7PB (tel. 071-499 6493).

TRANS-HIRE, Unit 16, 88 Clapham Park Rd, London SW4 7BX (tel. 081-978 1922).

EMBASSIES AND CONSULATES IN SPAIN
Australia: Paseo de la Castellana 143, 28003 Madrid (tel. (91) 279 8504).

Canada: Calle Nuñez de Balboa 35, 28001 Madrid (tel. (91) 431 4300); Vía Augusta 125, Atico 3, 08006 Barcelona (tel. (93) 209 0634).

UK: Calle Fernando El Santo 16, 28010 Madrid (tel. (91) 419 0200); Alameda de Urquijo 2, 8°, 48008 Bilbao, Vizcaya (tel. (94) 415 7600/7711) Paseo de Pereda 27, 39004 Santander (tel. (942) 220 000); Plaza de Compostela 23, 6° izq, 36201 Vigo, Pontevedra (tel. (986) 437 133).

United States: Calle Serrano 75, 28006 Madrid (tel. (91) 276 3600/3400); Avenida de Ejército 11, 48014 Bilbao, Vizcaya (tel. (94) 435 8300).

SPANISH EMBASSIES AND CONSULATES WORLDWIDE
UK: *Embassy*, Portland House, 16th Flr, Stag Place, London SW1E 5SE (tel. 071-235 5555; fax 071-235 9905). *Consulate*, 20 Draycott Place, London SW3 (tel. 071-581 5921/6; fax 071-589 5842); Suite 1a, Brook House, 70 Spring Gardens, Manchester M2 2BQ (tel. 061-236 1233); 63 North Castle St, Edinburgh EH2 3LJ (tel. 031-220 1843).

USA: *Embassy*, 2700 Fifteenth St NW, Washington DC 2009 (tel. 265 0190). *Consulates*, 150 East 58th Street, 16th Floor, New York, NY 10155 (tel. 355 4080); 2700 Fifteenth St NW, Washington DC 2009 (tel. 265 0191). There are also consulates in Boston, Chicago, Houston, Los Angeles, Miami, New Orleans and San Francisco.

Canada: *Embassy*, 350 Sparks Street, Suite 802, Ottawa, Ontario K1R 75B (tel.

237 2193). *Consulate*, 1 West Mount Square, Apartment 14, Wood Avenue, Montreal 832 2P9 (tel. 935 5235).
Australia: *Embassy*, 15 Arkana Street, Yarralumla, Canberra, ACT 2600 (tel. 733 555). *Consulate*, 19th Floor, Westfield Towers, 100 William Street, Sydney, NSW 2000 (tel. 358 5455).

SPANISH TOURIST OFFICES WORLDWIDE
UK: 57–58 St James Street, London SW1A 1LD (tel. 071-499 0901). (NB. Write for information, this office no longer handles telephone enquiries.)
USA: 665 Fifth Avenue, New York, NY 10022 (tel. 759 8822). There are also tourist offices in Chicago, Houston, Beverly Hills, and San Agustín, Florida.
Canada: 60 Bloor Street West, 201 Toronto, Ontario M4V 3B8 (tel. 961 3131).
Australia: International House, Suite 44, 104 Bathurst Street, (PO Box A-9675), Sydney, New South Wales (tel. 264 7966).

TOURIST AUTHORITIES IN SPAIN
Ministerio de Transportes, Turismo y Communicaciones, c/ María de Molino 50, 28006 Madrid (tel. 411 60 11).
Instituto Nacional de Promoción del Turismo, c/ María de Molino 50, 28006 Madrid (tel. 411 40 14).
Regional (north-west):
Comunidad Autónoma de Principado de Asturias, Consejería de Obras Públicas, Turismo, Transportes y Communicaciones, c/ Gil de Jaz 10, 4°, 33004 Oviedo (tel. (985) 25 46 11).
Diputación Regional de Cantabria, Consejeria de Industria, Transportes, Comunicaciones y Turismo, Palacio de la Diputación Regional, c/ Casimiro Sáinz 4, 39003 Santander (tel. (942) 31 27 61).
Junta de Castilla y León, Consejeria de Transportes, Turismo y Comercio, c/ Garcia Morato 36, 47008 Valladolid (tel. (983) 34 26 55).
Junta de Galicia, Consejería de Turismo, Juventud y Deportes, Plaza de Pontevedra 22, 2°, 15003 La Coruña (tel. (981) 22 00 43).
Comunidad Autónoma de La Rioja, Consejería de Industria, Comercio y Turismo, c/ Portales 1, 1°, Logroño (tel. (941) 22 76 54).
Diputación Foral de Navarra, Departamento de Industria, Comercio y Turismo, Av de San Ignacio 1, 31002 Pamplona (tel. (948) 22 72 00).
Gobierno Vasco, Departamento de Política Territorial, Transporte y Turismo, c/ Duque de Wellington 2, 01011 Vitoria (Alava) (tel. (945) 24 60 00).

TRAVEL AND TOUR OPERATORS
The Alternative Travel Group, 69–71 Banbury Rd, Oxford OX2 6PE (tel. (0865) 310 244; fax (0865) 310 299).
British Rail Continental Ltd, Ticket and Information Office, PO Box 303, Victoria Station, London SW1V 1JY (tel. 071–834 2345).
Brittany Ferries, Millbay Docks, Plymouth PL1 3EF (tel. (0752) 21321).
Casas Cantabricas, 31 Arbury Rd, Cambridge CB4 2JB (tel.(0223) 328 721; fax (0223) 322 711).
Iberia Airlines, 130 Regent St, London W1R 5RG (tel. 071-437 5622); fax 071-434

3375). Birmingham (tel. 021-643 1953); Manchester (tel. 061-436 6444).

Keytel International, 402 Edgware Rd, London W2 1ED (tel. 071–402 8182; fax 071-724 9503).

Magic of Spain, 227 Shepherd's Bush Rd, London W6 7AS (tel. 081-748 7575; fax 081-748 3731).

Mundi Colour, 276 Vauxhall Bridge Road, London SW1V 1BE (tel. 071–834 3492; fax 071-976 6763).

Secret Spain, Model Farm, Rattlesden, nr Bury St Edmunds, Suffolk IP30 0SY (tel. (0449) 737 664; fax (0449) 737 850).

Spanish National Railways (RENFE), Central Agency for Europe, 1–3 Av Marceau, 75116 Paris, France (tel. 47 23 52 00/1 or 47 23 63 60; fax 47 20 88 33).

Index